Joseph Gillow

# The Haydock papers

a glimpse into English Catholic life under the shade of persecution and in the dawn

of freedom

Joseph Gillow

**The Haydock papers**
*a glimpse into English Catholic life under the shade of persecution and in the dawn of freedom*

ISBN/EAN: 9783741157998

Manufactured in Europe, USA, Canada, Australia, Japa

Cover: Foto © Lupo / pixelio.de

Manufactured and distributed by brebook publishing software (www.brebook.com)

Joseph Gillow

# The Haydock papers

# THE
# HAYDOCK PAPERS:

### A GLIMPSE INTO

## ENGLISH CATHOLIC LIFE

*UNDER THE SHADE OF PERSECUTION AND IN THE DAWN OF FREEDOM.*

BY

## JOSEPH GILLOW.

LONDON : BURNS & OATES, LIMITED,
28 ORCHARD STREET, W., AND 63 PATERNOSTER ROW, E.C.
NEW YORK : 9 BARCLAY STREET.
1888.

" Not only this, but sundry other things
The author from Time's ruins hath composed,
Led by affection, whence endeavour springs,
And this his love, his labours have disclosed,
To gratify that nation is his ground
To whom he thinks his best endeavours bound."

*S. V. to Richard Verstegan,*
*Restitution of Decayed Intelligence,* 1605.

## Preface.

THE pleasure with which I read, in a recent number of *Merry England*, Monsignor Gradwell's "First journey to Ushaw Fifty Years Ago," induced me to hunt up a long-neglected series of MSS. in which, I recollected, was an account of a similar journey to the great Northern College shortly after its establishment, now fast approaching its centenary. As I turned over the papers, my interest increased with the perusal of each document, and it was not until I had examined the entire collection that I could lay it aside.

I longed to share with others some of the impressions I had gathered, but I felt that the administration of the "eighth sacrament in a dose of birch wine" had lamentably failed to develop in me, as it did in Monsignor Gradwell, the facile pen necessary to grace traditionary lore. I determined, however, to endeavour to compensate for my deficiency by drawing further upon the MSS. than I had first proposed, and by adding to my "Journey to Crook-Hall" extracts from a number of letters from Douay College, Old Hall Green, the Convents at Hammersmith and Spetisbury, and other correspondence. I have also included original narratives of the suppression of the colleges at Douay and S. Omer during the French Revolution, and of the establishment of the colleges at Ushaw and Old Hall Green. The catalogue, with biographical notices, of the last one hundred and three members of Douay College, supplies a considerable amount of useful information. I have likewise added the histories of a number of chapels and missionary stations in Lancashire, Cumberland, and Yorkshire, which present us with a kind of panorama of the difficulties and progress of Catholicity in this country from the days of Henry VIII. to the present time.

I recognised at a glance that a selection from the original sketches accompanying the collection, supplemented by portraits and other illustrations in my possession, would greatly enhance the value of the narratives, one of which describes the flight of the English Augustinian nuns from their convent of S. Monica at Louvain, with their subsequent settlements at Hammersmith and Spetisbury.

Before introducing the writers of these papers, I thought a brief notice of their ancestry, with the quaint traditions connected with the Haydocks, would give double interest to the closing records of a truly historical family, for I may say with Dryden—

> " So much religion in *their* name doth dwell,
>   Their souls must needs with piety excell.
>   Thus names, like (well-wrought) pictures drawn of old,
>   Their owners' nature and their story told."

J. G.

# The Haydocks of Cottam.

" My brain I'll prove the female to my soul ;
My soul, the father : and these two beget
A generation of still breeding thoughts."—
*Richard II.*

The Haydocks are inseparably associated with the history and traditions of Lancashire. Indeed, they may be regarded as a typical Catholic family, true to the faith through prosperity and adversity, and stoutly guarding it with that "hedge of oak" which the Lancashire historian says is the origin of the name.

Haydock and Cottam were portions of the possessions of the Haydocks from the most remote period. Hugh de Haydock held these manors in the thirteenth century, about which time the family and estates were divided. The elder branch, in the reign of King John, was represented by Sir Gilbert Haydock, who founded a chantry in Winwick parish in 1330, and was a great benefactor to the Priory of Burscough. Joan, the daughter and heiress of his descendant, Sir Gilbert Haydock, married Sir Peter Legh, of Lyme, in the reign of Henry V., and constituted him in her right lord of Haydock, Lowton, Poulton-with-Fearnhead, Bradley in Burtonwood, and other extensive territories. She afterwards became the wife of Sir Richard Molyneux, of Sefton, ancestor of the Earls of Sefton. In the same reign, Gilbert Haydock, lord of the manor of Cottam, was united to Isabel, daughter of William de Hoghton, of Hoghton and English Lea. Being related in the fourth degree, they were married by the special dispensation of his holiness, Martin V., dated Rome, Feb. 16, 1422. After almost half a century of conjugal happiness, a commission was granted in 1466 to Robert, Abbot of Cockersand, to veil Isabel, widow of Gilbert Haydock. Their son and heir, Richard, espoused Eleanor, daughter of Sir

A

William Ashton, of Croston, in 1455, and succeeding generations were intermarried with the families of Clifton of Clifton, Heton of Heton, Brown of Ribbleton, Osbaldeston of Osbaldeston, Hothersall of Hothersall, Haighton of Haighton, and other lead-ing Catholic families of the county of Lancaster.

THE GREAT OAK AT COTTAM.

## Cottam Hall.

> " No memory of its former state,
>   No record of its fame,
> A broken wall, a fallen tower,
> A half-forgotten name."
>
> *L. E. Landon.*

Cottam Hall was one of those quaint mansions, the growth of centuries, so pleasing to the lovers of the picturesque. To the south it presented three gables in the post and pan style, a fine remnant of the half-timbered houses of the fourteenth century. At the north-western corner of the house stood a lofty stone erection, with a flat, leaded roof. This was probably the portion of the house described in the marriage settlement of William Haydock and Jane Anderton, in 1670, as "the hall, the buildings over the hall, the chamber at the higher end of the hall, the buttery, the boarded chamber with a little closett, and a chamber over the entry." The banqueting-hall was a spacious apartment, having at one end a huge stone fire-place stretching from one side to the other. A moat surrounded the mansion, which was approached through an extensive and well-wooded park by a long avenue from the Tagg, on the eastern side, and a shorter drive from Woodplumpton on the north. When the building was removed in the early part of this century, and a farmstead erected to the south-west, a secret hiding-place was revealed, adjoining the ancient domestic chapel, and in it were found a few articles of altar furniture and a skeleton. The history of the latter is as follows :

## The Pilgrimage of Grace.

"How bloodily the sun begins to peer
Above yon busky hill ! "

*Henry IV.*

In 1536, the people of the northern counties, where the corruption of the Court had not penetrated, banded themselves together and raised a great army of thirty thousand men in defence of their faith, their ancient rights, and the dissolved monasteries. The nominal command was entrusted to Robert Aske, whose name revived the memory of the following lines in the ancient prophecies of Merlin, which were frequently sung in the army as an ambiguous prediction of their expedition and its chief :—

> " Forthe shall come a worme, an *Aske* with one eye,
>   He shall be the chiefe of the mainye ;
>   He shall gather of chivalrie a full fair flocke
>   Half capon and half cocke,
>   The chicken shell the capon slay,
>   And after thatte shall be no May."

From the borders of Scotland far into the fens of Lincolnshire, and to the west coast of Lancashire, the inhabitants generally bound themselves by oath to stand by each other, " for the love which they bore to Almighty God, His Faith, the holy Church, and the maintenance thereof." They complained chiefly of the suppression of the monasteries, of the Statute of Uses, of the introduction into the Council of such men as Cromwell and Rich, and of the preferment of the archbishops of Canterbury and Dublin, and of the bishops of Rochester, Salisbury, and St. David's, whose chief aim was to subvert the Church of Christ. The enterprise was termed " the pilgrimage of grace," and their banners were painted with the image of Christ Crucified, and with the chalice and host, the emblems of their belief. Wherever the pilgrims appeared, the people flocked to their standards, and the ejected monks were replaced in the monasteries. Their formidable appearance alarmed the king, who eventually offered them an unlimited pardon, with an| understanding that their grievances should be shortly discussed in the Parliament to be assembled at York. But the people in their simplicity were no match for the arbitrary and unscrupulous monarch and his ravenous advisers. After the army had been disbanded, Henry refused to keep his promise, arrested the leaders, and recommenced his plunder of the monastries. John Paslew, the last abbot of the Cistercian abbey of Whalley, with two of his monks, William Haydock and John Eastgate, had been in the foremost ranks of the popular outburst, and for this they were arraigned and convicted of high treason at the spring assizes holden at Lancaster in 1537. The abbot was executed, March 10, 1537, upon a gallows erected on a gentle elevation in a field called Holehouses, immediately facing Pendle Hill and the house of his birth near Whalley. Eastgate suffered with him, and their bodies were dismembered, and their quarters set up in various towns in Lancashire. William Haydock was hanged two days later in a field adjoining the abbey known by the name of *Le Impe-yard*, which signifies a nursery for young trees—the tree of faith that grew so strong in the Haydock family. His body for some reason was allowed to continue suspended on the gibbet entire, and ultimately was secured and secretly removed by his nephew and namesake to Cottam Hall, where it remained until its discovery when the hall was pulled down in the early part of this century.

William Trafford, abbot of the neighbouring Cistercian monastery of Salley, suffered in the same cause at Lancaster, on the same day as the abbot of Whalley. "Now thus!" went the flail, the motto and badge of the Traffords, ever ready, as we shall see, to be flung from right to left in threshing the wheat of this world, whilst keeping a shrewd eye on the next.

He was the second son of Sir John Trafford, of Trafford, and Elizabeth, daughter of Sir Thomas Assheton, of Ashton-under-Lyne, and was thus a relative of William Haydock, the monk of Whalley, whose grandmother, Eleanor, was the daughter of Sir Richard Assheton of Croston. The wife of Vivian Haydock's son, William, was the daughter of Sir Richard Hoghton, whose first wife was the daughter and co-heiress of Sir Thomas Assheton, of Ashton-under-Lyne. In later generations the Traffords were twice allied with the heiresses of the Asshetons, whose estate of Croston thus became the property of their family.

## 𝔗𝔥𝔢 𝔓𝔯𝔬𝔭𝔥𝔢𝔠𝔶.

*Tristitia vestra vertetur in gaudium*

Of the many traditions attaching to the family, none is more curious than that relating to the prophecy said to have been made by the mother of the martyr, George Haydock, shortly after his birth, in the reign of Queen Mary. While the saintly wife of Vivian Haydock lay on her bed of sickness for the last time, to add to the gloom which pervaded the moated and semi-fortified manor-house of Cottam, the intelligence arrived that Mary was dead, and the daughter of Anne Boleyn proclaimed Queen. There by his wife's bedside stood the squire, gazing into futurity, which was to find him a widower, a priest, a fugitive for conscience' sake, hunted to death along with his children in the land of his birth. He had seen the blood of his great uncle, William Haydock, ruthlessly shed with that of his abbot in front of Whalley Abbey by order of Henry VIII. He had seen lust linked with avarice spreading desolation over the land, and he had watched a new doctrine, the offspring of licentiousness, grow up and wax strong, whilst legitimate religion was trampled under foot. His wife, divining his thoughts, raised her feeble frame, and, pointing to the motto beneath the Haydock arms embroidered on the arras at the foot of the bed, slowly and distinctly pronounced the prophetic words, *Tristitia vestra vertetur in gaudium ;* then, clasping the babe by her side, she lay a corpse in her husband's arms

Little could Vivian Haydock foresee how his sorrow should be turned into joy. He was but at the outset of a long reign of unexampled persecution and cruelty, in which he was to drink to the very dregs, both of his own personal sufferings and of those of his family. But the prophecy foretold not the joy of this world ; it was the crown for which martyrs suffer, and that was promised to every generation of " the fugitive's " descendants, from that hour until the family became extinct.

> " Religion, source of smiling peace,
> Thou giv'st us joy that will not cease."
>
> *Haydock's Hymn on Religion.*

## Cardinal Allen.

"He was a scholar, and a ripe and good one ;
Exceeding wise, fair spoken, and persuading."

*Henry VIII.*

A few years after Mrs. Haydock's death, William Allen, afterwards Cardinal, came over to England, and during his three
years' stay, between 1562, and 1565, visited his friends and relatives in Lancashire. Mrs. Haydock and the wife of Dr. Allen's
brother George were sisters, daughters of William Westby, of
Westby, Co. York, and Mowbreck, Co. Lancaster, one of
the finest and most staunch Catholic gentlemen then resident in
Lancashire. Many were the consultations Dr. Allen held with
Vivian Haydock on the threatened extermination of religion in
the country. In the old manor-house at Cottam, and in the
lordly tower at Hoghton, the newly erected seat of their common
friend, Thomas Hoghton, they reviewed the process by which the
nation was being robbed of its birthright, and discussed pro-
posals for averting so disastrous an event. It was there that
Vivian Haydock was inspired with the determination to resign
his worldly position, as soon as his eldest son William should be
old enough to take his place, and to devote the remainder of his
life and energies to the preservation of the Church in England.
In the year 1568, the council, alarmed at the steadfast refusal of
the people of Lancashire to embrace the new religion, sent down
the Dean of St. Paul's to preach in the county, and ordered
Downham, the bishop of Chester, to make a visitation of his
diocese. Their message of peace was accompanied by all the
terrors of the penal laws, and a number of the leading gentry
were summoned to appear before the Earl of Derby, and other
ecclesiastical inquistors, at Lathom. The most "obstinate" of
these gentlemen were then sent to Chester to be kept under surveillance by its Christian bishop. Amongst them was John
Westby of Mowbreck Hall, on whom, the bishop writes to Cecil

under date Nov. 1, 1568, no impression could be made (*Dom. Eliz.* vol. xlviii. 36). The stringent measures now enforced by the Lancashire ecclesiastical inquisitors, the Bishop of Chester, and Bishop Young, the lord president of the North, made it clear that it would be almost impossible for prominent men to preserve their conscience and observe their religion in their native country. Under these circumstances, Vivian Haydock advised his friend, Thomas Hoghton, to withdraw to the Continent as he himself intended. In 1569, Hoghton secretly sailed for Antwerp, from his seat by the Ribble, called The Lea, a short distance from Cottam Hall. This hamlet or manor was anciently divided into English and French Lea, the Hoghtons being lords of the former, and the Haydocks of the latter. Thomas Hoghton's half-sister Bryde, daughter of Sir Richard Hoghton by his third wife, Elizabeth, daughter of a gentleman of Balderstone, John Gregson (whose family name was really Normanton' of Normanton, Co. York), became the wife of Vivian Haydock's eldest son William. The story of Hoghton's departure from Merry England is told in an ancient ballad formerly sung in Lancashire, which shall be introduced with the following prelude:

### The Three Weavers of Hoghton Bottoms.

> Backards and forards th'weyver flings
> Oo's shottle atween th' parted strings ;
> Troddle and sley keep o at wark,
> Reeds, healds, an' cogs, weft an' warp.

At the foot of the isolated hill rising above Hoghton Bottoms stood the ancient manor-house of the Hoghtons, partially dismantled of its timbers, and stript of its quondam grandeur ; for the lord of Hoghton had recently replaced it by the imposing building which still rears its majestic towers on the summit of Hoghton hill.

> " E'er since the Hoghtons from this hill took name,
> Who with the stiff, unbridled Saxons came"

are lines in the poetic address with which James the First was welcomed on his visit to Hoghton Tower in 1617.

The Tower was erected by Thomas Hoghton between the years 1563 and 1565, and the festivities at its formal opening in the latter year were graced by the presence of the future cardinal William Allen. A voice, which for twenty years had been silent sommoned the guests to solemn mass in the domestic chapel. It was the knell from the suppressed chantry of Ashton-under-Lyne—the bell with the legend inscribed by its donor, Sir Thomas Assheton—*Benedicta sit Sancta Trinitas.* The manor of Ashton was a grant to Sir John de Assheton, in 1412, from the Benedictine Bishop of Durham, Thomas Langley ; and Thomas Hoghton's father, Sir Richard, married one of the co-heiresses of the Assheton family.

> " ' Come to thy God in Time,'
> Sad grew the boding chime ;
> ' Come to thy God at last,'
> Boomed heavy on the blast."
>
> *R. S. Hawker.*

·    ·    ·    ·    ·    ·

Again the bell is sleeping, for the penal laws of Elizabeth forbid the celebration of the ancient rites, and the lord of Hoghton is an exile for his faith in a foreign land.

Within the half-ruined manor-house at Hoghton Bottoms sit three weavers at their looms, in a large room at the basement, with a clay floor, and long low windows of many mullions on two sides of the chamber. Such is the dandy-shop of the brothers Anderton. They are bachelors and advanced in years, and, though their occupation is humble, their thrift has made them men of means. A much younger man sits pensively by the fire, resting his head on his hands ; he is their youngest brother, just returned from the Netherlands—Roger Anderton, late butler to the lord of Hoghton. He had accompanied his master into exile, and had remained to the last his faithful servant.

Merrily sing the weavers to the racket of their looms, each verse of their ballad concluding with the chorus—

> Nickety nackety,
> Mondy come Saturdy,
> Pickin, sley, and troddle,
> Thrutchin o' mi noddle.

As they finish, the distressed butler raises his head, and thus addresses his brothers, "Sitha! broder Jock, owd thi shottle, Huan, stop thi troddle, Jim, hark ye!" and starting from his seat, breaks forth into the following lament :—

### The Blessed Conscience.

> Apollo, wyth hys radiant beames,
>   Inflam'd ye ayr soe fayr,
> Phaëton wyth hys fierie teames
>   Ye heat of warrs dyd beare.
> Ye daye was hot, ye eyv'nynge coole,
>   And pleasures dyd abounde ;
> Medes, wyth manie a crystal poole,
>   Dyd yeelde a joyful sounde.
>
> Thys fragrant tyme to pleasures prest,
>   Myself for to solàce,
> I walkèd forthe, as I thought best,
>   Into a pryvate place.
> And as I wentt, myselfe alone,
>   Ther cam to my presence
> A frende, who sem'd to mak grate moane,
>   And sayde, "Goe, gett yo hence."
>
> "Alas ! gode syr, what ys ye cause
>   Yo thys have sayde to mee ?"

" Indede," he sayde, " ye Prynce's lawes
   Wyl beare noe more wyth thee :
For Bysshopp Yonge wyl sumon thee,
   You must to hys prèsence.;
For yn thys londe yo canot lyve
   And kepe yor conscyènce."

" I am told I must not ryde,
   What ys my best to doe ? "
" Gode syr, here yo must not abyde,
   Unless to churche yo goe :
Or else to Preston yo must wende,
   For here ys no resydènce ;
For yn thys londe yo hav noe frende
   To kepe yor conscyènce."

Then dyd I thynke ytt was ye best
   For mee yn tyme provyde :
For Bysshopp Yonge wulde mee molesta,
   Yf here I shoulde abyde.
Then dyd I cause my men prepare,
   A shipp for my defence ;
For yn thys londe I culde not fare
   And kepe my conscyènce.

When my shipp that ytt was hired,
   My men retorn'd agayne ;
Ye tyme was almost ful expired,
   That here I shulde remayne ;
To Preston town I shulde hav gone
   To mak recognyzance ;
For other helpps perceyved I none,
   But kepe my conscyènce.

To lovelie Lea then I mee hied,
   And Hoghton bade fayrwell :
Ytt was more tyme for mee to ryde,
   Than longer ther to dwel.
I durst not trustt my dearest frende,
   Butt secretlie stole hence,
To take ye fortune God shulde sende,
   And kepe my conscyènce.

When to ye sea I came untyl
  And passed by ye Gate,
My cattle all, wyth belloes shryl,
  As yf thei mourn'd my fate,
Did lepe and roar, as if thei wulde
  Understonde my dyligence :
It seem'd my cause thei understode
  Thro' God's gode provydence.

At Hoghton hygh, which is a bower
  Of sports and lordly pleasure,
I wept, and lefte that loftie tower
  Wich was my chiefest treasure.
To save my soul and lose ye reste,
  Yt was my trew pretence :
Lyke fryghted bird, I lefte my neste
  To kepe my conscyènce.

Thus took I ther my leave, alas !
  And rode to ye sea-syde ;
Ynto ye shipp I hied apace,
  Wich dyd for mee abyde.
With syghs I sail'd from merrie Englande,
  I asked of none lycènce :
Wherfor my estate fell from my hande,
  And was forfeitt to my Prynce.

Thus merrie England hav I lefte,
  And cutt ye raging sea,
Wheroff ye waves hav mee bereft
  Of my soe deare coontrie.
Wyth sturdie storms and blustring blast
  We were yn grate suspense ;
Ful sixteen dayes and nyghts thei last,
  And all for my conscyènce.

When on ye shore I was arrived,
  Thro' Fraunce I toke my waye,
And unto Antwerpe I mee hied,
  Yn hope to make my staye.

When to ye citie I dyd come,
  I thought that my absence
Woulde to my men be cumbersome,
  Tho' thei made no offence.

Att Hoghton, where I used to reste,
  Of men I hadd great store,
Ful twentie gentlemen att least,
  Of yeomen gode threescore.
And of them all, I brought but twoe
  Wyth mee, when I cam thence.
I lefte them all ye worlde knows how
  To kepe my conscyènce !

But when my men cam to mee still,
  Lord ! how rejoycèd I,
To see them wyth so gode a wyll
  To leave theyr own coontrie ?
Both friends and kyn thei dyd forsake,
  And all for my presènce ;
Alyv or dead, amends I'll make,
  And gyve them recompence.

But fortune hadd mee soe berefte,
  Of all my godes and landes,
That for my men was nothing lefte
  But att my brethren's handes.
Then dyd I thinke ye trewthe to prove
  Whilst I was in absence,
That I might trie theyr constant love
  And kepe my conscyènce

When to my brethren I hadd sent,
  Ye welcome that thei made
Was false reports mee to present,
  Wych made my conscyence sad.
My brethren all dyd thus me cross,
  And lyttle regard my fall,
Save onlie one—that rued my loss—
  That is Richard, of Parke Hall,

He was ye comforte that I hadd ;
 I proved hys dyligence ;
He was as just, as thei were badd,
 Wych cheer'd my conscyènce.
When thys report of them I heard,
 My heart was sore wyth greefe,
Yn that my purpose was soe marr'd
 My men should want reliefe.

Gode cause I hadd to love my men,
 And them to recompence ;
Theyr lyves thei ventured, I know when,
 And lefte theyr deare parents.
Then to come home straightwaye I meant,
 My men for to relieve ;
My brethren sought thys to prevent,
 And summs of golde dyd gyve.

A thousande marks thei offered then,
 To hynder my lycènse ;
That I should not come home agayne,
 To kepe my conscyènce.
But if that day I once hadd seen,
 My landes to hav agayne,
And that my Prynce had changèd been
 I wulde not mee hav stay'n.

I shulde my men soe wel hav payde,
 Thro' God's gode provydence,
That thei should ne'er hav bene afrayde
 To lose theyr due expense.
Lovlie Lea and Hoghton Tower
 Shulde open be to all ;
Itt shulde be my pride and power,
 Myselfe theyr hoste to call.

But nowe my lyfe ys att an ende,
 And death ys att ye dore,
That gryslie ghost hys bowe doth bende,
 And thro' my bodie gore ;

Wych nature nowe must yielde to claye,
  And death wyl take mee hence ;
And nowe I shal goe wher I may
  Enjoy my conscyènce.

Fayr Englande ! nowe ten tymes adieu.
  And frendes that theryn dwel;
Fayrwel, my broder Richard trewe,
  Whom I dyd love soe wel.
Fayrwel, fayrwel ! gode people all,
  And learne experience ;
Love not too much ye golden ball,
  But kepe your conscyènce !

All yo who nowe thys songe shal heare,
  Helpp mee for to bewayl,
Ye wyght, who scarcelie hadd hys peere,
  Tyll death dyd hym assayl.
Hys life a myrour was to all,
  Hys death wythout offence ;
Confessor, then, lett us hym call,
  O blessed conscyènce !

## ﬄalgrí le ﬄort.

  " Fayr Englande ! nowe ten tymes adieu,
    And frendes that theryn dwel ;
  Fayrwel, my broder Richard trewe,
    Whom I dyd love soe wel "

                        *Hoghton Ballad.*

The lord of Hoghton's faithful brother, Richard, of Park Hall,
in Charnock Richard, was the son of Sir Richard Hoghton by
his fourth wife, Anne, daughter of Roger Browne, though he was
born out of wedlock.  He founded the family of Hoghton of
Park Hall, where his descendants resided till the family assumed
the name of Dalton.  Richard's great grandson, William Hogh-

ton, married one of the two daughters and co-heiresses of Robert Dalton, of Thurnham Hall, and his son, John Hoghton, removed to Thurnham upon the death of Robert Dalton in 1703, and about 1710 adopted the name and arms of Dalton. True to the faith to the last, the family became extinct on the death of Miss Dalton in 1861, and the estates are now enjoyed by Sir Gerald Dalton-Fitzgerald, Bart.

Richard Hoghton managed the exile's estates, and his love for his brother is shown in the journey he made to Antwerp to comfort and advise him. The original royal license for this journey is dated March 17, 1576. From this document, bearing the, signature of Elizabeth herself, and that of her secretary, Windebank, it appears that Richard Hoghton secured the assistance of John Fleetwood, of Calwich, in Staffordshire, a staunch Catholic, as, indeed, was every one of his descendants, to use his influence with his nephew, William Fleetwood, the Recorder of London, to obtain the Queen's permission for the faithful brother " to departe out of this or Realme of Englande, unto the parts beyonde the seas unto the Towne of Antwerpe, and there to remayne the space of two monethes next after his departure from heare ; To the intent to advise, persuade, and counsell Thomas Houghton, late of Houghton, in the countie of Lancaster, esquire (who, as we are informed, by occasion of synister and evill counsell, is departed out of this or Realme, without our Lycence), to retorne unto this our Realme, and to submitt hymselfe unto us and or Lawes, according to the dewtye of a good subject. Forasmuch as the said John Fleetwood and William Fleetwood standt bound unto us for and with the said Richard Houghton in the some of two hundreth poundes of Lawfull money of Englande that he, the saide Richard Houghton, within two monethes next after his departure forthe of this or Realme, shall retorne unto the same agayne (yf God spare hym lyffe). And that, in the meane tyme, the said Richard shall not doe, or attempt any Acte or thinge, Acts or things against us or our Realme." The license further permits him to be attended by one servant, and to take with him £20 for his expenses.

The lord of Hoghton has himself explained why he could not return—

> " For yn thys londe I could not fare,
> And kepe my conscyence."

He died at Liége, and was buried in .the church of S. Gervais, where a handsome monument was erected to his memory, bearing the following inscription, surmounted by the arms of the Hoghtons, quartered with those of Assheton, and the appropriate motto of the family—*Malgré le Tort*:—

" Hic e regione sepultus est vir Illustris D. Thomas Houghton, Anglus, qui post decem an. exiliū spontaneum variasque patrimonii et rerum oium direptiones propter Cath. fidei confessionem a sectariis illatas, obijt 4 Non. Jun. 1580. Ætat. 63."

In the archives of the See of Westminster is an original holograph by Cardinal Allen, dated June 25, 1580, stating that £100, deposited in his hands by the executors of Thomas Hoghton, " of godly memory," was left by the exile " to bye a payre of organs, one fayr table, and as many bookes of musick as should cost 7li., which he appoynted to be given to the churche of Preston, when the time should serve." In accordance with the donor's wishes, Cardinal Allen consented to receive the money, and to use it in the English College then at Rheims, for the benefit of the poor students under his government, " so long as this present schisme of our coontry of England dureth by Goddes sufferance ; with this intention, to employ the same summe wholy, when God shall have mercy on our coontrey, and restore the same to the Catholike faith and service, upon a payre of organs, one table, and certayne singing bookes, in the parish churche of Preston according to the trewe meaning of Mr. Hoghton, and the pourport of the forsayde article subscribed with his hand."

By his wife, Catherine, daughter of Sir Thomas Gerard, of Bryn, Thomas Hoghton had a son and namesake, whose history

B

is as sad as his own, and a daughter, Jane, his ultimate heiress, who became the wife of James Bradshaigh, of The Haigh, Esq. Mr. Bradshaigh's son, Roger, was the father of five eminent priests—three Jesuits and two seculars.    His eldest son and heir, James, a remarkably learned and pious man, unhappily died in the minority of his son, who was taken in ward by the Earl of Derby, and brought up a Protestant ; and thus one of the finest Catholic families was robbed of its faith.    Sir Roger Bradshaigh was the first Protestant who possessed Haigh Hall, which is now the residence of his representative in the female line, the Earl of Crawford and Balcarres.

Thomas Hoghton, the exile's son, was entrusted to Dr. Allen's care at Douay Collage.    On March 13, 1577, the diary says : " Mr. Allen set out to Louvain ; with him went Mr. Otway, who came to us a little while ago with the express purpose of conducting young Thomas Hoghton, a student here, into Brabant, to his very illustrious father, Mr. Hoghton." Elsewhere the diary records that he had matriculated in the University of Douay, but does not mention the date of his ordination.    His priesthood debarred him from his rightful inheritance, and as soon as he arrived in Lancashire, he was thrown into Salford gaol. There his name appears in the list of priests returned to the Council by Edmund Trafford and Robert Worsley on April 13, 1582. He was one of those who " do still contynue in their obstinate opynions, neyther do wee see anye likelyhoode of conformytie in any of them." (" P.R.O., Dom. Eliz.," Vol. cliii., No. 6.)    His name continues in the lists of recusants at Salford until January 23, 1584. after which it is lost sight of, and, in all probability, he went to swell the great band of confessors of the faith who perished in prison unrecorded.

Faithful Richard, of Park Hall, who seems at this time to have resided at the Tower, was arrested by Edmund Trafford immediately after Fr. Campion's apprehension, in the summer of 1581. The Council ordered that he and his wife, Mary, daughter of

Ralph Rishton, of Pontalgh Hall, Esq., sister of the priest, Edward Rishton, then prisoner in the Tower of London, be re-examined touching Campion's being at Hoghton Tower, with Ralph Emerson, his man, and his books ; also touching the books sent down by Rishton, and dispersed in Lancashire. It appears from a note in the Council-book (1581, p. 499) that a number of papers were seized in the search at Hoghton Tower. Though Mr. Hoghton survived this imprisonment, he was pursued with relentless persecution to the end of his life. In October, 1592, a report was sent to Lord Burghley that "Mr. Richarde Hoghton, of the Park Hall, hath kepte a Recusante scholmaster I thincke this twentie years. He hath had one after another, the name of one was Scholes, of the other Fawcett, as I remember, but I stande in doubte of the names." ("P.R.O., Dom. Eliz," Vol. ccxliii., No. 52.) His second wife was Catherine, daughter of George Rogerlye, of Park Hall, in Blackrod, Esq., by Margaret, daughter of William Skillicorne, of Prees Hall, Esq. She was the widow of Richard Tyldesley, of Garret Hall, Esq., and after Richard Hoghton's death, which is supposed to have occurred about 1623, she married, thirdly, John Osbaldeston, of Sunderland Hall, Esq., who died in 1629.

## The Fight at Lea Hall.

"Clubs, bills, and partisans ! strike !
beat them down !
Down with the Capulets ! down with the Montagues."

*Romeo and Juliet*

On the death of Thomas Hoghton, in 1580, his brother Alexander became the head of the family. He resided chiefly at The Lea, or Lea Hall, where he secretly maintained a priest to serve the domestic chapel and to attend to the spiritual wants of the neighbourhood. He did not long enjoy his heritage, for he died in Aug., 1581, and Thomas Hoghton, the younger, was the next possessor of the estates. At this period it was no uncommon custom in Lancashire to christen two brothers by the same name. He was half-brother to the exile, being the son of Sir Richard by his second wife.

This unfortunate lord of Hoghton was slain in a feud with Thomas Langton, baron of Newton, who was joined by Thomas Singleton, Esq., of Broughton Tower, a semi-fortified mansion situated within a few miles of Lea. The dispute was nominally over kine claimed by the widow Thomazene Singleton, of Stay- ning Grange. At the hour of midnight, on Nov. 20, 1589, the baron at the head of a large body of retainers, armed with "long picks, gunnes, long staves, welshe-hooks upon long staves, swords and dagges, bows and arrows and bills," attacked Thomas Hoghton at The Lea. "The crow is white !" was the watchword of the Langtons, as the lord of Hoghton with thirty men sallied forth from the gate-house in front of the hall to the cry of "Black-Black !" A bloody fray ensued, within sixty yards of the ancient manor-house, in which Thomas Hoghton was slain and the baron sore wounded. In consideration of this affair, Langton is said to have been forced to cede his manor of Walton-le-dale to the Hoghton family.

Thomas Hoghton's untimely death was a lasting misfortune to his decendants, for his son and heir, then but a minor, was given in ward to Sir Gilbert Gerard, Master of the Rolls, who married him to his daughter, whilst still under age, and brought him up a Protestant. *Malgrè le Tort !* the bell of Hoghton Tower may yet send forth a joyous peal.

His widow, the daughter of Henry Keighley, of Keighley, co. York, and Inskip Hall, co. Lancaster, Esq., (ancestor in the female line of the Dukes of Devonshire, who inherited the Keighley estates), was thus reported to the government in Oct., 1592, "Mrs. Hoghton, of the Lea, hathe kepte sithsince the deathe of her husbande one Richarde Blundell, Brother to

William Blundell, of Crosbie, armigr. who is an obstinate,
Papiste well acquainted with a number of Seminaries, and he
teacheth her children to singe and plaie upon the virginalls "
(" P.R.O. Dom. Eliz., vol ccxliii., No. 52). Her younger children
were thus all brought up Catholics, her second son William
being the founder of the Hoghtons of Grimsargh Hall. We shall
have to refer hereafter to her fourth son, Adam, in the tradition
of the Dun Cow Rib. Mrs. Hoghton subsequently became the
wife of Sir Richard Sherburne, of Stonyhurst, but died at The
Lea, Oct. 30, 1609, aged 60.

## 𝕿𝖍𝖊 𝕱𝖚𝖌𝖎𝖙𝖎𝖇𝖊.

" Though far from Albion's craggy shore,
    Divided by the dark blue main ;
A few brief rolling seasons o'er,
    Perchance I view her cliffs again."

*Byron.*

Some three years after Thomas Hoghton left England, Vivian
Haydock, accompanied by his son Richard, if not also by his
youngest son George, passed over to Douay, in 1573, and joined
Dr. Allen in his recently established college, Within two years,
having matriculated in the University of Douay, he was ordained
priest, and on Nov. 21. 1575, he set out from the college to risk
his life on the English mission. The strict watch kept by the
English Government was probably the cause of the temporary
postponement of his passage across the channel, for in the following February he was again at Douay for a few days. The high
opinion held by Dr. Allen, and all the professors at Douay, of
Vivian Haydock's prudence, integrity, and experience, induced
his appointment as procurator for the college in England, an
office which he undertook in 1581 to the general satisfaction of
the clergy. The Privy Council was aware of this, and made

great exertions to capture him. The examination of Jervais Pierpoint (" P.R.O., Dom. Eliz.," Vol. clxvii., No. 59. Jan. (?) 1584), refers to his having received £120 from Vivian Haydock, at Mr. Lauckland's in Derbyshire, for the seminary at Rheims.

It was here that Vivian Haydock met Fr. Edmund Campion, the martyr. The celebrated Jesuit, Mr. Simpson tells us, had been conducted by Gervase Pierrepoint to the house of his brother Henry Pierrepoint, of Holme Pierrepoint and Thoresby, in Nottinghamshire, ancestor of the Earls of Kingston. There he had remained till the Tuesday after Twelfth-day, 1581, when he and his guide left, and proceeded to Derbyshire, to the houses of Henry Sacheverell, Mr. Langford, Lady Foljambe, of Walton, and Mr. Powdrell. Fr. Campion then went into Yorkshire, and thence was conducted by Mr. More to Lancashire, where he visited the Worthingtons, of Blainscough Hall ; the Talbots, of Salesbury Hall; the Southworths, of Samlesbury Hall ; the Heskeths, of The Maynes; Mrs. Allen of Rossall Grange; the Hoghtons, at Lea Hall and Hoghton ; the Westbys, of Mowbreck Hall; the Rigmaydens, of Wedacre Hall ; and probably the Haydocks, at Cottam. At these houses he spent the time between Easter and Whitsuntide (Apr. 16), bestowing himself chiefly, according to Lord Burghley, at Mr. Talbot's and Mr. Southworth's, but according to Fr. Persons, at Thomas Worthington's and the house of his mother-in-law, Mrs. Allen, where he was fully occupied in preaching to the crowds that pressed to have conference with him. "Even up to my time' (1660), says Fr. Henry More in his history, "Campion's memory was popular in the North, where they still recollected his sermons on the Hail Mary, on the Ten Lepers, on the King who went a journey, on the Last Judgment, and others, which people were so greedy of hearing that very many persons of quality spent whole nights in neighbouring barns, so that they might be early at the place next day. They were drawn, not so much by his admirable eloquence and accent, as by his fire, and by a certain hidden force which they considered could only flow from the Holy Spirit."

"Hys native flowres were myxte with hearbe of grace,
His mylde behaveour tempered well wyth skyll ;
A lowlye mynde possest a learned place.
A sugred speache, a rare and vertuous wyll.
A saynt lyke mĒ was sett in earth belowe
The seede of trewth yn hearyng harts to sowe."

*Walpole's Epitaph on Campion.*

He preached daily except when he sometimes withdrew him-self to write his book, *De Hæresi Desperata* (which afterwards appeared as his *Decem Rationes*), and perhaps to avoid the pur-suivants, who were always on his tract. At Blainscough Hall he was saved from apprehension by a maid-servant, who in affected anger pushed him into a pond, and thus effectually disguised him, as the Abbé Dubois once disguised the Regent Orleans at a low masquerade by kicking him ; a process which made the regent angrily exclaim, *"Abbé, tu me déguises trop."*

It is not to be supposed, as Mr. Simpson remarks, that the excitement caused by the Jesuit's preaching escaped the notice of the Government. It induced them to use greater severity to the Catholics in prison, and to search with greater strictness for those not yet apprehended. A few months later, Campion was arrested, and the Earl of Derby apprehended Sir John South-worth, of Samlesbury Hall, his son-in-law, Bartholomew Hesketh, of Aughton (whose half-sister, Jane, was the wife of Alexander Hoghton, of Hoghton Tower and Lea Hall) ; William Hesketh of The Maynes (Cardinal Allen's brother-in-law); John Westby, of Mowbreck (son-in-law to Sir John Southworth and brother-in-law to Vivian Haydock) ; and Richard Hoghton, of Park Hall. Thus Vivian Haydock was hunted from place to place, and at length the constitution of the old man gave way, and whilst staying at Mowbreck Hall, he received a shock which speedily laid him in his grave.

## Allhallowe'en.

"If you for me now do not pray,
The utmost farthing I must pay :
The time is hid, when I'll be rid,
Haste then to pity me."

*Haydock's Hymn for All Souls.*

On the mystic evening of the last day of October, All Hallows' Eve, it was an ancient belief that supernatural influence prevailed, and spirits, visible and invisible, revisited the scenes of their earthly existence. From Layton Hill to Pendle, Parlick Pike and Beacon Fell, brightly shone the *Tien-lowe*, the "sacred fire" of the Druids. On every hill throughout the Fylde, men stood in circles, raising aloft platted wisps of blazing straw on forks, to ward off the *bar-gheist*, or boggart. But in Catholic times the custom was observed with different meaning ; it was to beg intercession for the souls of the faithful departed— the "mournful fire," reminding the faithful to pray for the souls in purgatory.

On this evening also were baked the *Somas cakes*—oatmeal cakes of small size—in preparation for distribution to the children who went from house to house on All Souls Day. These cakes are said to have been made by the Jews in honour of the Queen of Heaven. In Christian times *somas* was understood to be intended for "souls mass," but the origin of the custom dates from early English times, and probably the word derived from *seoma*, meaning fetters or restraint, the cakes being an offering to propitiate the wandering spirits. Thus this signification was readily applied to purgatory by the early English Christians.

In the days of persecution Catholics took advantage of this celebration, which was carried on to a late hour, to secretly assemble in their chapels at midnight, without suspicion, in readiness to hear Mass on the feast of All-hallows.

Tradition attributes to this evening the scene of the tragic death of Vivian Haydock, and the legend is still preserved in the Fylde under the title of—

## The Gory Head of Mowbreck Hall.

" A horrid spectre rises to my sight,
  Close by my side, and plain and palpable,
  In all good seeming and close circumstance,
  As man meets man."

*Ethurwald.*

On the hallowe'en preceding the arrest of his son George, Vivian Haydock stood, robed in his vestments, at the foot of the altar in the domestic chapel at Mowbreck, awaiting the clock to strike twelve. As the bell tolled the hour of midnight, the "fugitive" beheld the decapitated head of his favourite son slowly rising above the altar, whose blood-stained lips seemed to repeat those memorable words, *Tristitia vestra vertetur in gaudium.* Swooning at the horrible apparition, the old man was carried to his secret chamber; and when the little children called on All Souls for their somas cakes, to their customary acknowledgment of "Pray God be merciful to the suffering souls in purgatory," they added—"God be merciful to the soul of Vivian Haydock." His body was borne to its last resting-place, and laid beneath the chapel at Cottam Hall by his son, Dr. Richard Haydock.

## The Douay Collegian.

" O faith, thou wonder-working principle,
  Eternal substance of our present hope,
  Thou evidence of things invisible !
  What cannot man sustain sustain'd by thee ? "

*H. More's Daniel.*

The martyr, George Haydock, to whom the premonitory apparition in the foregoing legend refers, probably accompanied his father to Douay in 1573, but seems to have returned to England for a short time on account of his health, for in June, 1577, we learn from the diary that he was readmitted into the college. In 1578 he was sent with others to colonise the English college at Rome, and was present at its formal erection, April 23, 1579. At Rome he was ordained deacon, but his health giving way under the heat of the climate, it was thought advisable that he should return to Rheims to be ordained priest. Before leaving the Eternal City he went to kiss the feet of the pontiff, who received him graciously, wished him God speed in his mission, and supplied him with the necessary funds for his journey. This was in Sept., 1581, and, on Nov. 2, he arrived at Rheims. On Dec. 21, he was ordained priest, and on Jan. 4, 1582, he celebrated his first Mass. Twelve days later he left the college for the English mission.

> " He came by vow. The cawse, to conquyre synne.
>     His armour, praier. The word his terdge and shielde.
>   His cumfort heaven, his spoile our sowles to wynne.
>     The devyll his foe, the wicked worlde his fielde.
>   His triumphe joy. His wage aeternall blysse.
>     His capteine Christe, wich ever durying ys."
>
> *Fr. Henry Walpole's Epitaph on Campion.*

He had scarcely arrived in London when he was betrayed by an old acquaintance into the hands of the pursuivants. This man, Hankinson, was the son of one of Vivian Haydock's tenants at Hollowforth or Lea, and, being of an unsettled disposition, had proceeded to London, where he had rendered assistance to the squire's son on the occasion of his return to Douay. In the meantime, Hankinson had become a pervert, and not suspecting the change, the martyr made straight for his house, and told him all about himself and his intentions. The traitor at once made secret arrangement with Norris and Slade, two pursuivants of the very worst stamp, that they should lie in wait near his house in St. Paul's churchyard, and seize the young

priest as he came out. With this they readily complied, on
Feb. 6, 1582, and carried their prisoner into the cathedral, where
one of the Calvinist ministers conferred with him, and offered
him liberty without further trouble if he would conform to their
new religion.

> " Religion there was treason to the quene,
> Preachyng of penaunce warre agaynst the land,
> Priests were such dayngerouse men, as hath not bene,
> Praiers and beedes were fyght and force of hand.
> Cases of cõscience bane unto the state,
> So blynde ys errour, so false a wittnes hate."
>
> *Fr. H. Walpole's Epitaph on Campion.*

In consequence of Mr. Haydock's steadfast refusal to entertain
anything approaching abjuration of his faith, he was led to a
restaurant or inn, wherein he had been accustomed to take his
meals. There they met with another priest, Arthur Pitts, dining
with Mr. William Jenison, a law-student. The former was instantly recognised by Slade, for he had been a student with him
at the English college at Rome—the one studying letters, and
the other deceit. They were all three led off to appear before
Popham, the queen's attorney ; but in the meantime, whilst awaiting his arrival, they were surrounded by a concourse of Templars
studying the law in that college, and a keen dispute was carried
on for nearly an hour on the subject of religion. At length, on
Popham's appearance, the prisoners underwent their examination, of which Mr. Haydock has left a circumstantial account as
regards his own in a letter to a fellow-prisoner. He was then
conveyed to the Gatehouse for the night, and on the morrow to
the Star Chamber, to appear before Cecil, the high treasurer
who committed him to the Tower with Mr. Pitts, where they
were received by Sir William George, then in command of the
gate-wardens. This ruffian heaped every kind of abuse upon
the defenceless prisoners, passing Mr. Haydock at length to the
mercy of a man who proved himself to be still more depraved.

It appears that on his arrest, Norris offered to release the young priest if he would give him some pieces of gold. Inexperienced in the artifices of such men, Mr. Haydock drew forth his purse and paid the pursuivant what he demanded. But the scoundrel, perceiving that he had a considerable sum left, set his mind upon the remainder, and refused to keep his plighted word. He then listened attentively at the examinations to learn to what prison the priest should be consigned, and going by a short cut to the lieutenant of the Tower, Sir Owen Hopton, advised him of the gold remaining on Mr. Haydock's person, in the hope that he might be allowed some share of the plunder. Hopton, therefore, consigned his prisoner to a remote dungeon, and forbade all access to him, so that the robbery might not become known. Thus for fifteen months Mr. Haydock was detained in a most wretched condition, seeing no one but his gaoler, except on one occasion when a priest contrived to get into his cell and to fortify him with the Holy Eucharist.

Shortly before his martyrdom he was removed to another cell, where access to him was occasionally permitted, and he was enabled secretly to receive the sacraments. Those who saw him were greatly edified by his humility and patience, for besides the inflictions of his prison, he was suffering from a return of the lingering disease contracted in Italy, which grievously tormented him by day and night, frequently causing violent cramps of an hour's duration in his stomach and limbs.

At length, on Jan. 18, 1584, he was brought before the recorder of London, Sir William Fleetwood, who received him with most outrageous language, unfit for publication, and allowed his fury to attain such a pitch as to stretch forth his fist to strike the poor young priest, whose only remark was—" Use your might, for in behalf of the Catholic faith I will cheerfully suffer anything."

> " The martyr smil'd beneath avenging power,
> And braved the tyrant in his torturing hour !"
>
> *T. Campbell, Pleasures of Hope.*

His constancy being apparent, it was resolved to make away with him, and accordingly those murderous questions were put —what he thought of the Pope, and what of the Queen—what authority ought, in his opinion, to be granted to the one, and what to the other? To this the martyr courageously answered in well-chosen words, that the Roman Pontiff possessed supreme and full power of ruling the universal church of Christ upon earth, and that the Queen was incompetent to hold this priestly dignity and authority, nor could that holy office be filled by a woman. This was enough, but to render him more odious to her majesty and the council, he was pressed till he reluctantly consented (as he himself afterwards frankly confessed) to declare that the Queen was a heretic, and, without repentance, was in danger of being eternally lost. Then in triumph he was committed, the day being the feast of St. Peter's Chair. The thought that he should be doomed for maintaining the authority of the chair on this very day was a source of great satisfaction to the martyr.

> " Remember you that wulde oppresse the cawse,
>    The churche ys Christe's, his honour can not dye,
> Thowgh hell it selfe wreste her gryslye iawes,
>    And ioyne yn leage wyth schisme and hæresie,
> Thowgh crafte devise and cruell rage oppresse,
>    Yet skyle wyll wryte, and martyrdome confesse."
>
> *Fr. H. Walpole's Epitaph on Campion.*

## The Plunder of Rossall Grange.

" Homo homine lupus."
*Fleetwood Motto.*

The extraordinary exhibition of animosity displayed by the recorder, Sir William Fleetwood, on the occasion of George Haydock's commitment, may undoubtedly be accounted for to some extent, from the fact of his being own cousin to Edmund Fleet-

wood, son of Thomas Fleetwood, of Vach, Co. Bucks, who was
at that very time endeavouring to encompass the Allens and
their relatives in the meshes of the penal laws in order to obtain
possession of their estate at Rossall, of which his father had purchased the reversion.  Rossall had formerly been a grange belonging to the suppressed abbey of Dieulacres, and from an
early period it had been held under·long leases by the Allen
family, one of whom had been abbot of that monastery.  On
March 13, 1553, Edward VI. granted Rossall to Thomas Fleetwood, subject to the unexpired lease of the Allens, which had
still many years to run at the time of its seizure.  George Haydock's widowed aunt, Mrs. Allen, the Cardinal's sister-in-law,
was then residing at the Grange with her daughters.  On the
very day the martyr suffered, the mansion was entered and
plundered by Edmund Trafford, of Trafford, sheriff of the
county of Lancaster, acting in collusion with Edmund Fleetwood.  Finding the portrait of the eminent Cardinal hanging on
the wall in the dining-hall, the intruders hurled innumerable
revilings and bloodthirsty speeches against him, and defacing
his portrait with their knives and daggers, finally threw it down
upon the floor and trampled it under foot.  Fleetwood then took
possession of the estate, and over the entrance to Rossall Grange
set up the wolf, in place of the three conies, with the ominous
motto of the Fleetwoods—*Homo Homine Lupus.*

This robbery was confirmed by a most scandalously conducted trial at Manchester, a mere mockery of the law, at which
Fleetwood himself was appointed foreman of the packed jury
by the iniquitous Trafford in virtue of his office of sheriff.

## 𝔑oᵐ, 𝔱𝔥𝔲𝔰 !

"And now behold how hunger haunts with cheeks both pale and leane,
This bloudy butcher furious Mars, and all his wicked traine;
And greedy spoile, spares not to spill, to pray on others good,
Ravening Rape with maid and wife runs headlong to the wood."

*Robinson's Verses upon Sir Edmond Trafford.*

Fifty years before, William Trafford, Abbot of Salley, stood side by side in the dock at Lancaster with William Haydock, monk of Whalley. Now the Trafford flail reverses. Dr. Bridgewater, in his *Concertatio*, graphically describes the thrasher. Sir Edmund Trafford, he tells us, was selected by the council as sheriff of the county because he was so thoroughly imbued with the perfidy of Calvin, and the frenzy of Beza, that it might be said he was merely waiting for this very opportunity systematically to pursue with insults and to despoil of their property all those who remained staunch to the ancient faith. For the furious hate of this inhuman wretch was all the more fiercely stirred by the fact that he saw offered to him such a prospect of increasing his slender means out of the property of Catholics, and of adorning his house with various articles of furniture filched from their houses. For though, as far as his own fortune went, he could scarcely be called a gentleman, still with other people's gold, no matter how wrongfully come by, he might rightly be called and accounted a knight. This reward he eventually received at York, April 17, 1603; and as a second wife, Cecil, Lord Burghly, the arch-persecutor, gave him his daughter Mildred. It is significant that Sir Edmund's daughter Elizabeth married Richard Fleetwood of Penwortham.

Happily the flail took the opposite direction in the next generation with the return of Sir Cecil Trafford, knighted at Hoghton Tower, to the faith of his ancestors.

Shortly before the plunder of Rossall, Edmund Trafford went

on a similar errand to Blainscough Hall, the seat of Thomas Worthington, who had married the martyr's cousin, Mary Allen. About the same time he made a raid on Cottam Hall, the seat of William Haydock, the martyr's eldest brother, and there he seized their only sister, Aloysia Haydock, "a maiden truly worthy of the noble race of Haydock," says Dr. Bridgewater, "which has the glory of producing two confessors, the father and elder son, and one martyr, George Haydock, the younger son, all of them most holy priests of Christ." Poor girl! though subject to frequent epileptic fits, of which the robber was aware, and saw with his own eyes, she was hurried to Salford gaol for refusing to join him in his scurrilous abuse of Christ's Vicar. And her sorrow too was soon turned into eternal joy—*Tristitia vestra vertetur in gaudium.*

With this brave girl was sent to the same gaol Elizabeth Hankinson, the sister of the Iscariot who betrayed the martyr. It is curious to find in the records of the prison that at this very time it held so many relatives of the Allen and Haydock families—old Sir John Southworth, the brother-in-law of George Haydock's uncle John Westby, Thomas Woods, priest, and Thomas Hoghton, priest. The martyr's cousin, William Hesketh of Little Poulton Hall, whose mother was a Westby, was imprisoned in the Fleet, where the young priest had visited him on his arrival in London, and learned for the first time the intelligence of his father's sudden death at Mowbreck Hall. It was William Hesketh who married Cardinal Allen's sister Elizabeth, and it was in his name that an unsuccessful action was brought in the Duchy of Lancaster court by Bartholomew Hesketh, June 29, 1585, to recover some of the property seized at the plunder of Rossall Grange.

## The Martyrdom.

" The towre saies, the trewth he dyd defende,
   The barre beares wittnes of his gyltelesse mynde,
Tiburne doth tell, he made a pacient end,
   In everie gate his martyrdom we fynde,
   In vayne yoᵘ wroghte, that wuld obscure his name,
   For heaven and earthe wyll styll recorde the same."

*Fr. H Walpole, Epitaph on Campion.*

On the feast of the Epiphany, 1584, the day on which the
martyr had been apprehended two years before, he was brought
from the Tower to Westminster Hall. There he was arraigned
for high treason, with four other priests, and on the following
day, the feast of St. Dorothy, to whom he had a special devotion,
he was condemned. This coincidence he carefully noted in the
calendar of his breviary previous to presenting it to his fellow-
prisoner, the venerable archbishop of Armagh.

After receiving sentence of death for being a priest, the
martyr returned to his cell filled with a gladness beyond expression, and thanking God from his soul for granting him so great a
privilege. The description of his barbarous execution at Tyburn,
a few days later, Feb. 12, 1584, and the circumstances attending
it, will be found related in Bishop Challoner's "Memoirs of
Missionary Priests" with sufficient exactitude, and need not here
be repeated. One fact more, however, may be added with advantage.

## The Handwriting on the Prison Wall.

" The day shall come, a great and happy day,
   When vice shall yield its arbitrary sway."

*Bishop John Briggs, MS.*

Whilst all alone in his loathsome dungeon, and no admittance
being granted to anyone, the martyr took pleasure in drawing
the name and ensigns of the Roman pontiff with a꜀ piece of

chalk, and carving them with some sharp instrument, on the wall of the prison. Afterwards he added the following inscription, "Gregory XIII., on earth the supreme head of the whole Catholic Church," and though he was soundly rated for it by the warder, declined to efface it. Elsewhere he inscribed his family motto, and it is exceedingly curious that a hundred years later, Fr. Corker, O.S.B., relates in his "Remonstrance of Piety and Innocence," that the holy confessor, Fr. Thomas Jenison, S.J., relieved the weary hours of his imprisonment by extracting the following double chronogram (1686), out of this inscription, found in his cell at Newgate, apparently in the hope that the prophecy would be accomplished in the joyful restoration of re. ligion under the rule of the Catholic sovereign, James II.:—

tRIstItIa VestRa VertetVr In gaVDIVM aLLeLVIa, yoVr sorroVV shaL be MaDe Very JoyfVLL VNto yoV.

## The Skull at Mawdesley.

"Now no more shall pain or tears
    Crush his heart or bow his spirit ;
Now no more shall earthly fears
    Cloud the joys he doth inherit."

*Hymn to St. Francis of Assisi.*

It was probably the martyr's cousin, William Hesketh, discharged from the Fleet in 1582, who obtained possession of his head, which was religiously preserved by the family in the chapel at Cottam till the estate passed into other hands. The skull was then taken to Mawdesley, the seat of Thomas Finch, gentleman, who married one of the sisters of the last squire of Cottam. There, in its faded velvet bag, it still remains in the priest's hiding-place adjoining the chapel at the top of the house. This quaint old building has been the residence of the family for centuries. It was erected in the sixteenth century, and the family can point with pride to its martyr, John Finch, the layman executed at Lancaster, April 20, 1584. In the secluded burial-ground attached to the little chapel at Fernyhalgh, is a monument erected to the memory of the Reverend James Finch, the last of the English Carthusian monks, who died March 3, 1821, aged 72—

> " Good Christian, on this stone shed not a tear,
> For virtue lies entomb'd, enshrouded here."

## Parsons' Coachman.

> " Do not our great reformers use
> This Sidrophel to forbode news ?"
>
> *Butler.*

The martyr's elder brother Richard is frequently referred to in documents in the State Paper Office, and in the records of English Catholic affairs on the continent. He was born about 1552, and went to Douay College with his father Vivian Haydock, in 1573. Four years later he was ordained priest, and accompanied the professors and students when the college was transferred to Rheims in 1578. He was one of the first selected by Dr. Allen to commence the establishment of an English college at Rome. When Dr. Clenock's partiality for his Welsh countrymen created dissensions in the college, which terminated in its being placed under the direction of the Jesuits, Dr. Haydock was one of the most prominent actors. His name appears second in the list of those who took the college oath at its final settlement and formal opening, April 23, 1579. There he completed his studies and took his degree of D.D. On the following November 4, he left the college for the English mission, having previously been presented by Dr. Allen to his Holiness, who gave him his blessing and liberally provided him with funds for his dangerous journey. The English Government was shortly apprised, by one of its numerous spies on the continent, that

" Doctor Haddock with three other priests have passed this way."
In his letter, now amongst the state papers (*Dom. Elis.* cli. No.
74, 1581), the informer, in furtherance of his profession, pretended to have heard a report that Father Parsons' gold had
animated them to some villainous attempt against her Majesy's
person.    He cunningly added, " I cannott believe that suche
wickednes can be fostered in the spiritte of these youthes (for
they are yonge), notwithstanding be warie and very circumspect
that if this Haddock come to England you now non of yoᵗʰ
come into his company, for Parsons' wrath be devilishe and have
extravagant drifte and bad ends."

    In 1582 the council received another information (*Dom. Elis.*
vol. cliv. No. 76), "Richard Hadocke, preeste, who keepithe
wᵗʰ his brother at Cottam Hall, two myles from Preston in
Lankᵉ or with his Uncᶦ three miles from his brother's house.
His unckell's name is John Westbye, and the house where he
dwellethe is called Moorbrydge Hall in Lanckᵉ.    Dr. Allen is
unckell unto the said Hadocke and to George Hadocke prisoner
in the Tower."    It has already been said that the doctor's eldest
brother, William, married the daughter of Sir Richard Hoghton,
of Hoghton Tower.    He was a great sufferer for the faith, and
his name prominently figures in the records of the Lancashire
recusants.    In 1584, the year of so much trouble to his family,
he was one of those Lancashire gentlemen who had awarded to
them, in virtue of their recusancy, the exclusive privilege of fur-
nishing each a light horseman with accoutrements for the service
of her Majesty.    At a later period (*Dom. Elis.* vol. cclxvi., No. 80,
Feb. 1598), he was assessed £5 towards the expense of raising
troops for service in Ireland on the same account, and throughout his life he was subjected to all those cruel impositions and
penalties under the penal laws devised by a tyrannical government to stamp out the faith of the people and to establish a new
religion.    In an information about the keeping of schoolmasters
in Lancashire (*Dom. Elis.* vol. ccxliii., No. 52., Oct. 1592), the

following occurs, " Mr. Haddocke of Cottam, he is of Allens Kynrid, kepte a Recusante scholemaster many yeares whose name as of the others I can learne when I come into Lancashire."

According to the diary of the English college at Rome, Dr. Haydock at some period of his career in England suffered imprisonment for the faith. After ten years of missionary labour in England and Ireland, playing hide and seek with the pursuivants, the doctor returned to the continent and was invited to Rome by Cardinal Allen, who appointed him his domestic chaplain. This position he retained till the cardinal's death in 1594 when he was recommended for a benefice by the Spanish ambassador, El Duque de Sessa. He remained in Italy for some years, in close friendship with Fr. Persons, S.J., whose confidence he enjoyed. In 1595 the English government was informed by Thomas Wilson, one of its spies (*Dom. Eliz.* vol. ccli., No. 90), that two years before there had been a consultation at Rome between the Duke of Sissons, Ambassador of Spain, Cardinal Aldobrandini, Protector of England, the Jesuit General Aquaviva, Fr. Persons, Prefect of the English mission, S.J., and others, about the restoration of the hierarchy in England. The spy professed that Blackwell, the archpriest, was selected for the archbishopric of York, with an annual pension of 4,000 crowns from Spain; Dr. Haydock was to fill the princely See of Durham, and a third bishop was proposed for Carlisle, the two latter to have pensions of 2,000 crowns. The drift of the device was to stop the entrance of the King of Scots into England, and to form a strong party for the Infanta. But this, the spy added, was abandoned through the objections of an English priest, and some other plan proposed.

Another document in the Record Office (*Dom. Eliz.* vol. xxxiv. *Addenda.* n. 42, II, Oct. 1601) again reveals the attention paid by the spies to Dr. Haydock, who is represented to Cecil as " Parsons' coachman, for that he keepeth his coach and horses, and are at his sole command, but sayeth or may say, *Hos ego versiculos feci tulit alter honores.* For it is well known unto the world that Dr. Haddocks is not able to keep a coach and two horses at Rome, for it is very chargeable, and his living small, besides two men to attend him, but the poor scholars pay for all, and whereas the college formerly was well able to maintain seventy scholars, now it is not able to maintain fifty, although the living or revenues is rather increased than decreased ; only except that Parsons, in despite and revenge of the scholars, sold away a great vineyard, the goodliest in Rome, both in vines, walks, fruits, houses, waters, and other necessaries whatsoever, and a thousand crowns under the value as would have been given for the same. The said Mr. Doctor is president of the council at the college, and generally every afternoon do they sit to deliberate of all causes. The councillors' names are these following : Parsons, judge, Walpole, Stephens, Smythe, Owen, Dr. Haydock, Mr. Thomas Fitzherbert, Mr. Roger Baines, and Mr. Sweete, when he was there. When the case is litigious then Father Harrison is sent for to censure his opinion in the same. They cannot well agree among themselves who should be cardinal, some will have Fr. Parsons, Mr. Fitzherbert, Mr. Mumpsons, or Dr. Haddock, but the pope will take an order for making of English cardinals, for he is well persuaded of their sedition and ... tion bishoprics will not serve their turns, but must presently become cardinals."

Soon after this Dr. Haydock left Rome for Douay College, where he arrived Oct. 26th, 1602. He then proceeded to Lancashire, and thence, perhaps, to Ireland, where he held the dignity of Dean of Dublin, for in the archives of the See of Westminster (vol. III., p. 311) is a memorial to the pope, dated 1602, to which among other autograph signatures is appended that of " Richardus Hadocus, sacræ theologiæ doctor et Dubliniensis decanus." Filled with a desire to visit Rome once more, he returned to Douay, June 3rd, 1603, and began his journey thence in company with Dr. Harrison, procurator of the college, who was commissioned to lay before His Holiness the poverty of the college at that time. Dr. Haydock arrived at the English College at Rome on the following Aug. 27th. The pilgrim-book of the hospice in connection with the college states that he received with his servant ten days' hospitality.

The remainder of his life was spent in Rome, during which time he translated from the Italian Cardinal Bellarmine's large catechism into English. He then sent it to Douay for publication in 1604. Worn out with continual labour and suffering, he died at a comparatively early age in the year 1605, and was probably buried, as directed in his will, at the foot of the altar of our Lady in the church of St. Thomas of Canterbury, attached to the English college at Rome. In his will, written in Latin, he made bequests to St. Ursula's Augustinian Convent at Louvain, to his maternal aunt, Elizabeth Allen, and to his relatives, Catherine Allen, Fr. Thomas Talbot, S.J., Thomas Worthington of Blainscough, Esq., Dr. Thomas Worthington, president of Douay College, &c. He made the English College, Rome, his residuary legatee, and desired a marble slab to be placed over his remains, inscribed with his name and degree, his arms and the Haydock motto—*Tristitia vestra vertetur in gaudium*—

> " Oh, that posterity
> Could learn from him but this, that loves his wound,
> There is no pain at all in dying well,
> For none are lost but those that make their hell ! "     *Valentinian.*

## The Restoration of the English Benedictine Congregation.

> " Which force to Bennet eke they give, that help enough may be,
> By saints in every place. What dost thou omitted see ? "     *Anon.*

Another ecclesiastical member of the Cottam family is conspicuous for the part he took in the restoration of the venerable Benedictine congregation in England. Dom Robert Haydock, who used the *alias* of Benson on the mission, was professed in the monastery of St. Martin at Compostella. In 1607 he arrived in London, where he. had the reputation of being one of the most learned and spiritually wise of those who had been brought up in Spain. He became the superior of the monks on the mission in England belonging to the Spanish congregation, and in that capacity was elected one of the nine definitors to draw up the terms of the union of the three congregations then in England, the Italian, the Spanish, and the old English congrega. tion. This was approved by Paul V., and the new congregation was constituted in 1619, by the brief *Ex Incumbenti*. At the chapter of 1625, Dom Robert Haydock was elected provincial of York, an office which he held till 1629. In 1633 he was elected the first cathedral prior of Durham, under the new con- stitution, and in this dignity he was confirmed by the bull of Urban VIII., dated July 4, in that year. It was in this year that Charles I. visited Durham on his way to Scotland, when he was entertained by Bishop Morton, whose expenses in one day amounted to £1500. Having laboured with great fruit on the mission, the venerable prior died in Staffordshire, full of years, Feb. 8, 1650.

> " He sleeps in yonder nameless ground,
> A cross hath marked the stone—
> Pray ye, his soul in death hath found
> The peace to life unknown ! "        *R. S .Hawker.*

## Mag Shelton, the Witch of Woodplumpton.

> '' By the pricking of my thumbs,
> Something wicked this way comes :—
> Open locks, whoever knocks."        *Macbeth.*

He have now arrived at a period when the Haydocks are again brought under notice by one of the numerous traditions connected with the Fylde. In the 17th century there lived in these parts a famous witch commonly known by the name of Mag Shelton, though her real name was Margery Hilton. This hag resided alone in a wretched hovel called Cuckoo Hall, situated in a solitary part of Wesham, adjoining the footpath leading from Kirkham to Singleton.

> " It was a lodge of ample size,
> But strange of structure and device ;
> Of such materials as around
> The workman's hand had readiest found." *Lady of the Lake.*

Her neighbours regarded her with dread. Even to this day oral traditions of her extraordinary pranks are retained by the country folk. Her food was haggis (in common use at that time in the Fylde), made of boiled groats mixed with thyme and parsley. So great was the superstition of the times, that almost every misfortune in the neighourhood was attributed to the evil doings of Mag Shelton. Farmers complained of their milk being turned sour, of their cattle being lamed, and of their cows being milked. On one occasion she was met by a countryman driving a goose before her. The path was narrow, and as the goose did not get out of the way, the lout struck the seeming bird with his stick, when lo ! to his amazement, it was changed into a broken pitcher, with milk flowing on every side. It was thus the witch conveyed the stolen milk to her abode. On another occasion she was foiled by a powerful spell, the contrivance of a maiden, whose father suspected that his cow had been bewitched. With kindly words the girl inveigled the unsuspecting hag into the farm, and seated her cosily in the " ingle neuk." Under the "squab " where the witch sat, a bodkin, crossed with two weavers' healds, was laid, so that Mag, once seated, was powerless to rise. '' Oo shonna shift naa, fayther, ti' oo's t'en 'or een oth coo," said the wench, as she heaped turf and wood on the fire till the flames roared fiercely up the chimney. The heat grew more and more intense, till the unhappy witch was nearly roasted. Her piteous

screams found no compassion until she had removed the enchant-
ment from the cow.

It is no wonder, therefore, that in course of time the extreme
aversion with which Mag Shelton was regarded, rendered her
position at Cuckoo Hall almost intolerable, and it was with
shrewd avidity that she took advantage of the following incident
to change her abode.

## The Witch's Compact.

" Hare, hare, God send thee care !
I am in hare's likeness now ;
But I shall be a woman even now—
Hare, hare, God send thee care."

*Scott, Letters on Demonology and Witchcraft.*

THE lord of Cottam at this period was an ardent follower of
the hounds, and one day, after fruitless search for sport, he
visited the witch, and complained that he could find no hares.
Cuckoo Hall was the property of the Haydocks, but passed to the
Cottams as part of the marriage settlement of the squire's sister.
Ultimately, it reverted to its original owners through the marriage of the heiress of the Cottams with George Haydock, whose
son, George Leo, the biblical annotator, has left a sketch of the
place as it appeared in 1793.  William Haydock, the hero of this
story, married Jane, daughter of Hugh Anderton of Euxton
Hall, by Margaret, daughter of Roger Kirkby, of Kirkby, Esq.,
and his portrait, in the act of caressing his favourite hound, is
still preserved with that of his wife.

In response to the squire's complaint, Mag Shelton agreed to
produce a hare on condition that he should provide her with a
cottage on his estate in Woodplumpton, near to Cottam Hall,
for she felt that she could no longer reside at Cuckoo Hall with
safety.  But this offer was accompanied with the proviso that a

certain black hound should not be let slip. The squire readily acquiesced, and, following the hag's instructions, proceeded with his dogs to the field behind her house, where he was told he would find what he wanted. Within a few minutes, a hare broke through the hedge and made across country in the direction of Plumpton. In the words of the "Stonyhurst Buck-Hunt," written in 1712 by Mr. Cottam, of Hurst Green, a connection of the squire :

> " The hounds uncoupled on the plain,
> A mortal war straight did proclaim."

It was a famous run, the hare always keeping just in front of the dogs, but, as evening came on the fear of losing the hare altogether made the squire forget his promise. The black hound was slipped, and gained fast upon its quarry, which now doubled and ran madly towards Wesham, barely saving its life by jumping through the witch's window.

> " Close on the hounds the hunter came,
> To cheer them on the vanished game."
>
> *Scott, Lady of the Lake, Canto. I. ix.*

Imprecations from the hovel brought back the witch's compact to the squire's remembrance. The black hound had snapped her heel as she disappeared through the lattice, and it was significant that ever afterwards Mag Shelton limped.

## The Boulder-stone at Woodplumpton.

> " The solemn dirge, ye owls, prepare,
> Ye bats, more hoarsely shriek,
> Croak, all ye ravens, round the bier,
> And all ye church-mice squeak."—*Anon.*

At length the time came when the witch was missed from her

accustomed haunts. Several days had passed without anyone seeing her. The squire ordered her door to be broken open, and Mag Shelton was discovered crushed to death between a barrel and the wall. The gossips unanimously declared that the devil had adopted this plan of claiming his own. She was buried by torchlight at the western end of the churchyard at Woodplumpton, close to the end of the footpath. But the restless spirit of Mag Shelton was not so easily pacified. Her corpse was found on the sod in the morning, and as often as it was interred it reappeared, till her spirit was laid by the priest at Cottam Hall. A huge boulder-stone was rolled over the grave, which even yet raises its massive body from its deep embedment, and calls the attention of the passers-by to the spot where Mag Shelton, the witch of Woodplumpton, lies buried.

## The Last Squire of Cottam.

" But to wanton me, to wanton me,
Ken ye which maist wad wanton me ?
To see King James at Edinburgh Cross,
Wi' fifty thousand foot and horse,
And the Usurper forced to flee;
Oh, this is what maist wad wanton me."

*Jacobite Song.*

William Haydock, born about 1671, was the eldest son of the hunting squire. He has the unenviable distinction of having brought to a close the residence of the family at Cottam Hall. The honest squire, as he was generally termed, was a staunch adherent of the exiled Stuarts. It was this that ruined the Haydocks, like so many other Catholic families in Lancashire, whose loyalty to the rightful heir to the throne was proof against the temptations of the usurper. He was a bachelor, and he devoted the whole of his energies and means to the furtherance of the cause that was nearest his heart. Thomas Tyldesley, the diarist, under date August 4, 1714, notes his going from his residence at Myerscough Lodge to meet a number of Jacobite squires—Ned Winckley, of Bannister Hall, the young lord of Rawcliffe (Richard Butler), Gabriel Hesketh, of White Hill, Henry Whittingham, of Whittingham, and Squire Haydock—of whom the last brought the news that Queen Anne died on the previous Sunday morning between seven and eight o'clock. Such were their joyful expectations of the restoration of the royal exiles that they forthwith indulged in a "pig-feast" to celebrate the event. Over the water-jug went the Fulham-ware cups, with a rose on the rim above the drinker's mouth, *sub rosa*, "To the king," across the water—

> " God bless the King ! I mean the Faith's Defender.
> God bless—no harm in blessing—the Pretender !
> Who that Pretender is, and who is King,
> God bless us all ! that's quite another thing."
>
> *John Byrom*

Then " Hie thee, Jamie, hame again," resounded through the hall.

The accession of the Elector of Hanover to the throne was not the first inversion of the family motto which Squire Haydock experienced. It was he who bred the steed which threw the Orange Prince, William III., and cost him his life on the 8th of March, 1702. Queen Anne, instead of the legitimate heir to the throne, replaced the Dutch intruder, and now the queen was succeeded by her cousin George. Poor Tyldesley did not live to see the failure of the Chevalier de St. George's struggle for his rights, for he died in January, 1715, leaving his friend, the honest squire of Cottam, the loser of the considerable sum he had lent him. In the following year, William Haydock was outlawed for the part he had taken in the Stuart rising, and he died shortly afterwards, either from wounds received at the battle of Preston, or from a broken heart at the ruin of his master's cause.

Shortly before he was declared an outlaw, the squire conveyed the manor of Cottam to John Shuttleworth, of Hodsock Park, Nottinghamshire, Esq., whose son and heir, George, had married Dorothy Haydock, one of the squire's three sisters and eventual co-heiresses. Her portrait bears the inscription, "1737, aged 57." The estate, according to the entail, should have passed in succession to his three brothers, Gilbert, Cuthbert, and Hugh, all of whom were priests. Their cousin, George Haydock, of Leach Hall, Bartle, in Woodplumpton, was the next heir, and executor to the squire's will, in which George's son, Gilbert, the testator's godson, received a bequest. On July 2, 1730, George Haydock conveyed his interest in the manor of Cottam for a small consideration to George Farington, of Worden Hall, in trust for Henry Farington of Preston, son and heir of Valentine Farington. Towàrds the close of the century, the estate was sold by the Faringtons to John Cross, grandfather to the late Col. W. Assheton Cross, of Redscar, and his brother, the present Viscount Cross. It was their father, William Cross, who pulled down the Hall in the early part of this century.

It is worthy of notice that the last squire, in his will, requested his executors to ratify and confirm a lease for three lives to Thomas Miller of a messuage in Cottam and a close of land in Ingol. From Thomas Miller descended the immortal bishop of Castabala, John Milner, vicar apostolic of the Midland District, who changed the orthography of his name when he went to Sedgley Park School.

## Catch-field.

> " Here, where girls unfearing play,
>   Sacrilage erst sought for prey ;
>   Scared the flock, the priest with scorn,
>   Plundered, to a gaol was borne."

*Edw. Wilcock.*

Tradition affirms that a priest of the family of Haydock was

taken in the middle of a field adjoining Cottam Hall, which is
known to this day by the name of Catch-field. The history is
as follows. Gilbert Haydock, born in 1678, was a younger
brother of the last squire. He was sent to Douay College at an
early age, where he was distinguished for his close application to
his studies, and for his equal progress in virtue and piety. He
took the college oath, Sept. 8th, 1703, and in the beginning of
1705, we learn from Bishop Dicconson's diary that he was one
of the six students then in the school of philosophy. The same
authority informs us that he passed through his defensions—in
Latin and Greek—with universal admiration, on the 3rd, 4th,
and 5th of August, in that year. Four or five Jesuits from the
university of Douay attended each day to dispute in Greek. On
December 16th, 1706, he was ordained sub-deacon at Cambrai,
and in 1708 he was ordained priest. In the following year he
was sent to the mission at Cottam Hall, where his apostolic zeal
and labours were attended with the happiest effects in the conversion and care of souls. In the spring following the unsuccessful rising in favour of the rightful heir to the throne, in 1715,
his brother was outlawed, a raid was made on Cottam Hall, and
Gilbert Haydock was seized in the middle of " catch-field " as he
was endeavouring to make his escape. He was consigned to
Lancaster Castle, where he endured several months' imprisonment. Whilst still a prisoner he was appointed chaplain to the
Augustinian nuns of the convent of St. Monica at Louvain,
where he arrived, after his discharge from prison, on August 1st,
1716.

Some entries in the Douay diary at this period are per-
tinent to the subject. On November 24th, 1715, is recorded
the victory of the Earl of Marr over the Earl of Argyle at Dum-
blane, and the defeat and capture of the Earl of Derwentwater at
Preston. Amongst the prisoners was James Mudford, a priest
and *alumnus* of Douay. Prayers were recited in the college, by
order of the president, Mr. Robert Witham, for the success of

James III. A little later it is stated that James embarked at Dunkirk on December 27th, 1715, and landed in Scotland on January 2nd, 1716. The event was celebrated at the college by a *Te Deum*. On the 22nd of February he returned to France, unable to cope with the forces sent against him, landing safe near Calais. The parliament had offered for him, dead or alive, £100,000. About 1718, President Witham went to Louvain to take Gilbert Haydock's place, whilst he went to England with two nuns of the family of the Earl of Derwentwater on business, lest the convent should suffer by losing their pension, which had been paid from the patrimony of the Earl.

Gilbert Haydock remained chaplain at Louvain till his death, greatly to the satisfaction and edification of the religious ladies, who, in their mortuary bill, bore testimony to his merit. " He was a truly pious and exemplary clergyman, and minutely exact in every duty; in the celebration of the divine mysteries, his fervour and piety frequently manifested themselves in a copious profusion of tears, and his charity to the poor in abundant alms. In a word, he was the mirror and pattern of every virtue becoming a christian and a clergyman." He bore a tender devotion to the Blessed Virgin, and every year, after a spiritual retreat of eight days, made a pilgrimage to her chapel on Mount Acuto. After an illness of fifteen days, which he bore with the most exemplary patience, and spent in preparing himself for eternity, he departed this life on the 22nd day of September, 1749, in the 68th year of his age, and the 42nd of his priesthood.

## The Distruction of Worksop Manor.

" 'Twas the last red ray of the setting sun,
    And it stream'd on the painted wall,
And told that another bright day was done,
    And had vanished beyond recall."

*F. C. Husenbeth.*

Cuthbert Haydock, another brother of the last squire, was

born, according to the Douay diary, in 1684. He went to the college with his brother Gilbert, and there they were subsequently joined by their younger brother Hugh. Cuthbert took the college oath Dec. 27th, 1703, and Hugh, who was born July 21st, 1689, followed his example on Nov. 3rd, 1711. Towards the close of 1712, the Dean of Mechlin and another ecclesiastic were commissioned to examine the president, professors, and students at Douay, the college having been falsely charged with Jansenist opinions. Hugh Haydock was one of the six youths questioned under the school of divinity, and helped by his lucid answers in writing to clear the college from the imputation. In due time both brothers were ordained priests. Cuthbert was sent to the mission on Mar. 26th, 1714. He was at first stationed at Mawdesley in Lancashire, but probably found it necessary to leave it when the persecution became so hot after the Stuart rising in 1715, for his name and residence were reported to the government in the following year (*Forfeited Estates, S. 95. P.R.O.* He lived for some time at Mawdesley with Thomas Finche, who had married his sister Mary. There he attended the Catholics of the district, and in the little sacristy, adjoining the chapel at the top of the house, some of his books remain to this day. Ultimately he was appointed chaplain to the Duke of Norfolk at Worksop Manor, in Nottinghamshire, not very far removed from the residence of his sister, Mrs. Shuttleworth, at Hodsock Park, where it is also said he spent some time as chaplain between his leaving Lancashire and settling at Worksop. There he lived forty years, beloved by all who knew him.

On Nov. 22nd, 1761, the ancient mansion at Worksop, on which £22,000 had been recently expended, was unfortunately burned to the ground, and the loss in paintings, statuary (including a part of the Arundelian collection), fine library, and furniture, was estimated at more than £100,000. It was commonly reported that " Mr. Haydock never looked up after." He died Jan. 11th, 1763, aged 78, just two months before Edward, ninth Duke of Norfolk, laid the foundation of a splendid new mansion which cost him £300,000. This edifice, which was a scene of almost regal magnificence, was destined in turn to be razed to the ground, when the Duke sold the estate to the Duke of Newcastle for £380,000.

Mr. Haydock was a staunch supporter of his *alma mater*, Douay College. The diary records that he took there six students of good family on July 18th, 1726. He was chosen a member of the old chapter in March, 1734, and was held in high estimation by all his brethren. He devised his estate to his nephew, Henry Finche, of Mawdesley, but that gentleman dying before the testator, Mr. Haydock annexed a codicil to his will dated October 20th, 1762, by which Mr. Finche's son and heir, James, became the residuary legatee, and the devisee of all his books and manuscripts.

> " Amidst this wreck, where thou hast made a shrine
> And temple more divinely desolate,
> Among thy mightier offerings here are mine,
> Ruins of years—though few, yet full of fate."
>
> *Byron.*

# The Tagg

" Oh, fair old house—how time doth honour thee,
   Giving thee what to-day may never gain,
   Of long respect and ancient poesy ;
   The yew-trees at thy door are black with years,
   And filled with memories of *bygone* days."

*L. E. Landon.*

ON the western side of the road diverging from Preston round by Tulketh Hall, the ancient residence of the Saxon family of Travers in close proximity to the spot where the Cistercian monks from Savigny rested during their erection of Furness Abbey, and continuing over Cadley Moor through Ingol and Cottam to Woodplumpton, stood the entrance gates to the shady avenue leading to Cottam Hall. Facing the north-east, in the angle formed by the road and the avenue, was a venerable time-worn building of quaint appearance, surrounded by a large garden stretching in the direction of the hall. This was The Tagg, the ancient dower-house of the Haydocks, the birthplace and residence of George Leo Haydock, the biblical annotator, who endearingly called it " Golden Tagg."

The grounds around the house were planned in the Dutch style by "old trusty Beaumont," gardener to James II., by whom it is said the gardens at Hampton Court were laid out. It was probably done for the step-mother of the last Squire Haydock about the time that Beaumont was engaged by Colonel James Graham and Sir Nicholas Sherburn to lay out their grounds at Levens Hall and Stonyhurst. In the corner abutting upon the hall gates was an ancient yew cut into the form of a summer-house, with a small pond in front of it, and another of considerable size stretching parallel with the avenue. All around were yew and other trees clipt into the fantastic forms of bygone times.

After the death of the outlawed squire, his cousin George, who resided at Leach Hall, Bartle Quarter, in Woodplumpton, an ancient erection with a tower and flat leaded roof, now replaced by the modern house called Bartle Hall, took no steps to secure the rights of his children to the lordship of Cottam. Indeed, as we have seen, he conveyed his interest in the manor for a small consideration to the Faringtons in 1730, probably being disheartened by the encumbrances on the estate, its complication by the last squire's outlawry, and the tenant-for-life interests of the three priests, Gilbert, Cuthbert, and Hugh.

George Haydock had a large family: Robert, of Leach Hall, born in 1692; William, of the Tagg; Cuthbert, born in 1696, who died in the following year ; Gilbert, born in 1699, godson to the last squire; and Jennet, wife of George Greene of Woodplumpton, the representative of the ancient family of Greene of Bowers House, Nateby.

The eldest son, Robert, succeeded his father at Leach Hall, and, by, his wife Elizabeth Eccles (a cousin of his brother William's wife), had a son Robert, born in 1724, also of Leach Hall, who married Alice, daughter of Robert Smith, of Larbreck, descended from the Smiths of Forton. The younger Robert's son and namesake, Robert Haydock, born in 1749, espoused his cousin Mary, daughter and eventual heiress of Ralph Fidler, of Lea, by Jennet, daughter of Robert Haydock, of Leach Hall. She was some four years older than her husband, who died Oct. 1st, 1826, aged 76, and she used to relate with pride to her children, how, when Prince Charlie passed through Sidgreaves Lane, Lea, she was lifted up by her father to see the Scots pass, some of whom were supplied by her family with food.

" How proud were we of our young prince,
  And of his native sway !
But all our hopes are past and gone
  Upon Culloden day."

*Jacobite Song.*

## Cottam Chapel.

" Old traditions linger here,
  Time-worn relics too are near ;
  Now and then—grave ramblers gaze,
  Pondering scenes of other days,—
  Scenes of fitting peaceful life,
  Scenes with persecution rife."

*Edward Wilcock, Occasional Verses.*

After the retreat of Prince Charles Edward to Scotland, an infuriated mob marched out of Preston, plundered the houses of Catholics on their way, and destroyed the chapel at Cottam.

During the long period of persecution, the Catholics of the district had worshipped in the domestic chapel at Cottam Hall, but some fifteen years before the death of the last Squire Haydock, when the hall passed into Protestant hands, the Rev. John Kendal, whose true name was Baine, rented a barn, with four acres of land in Cottam, from William Bilsborrow of Woodplumpton, yeoman, and fitted it up as a dwelling-house and chapel. This property had been demised and granted by William Haydock, Esq., about the year 1685, to John Bilsborrow, father of William Bilsborrow, for ninety-nine years, determinable on three lives at a nominal rental of seven shillings and eightpence. This can hardly be the site of the present chapel, which, though always known by the name of Cottam Chapel, is really in Woodplumpton. Adjoining this land, William Bilsborrow owned a freehold cottage and six acres of land in Woodplumpton. It is probable that after his death, when the lease of the Cottam property expired, the Woodplumpton land passed to Mr. Kendal, or his relative and name-

sake John Kendal of Fulwood ; for a document preserved at the
rectory says that after he purchased and repaired his property
in Woodplumpton, he left it in trust for procuring Mass twice
per month for the Catholics of the neighbourhood.   Either Mr.
Kendal or his relative, the Rev. Henry Kendal, who succeeded
him in the mission, erected a new chapel situated about a mile
to the north-east of Cottam Hall, a little nearer to the road than
the present one.

COTTAM CHAPEL.

On Nov. 3rd, 1734, John Harrison, a native of Cottam, born
Oct. 21st, 1714, took the college oath at Douay, and soon after
his ordination, came on the mission and was appointed to Cottam.
In 1745 his house and chapel were attacked by a mob from
Preston, and though "he resisted with intrepidity," both were
burnt down by the "no-popery" ruffians, and for two years
afterwards no Mass was said at Cottam.   Mr. Harrison removed

to Towneley, and served that mission for thirty years, until he was no longer able. When his infirmities incapacitated him from labour, he retired to the house of his brother Laurence in Preston, and died in Friargate, about Jan. 16th, 1780. Another priest at Cottam was the Rev. John Cowban, also a native of the Fylde and an *alumnus* of Douay College. He afterwards went to Crathorne, in Cleveland, where he died, Oct. 6th, 1777, having laboured over 40 years on the English mission. Probably he was Mr. Harrison's predecessor at Cottam. From the Bilsborrow Charity, issuing out of lands and tenements in Ashton-super-Ribble, devised by John Bilsborrow, son of the before-mentioned William Bilsborrow, of which the Haydocks of Leach Hall were the trustees, it would seem that a Mr. Smith was priest at Cottam in 1763 and 1765—perhaps the Rev. John Harrison's successor, and the restorer of the chapel and house. During the great election riot at Preston in 1768, the chapel was again nearly destroyed, with the priest's house, by a mob from the town, after which the mission seems to have been discontinued for a short time. Eventually Robert Haydock, of Leach Hall, with two other members of the congregation, succeeded in repairing the premises, and the bishop was persuaded to send another priest to Cottam. The Rev. John Lund came in 1769. He erected the present chapel in 1793, and was buried within it in 1812. He was succeeded by the Rev. Thomas Caton, a relative of Mrs. Haydock of the Tagg, who came on July 24th, 1812, died Aug. 14th, 1826, and was likewise buried within the chapel. Then came the Rev. Thomas Berry, a fellow-collegian of the Rev. George Leo Haydock and his brother Thomas, who, less fortunate than they, suffered imprisonment after Douay was seized by the revolutionists, and only secured his liberation with the rest of the collegians, Feb. 25th, 1795. Mr. Berry arrived at Cottam, Oct. 25th, 1826, and during his residence erected the priest's house adjoining the chapel. He left in 1845, and was succeeded by the Rev. John Dixon, who remained until April, 1852, when he retired on account of ill-health. The Rev. George J. A. Corless, D.D., then came from Thropton, and was the first *mission-ary-rector* of Cottam. To him, for his exertions in improving the chapel, adding a new sanctuary and sacristy, &c., the mission owes a debt of gratitude. He laid out the little burial-ground, and in the centre erected a handsome cemetery cross for his own resting-place, inscribed to his memory, with blanks for the inser-tion of the date of his demise. He died Nov. 1st, 1865, and there he was laid. The late Rev. Roger Taylor was then appointed to the mission, but his health breaking down, he resigned in 1867, and the Rev. Henry J. Thrower, who had supplied his place for twelve months, was installed in the mission by the late Bishop Goss. He has just been succeeded by the Rev. Francis Gillow.

## Newsham.

> " Affliction's sting may wound thee here,
> And proud ascendants lavish gall :
> But faith's keen eye beyond the bier
> Looks out and sees an end of all."
>
> *Flowers from the Holy Fathers.*

Facing the entrance to the pretty little chapel at Newshouse, Newsham, were two table-monuments, which have recently been desecrated by having their supports removed, in order to increase the width of the pathway, and to allow people to walk over and deface the inscriptions. The one covered the remains of the Haydocks of Leach Hall, and the other those of the Haydocks of the Tagg. The former bears the inscription—

> "Sacred to the memory of MARY HAYDOCK,
> wife of ROBERT HAYDOCK, of Bartell,
> who died the 15th August, 1809, aged 69.
> Also of the above ROBERT HAYDOCK,
> who departed this life, the 1st day of Oct., 1826,
> aged 76 years."

Their daughter and co-heiress, Jane Haydock, the last of the family, became the wife of William Smith, of Clock House, Lea and Forton, gent. She died Nov. 21st, 1865, aged 81, and was laid in the quiet little burial-ground attached to the chapel at Cottam, which succeeded the one in the home of her ancestors.

> " Let the old ancestral names
>    Which were bound to thee and thine,
> Kneel before the rising sun—
>    Worship at a newer shrine."
>
> *L. E. Landon.*

The history of Newhouse chapel is of considerable interest, for in it were united the missions at Bank Hall, Broughton, Midge Hall, Myrescough, Crow Hall, and The Hough, Newsham. It may be traced as follows:—

## Bank Hall.

> " They tore the banners that graced the hall ;
>    They plundered the chapel of pyx and pall."
>
> *J. R. Planché.*

Broughton Tower, abutting on Sharoe Green, in Broughton, was for centuries the seat of the knightly family of Singleton, which removed there from Singleton. It was a most devout family and at different times founded chauntries at Broughton, Goosnargh, and Fernyhalgh. On Jan. 8th, 1348-9, a license was granted by Archbishop Zouche to Thomas, son of Gilbert de Singleton, to have divine service by a fit chaplain within his manors of Brughton, Fernyhalgh, and Farmunholes for three years, without injury to the parish church of Preston in Amounderness.

But the lust of Henry VIII. changed all this. No longer was the saunce bell heard, and in the reign of his son Edward VI., the so-called Reformers swept off the bells and other fittings which still remained in the chantries. Though dismantled, Ladywell, in Fernyhalgh, was never deserted by the Catholics of the neighbourhood, and was even a place of pilgrimage for those at a distance. The site fell into Catholic hands, and a new chapel was erected:—

> " And aye the mass priest sings his song,
>     And patters many a prayer—
> And the Chantry Bell tolls loud and long,
>     And aye the lamp burns there."

In the reign of James II., Mr. Hugh Charnley, of Durton, by indenture dated March 16th, 1685, gave to George Leyburne, of Nateby Hall, Nicholas Wadsworth, of Haighton Hall, Cuthbert Hesketh, of White Hill, and Robert Shepherd, of Broughton, gentlemen, the site of the ancient well in trust for the mission at Ladywell, and—

> " Long beside the well there stood,
>     Now torn away, the sacred rood."
>
> *Edw. Wilcock.*

Though a new chapel was erected by the Rev. Anthony Lund, in 1793, at some little distance from the well, the original building, in a modernised form, still belongs to the mission, and the ancient chalice which the Irish chieftain presented as a memorial of his pilgrimage to Ladywell is still in use. It bears on its foot the inscription:—" Dosus Maguir Rex Fermanne me fi[ere]: fe[cit]: MCCCCCXXIX." It was his son, Fergus MacGuire, who with well-affected simplicity returned the following spirited message to Sir William Fitz William, the successor of Sir Henry Sidney in the government of Ireland in 1571, in reply to the intimation that a sheriff was to be sent into his district :—"Your sheriff shall be welcome, but let me know his price, that if my people should cut off his head, I may levy it upon the country."

It is indeed a pity that the old site, so lovely in its situation, and so hallowed by tradition, should not have been retained for the new chapel :—

> " Stranger ! Is there not a spell
> Stays thy steps at Ladywell ?
> Changed the lowly fane of yore,
> Gone the wondrous tree which bore
> Wilding fruit without a core,
> But the fountain faileth not
> Nor unloved the quiet spot."
>
> *Edw. Wilcock, Occasional Verses.*

Many were the sufferings the Singletons endured for their recusancy, and many the learned priests they gave to the Church. In a return to the council about 1585 (" P.R.O. Dom. Eliz. Vol. clxxxv. No. 85") is noted :—" Mr. Singeltonne, A Jesuit att Mr. Singeletonne of the Tower, 3 miles ffrom Prestonne, or els in the filde." On the large map of Lancashire, supplied to the same authority for the purpose of coercing the people to join the new religion ("Dom. Eliz. Vol. ccxxxv. No. 5. 1590"), appears the name of John Singleton de Singleton Tower, as also that of John Singleton de Schales (in Lonsdale hundred). When James I. invented that iniquitous system of appeasing the appetites of his parasites by granting them the benefit of the recusancy of Catholics, Edward Singleton, of Broughton Tower, was awarded to Charles Chambers as his prey, Mar. 21st, 1608 ("Dom. Eliz. Vol. xxxi. 82"). Dr. Challoner tells us how the Rev. Edward Bamber the martyr, during the days of the fanatical Cromwellians, made his escape from his keepers whilst lodging at a place beyond Preston on his journey to Lancaster gaol. Finding that his conductors were drunk, he found means in the dead of the night to lower himself out of a window in his shirt, for his clothes had been removed for safety's sake. In this state he was found by the master of Broughton Tower, who had been admonished that night in a dream that he should find him in a certain field. Fully possessed of the truth of the vision, he got up and found Mr. Bamber in the very spot. He conducted him to his house where he took every care of him.

About 1625, Thomas Singleton, the representative of the branch of the family seated at Bank Hall, sold that estate and went to reside at Scale Hall. The estate about this time appears to have been divided, for, in 1632, Hugo Crooke was living there and in that year paid his fines for recusancy, and in 1641, Richard Woodcock, of Walton-le-dale, was found in his *inquisition post mortem* to be possessed of some portion of the estate. Eventually a moiety of Bank Hall and estate was settled by the Rev. George Crooke, who served the mission there, in tail male upon his nephew John Crooke and his issue by Martha Preston, at the time of their marriage about 1695. The other moiety seems to have been given to the Church for the use of the mission. George Crooke died Mar. 2, 1709, and was succeeded in the mission by the Rev. Edward Kitchen, *alias* Smith, a Douay priest.

When the persecution was renewed with such vigour after the unsuccessful Stuart rising in 1715, Samuel Peploe, vicar of Preston, forwarded to the commissioners for Forfeited Estates, in 1716, the following "account of estates granted to superstitious uses in and about Preston co. Lancaster" (" P.R.O. Forfeited Estates, P. 134"). "Bank Hall in the chapelry of Broughton and parish of Preston. This estate is divided into two parts. One part was one Mr. George Crooke's freehold estate, who was a Romish priest, died about four or five years ago. He upon the marriage of his kinsman, John Crooke, with Martha Preston. settled that estate upon him the said John and his male issue by that marriage, about 18 or 20 years ago. Afterwards, at his death, he confirmed that settlement by his will, charging the estate with the payment of £200 to Mr. Layburne, of Nateby, now a rebel, which was only in trust to him for Romish priests. This, the wife of the said John Crooke has told me several times, and I know other people to whom I believe she has told the same. Mr. Thornton, of Preston, has or had a copy of George Crooke's will. John Crooke told Thomas Woods, of Broughton, that his estate was charged £200 to Mr. Layburne. Richard Withnell, late schoolmaster of Broughton, is a proper person to be examined. The other part of Bank Hall estate is Mr. Thomas (or his son John) Clayton, of Preston; this has been in lease many years. Mr. Smith, a Romish priest (whose true name is Edward Kitchen), lives in that part of the house at Bank Hall which belongs to this side of the estate, and has occupied and let the ground from time to time ; his life is in the lease as I am told. Thomas Moor, of Sandyford, in Woodplumpton, holds now about £5 or £6 per annum, which he took of Mr. Smith *alias* Kitchen in the name of William Shepherd. He has always paid his rent to Smith, only he paid it this summer to Dorothy Walton his housekeeper. William Gregson, of Broughton has likewise ground of Mr. Smith. The said Smith has also for many years paid me Easter dues and small tythes for these lands he has had in possession. I am told that Mr. John Clayton has entered on this tenement some days ago, pretending that he has bought Smith out of it. Clayton told the above mentioned Gregson so. Nicholas Moor, son of the said Thomas Moor, and Thomas Tounson, of Barton, have taken grounds of Mr. Smith, and paid him their rents."

William Shepherd, of Fernyhalgh in Broughton, gent., then residing at Croxteth, where his wife, Mary Blundell, probably had property, was one of the trustees for the secular missions of Fernyhalgh, Crow Hall, and Bank Hall. The Claytons were trustees for the clergy's moiety of Bank Hall estate. John Crook's eldest son and heir, George Crook, succeeded to the estate. His marriage settlement with Janet, daughter and co-heiress of Richard Blackburne, of Stockenbridge, gent., is dated Sep. 15, 1732. Their son John was succeeded by his namesake who was the father of John Crook, Esq., M.D., and his trustee Joseph Bushell, of Myrescough, Esq., sold the estate of Bank Hall, in the first half of this century, to John Wilson, of Preston, attorney-at-law, whose son now possesses it. The Wilsons erected a new house, some little distance from the old hall, and, in making alterations in the latter, discovered a secret chamber adjoining the room formerly used as a chapel, in which was a tabernacle, chalice, and other church furniture. These they handed over to Dr. Crook, who resided in Broughton until his death, Oct. 31, 1869, aged 65. The chapel would only be used by itinerant missioners after the establishment of a permanent mission at Newhouse.

## Midge Hall.

" Long its inmates have departed,
    Shelterless is now that bound,
  Where of yore the broken-hearted
    Holiest consolation found."

The Lonnde or Lund family were seated in Midghalgh, Mydysall, or Midgall, a hamlet in Myrescough, from time immemorial. Anthony Lundde died here in Oct., 1605. The residence of the family known as Midge Hall was a purchase of James Lund towards the end of the seventeenth century. His son and heir, Anthony, is frequently referred to in the Tyldesley Diary. There was a chapel in the house, which seems to have been pretty regularly served, though probably by itinerant missioners as there is no record of a resident priest.

On Sunday, July 25, 1714, Squire Tyldesley notes—" Went with Mrs. and lasses to Antony Lund's. Mr. Roger Brookhall

dind with us. Went to Natby, Dick Gornall with mee. Saw
cos. Gerard and his wife there." The Rev. Roger Brockholes,
younger son of John Brockholes, of Claughton Hall, Esq., was
then residing with his father, and, besides assisting the Rev.
Richard Taylor in the mission there, to which he succeeded,
frequently attended the chapels at Midge Hall and The Hough.
On Sunday, Sep. 5, in the same year, the diarist records, "Wee
went to Antony Lund's off Midghall ; Mr. Vavisor there. After
dinr cos. Hesketh and his wiffe, and son Threlfall and his wiffe
came to see us, and suped with us." Sir Walter Vavasour, of
Haslewood, Bart., was a Jesuit serving the mission in this district.
At this period he resided in Alston, perhaps with Richard Bilsborrow, who was outlawed for taking part with the Chevalier de
St. George in 1715, though it is pretty certain that Fr. Vavasour
frequently said mass in the domestic chapel at Hothersall
Hall, the seat of Thomas Hothersall, Esq., a cousin of the Haydocks. The latter's son, John Hothersall, was also "out" in
1715, for which he was outlawed, but made his escape and was
never apprehended, passing the remainder of his days in privacy
with his sister, Mrs. William Leckonby, of Leckonby House
Great Eccleston, to whom the estate of Hothersall passed. In
the Record Office is an information to the Commissioners for
Forfeited Estates by John Harrison, of Balderston, dated Nov.
24, 1716, relating to Father Vavasour's being at Preston at
the time of the Stuart rising :—"John Harrison did on Friday, 11 Nov., 1715, at Preston, see Mr. Vavasor (brother of Sir
Walter Vavasour) who is said to be a Jesuite, appear there openly
in the streets and particularly did see him go into the White
Bull Inne, in Church Gate Street, in company in the several
persons who had all or most of them cockades in their hatts—
that the said Mr. Vavasor had then a sword by his side, &c." On
the previous Oct. 17, George Green, the high constable of the
hundred of Amounderness, advised the commissioners that "Mr
Vavisor, who is a reputed priest, harboured in our town [Alston

cum-Hothersall]. Richard Bilsborrow is outlawed but his estate
was formerly mortgaged. John Hothersall (son to Thomas
Hothersall, Esq.) was in this late Rebellion and made his escape
and never since apprehended " —*( P.R.O., Forfeited Estates, B.* 62
*and L.* 4). Sir Walter afterwards succeeded Fr. James Thomson,
S.J., to the mission at Preston.

Anthony Lund died at Midge Hall in 1727, and was succeeded
by his son John, who was the father of the Rev. Anthony Lund,
of Ladywell, Fernyhalgh, and the Rev. John Lund, of Cottam.
The estate was sold by the Rev. Anthony Lund, who died at
Fernyhalgh, Sep. 20, 1811. During his lifetime this remarkable
old priest gave the sum of £4,550 to establish ecclesiastical education funds at Ushaw College, and also left the college several
estates. Around one of these a curious tradition has gathered.
As the estate formerly belonged to the Hoghtons, and as the
history is an example of the way in which traditions are sometimes manufactured, it may not be out of place to introduce the
story here.


## The Dun Cow Rib.

" By Saynt Peter and by Saynt Paul,
    If ould Meg has stown Dunholme's cow,
    Turn round riddle, shears and all."

On the moors around Whittingham, it is stated, there once
lived an old dun cow of enormous size. Though recognising no
owner, it gave milk to all comers, and that in no stinted quantity.
At last an old witch said she would take a pail which the dun
cow could not fill. She produced a riddle, and, after a vain
attempt to fill it, the beast died of vexation. Intense was the
grief of the country-folk at the loss of the cow, and to preserve

its memory Adam Hoghton hung one of its ribs over his door, where it remains to this day.

The history of Dun Cow Rib farm is as follows. The house was erected by Adam Hoghton, fourth son of Thomas Hoghton, of Hoghton Tower, who was slain at Lea. The second son William, founded the staunch Catholic family of Hoghton of Grimsargh Hall, whose descendants continued to reside there for four more generations, being allied with some of the best Catholic familes in Lancashire. Eventually, Grimsargh reverted to the elder branch at Hoghton Tower, which in the meantime had been robbed of its faith. Col. Fishwick, in his history of Goosnargh, states that two similar bones to the one at Dun Cow Rib were found within recent years at Grimsargh Hall.

Dun Cow Rib, situated in Half-penny Lane, Whittingham, near Longridge, is substantially built of stone, and is an interesting specimen of the architecture of a small country house of the early part of the 17th century. In the gable of the upper storey is one of those curious overhanging closets ; and a thick oaken bar draws out of the wall from one jamb to the other to fasten the front-door. Over the door is chained the " rib," and within the semi-circle thus formed, are the arms of the Hoghtons, with the initials and date " 1616—A.H." From the Hoghtons the property passed to another Catholic family, the Whittinghams of Whittingham Hall, and by them it was leased in 1677, 1680, 1692, and 1702, to a Catholic yeoman of the name of Robert Sturzaker, who was frequently fined for his recusancy. In these leases Dun Cow Rib is called Moor House. Robert Sturzaker's son and heir, William, resided here, and in 1703 purchased the freehold from John Barton, of Whittingham, yeoman, who had bought it from the Whittinghams. In 1717, in compliance with the Act of 1 Geo. I., William Sturzaker registered his estate as a Catholic non-juror, and returned Moor House and 4 acres free-hold besides leasehold estate. He was convicted of recusancy with his father at the Lancaster sessions, Jan. 15, 1717. He administered to his father's estate in 1731, and entailed his freehold and leasehold property on his nephew James Taylor, mercer and grocer, then living at Croston, who, in 1734, sold Moor House to John Fishwick, of Bulsnape, in Goosnargh, afterwards of Liverpool, gent. Some time later Moor House became the property of John Lund, of Midge Hall, who conveyed it to his son and heir, the Rev. Anthony Lund, May 12, 1772.

The Rev. Anthony Lund was the priest at Ladywell, Fernyhalgh, with which is associated a legend similar in some degree to that connected with the building of Durham Cathedral. The old priest's heart was in the establishment of St. Cuthbert's College, near Durham, and, in 1808, the year in which the new college was erected, he settled upon it the estate, which he probably called Dun Cow Rib, to remain as a reminder of the legend attached to St. Cuthbert's Cathedral.

We are told by Raine, in his history of St. Cuthbert, that it had been announced by the Saint that it was his determination to repose in Dunholme, but no one of his followers had ever heard of the place. In this state of suspense, a female was heard inquiring of a home-wending milk-maid if she could direct her to her cow, which had strayed from its accustomed haunts. "Down in Dunholme," was the reply, and the overjoyed monks, hearing the name, soon found the place. This is the tale which is told as explanatory of the sculpture of the two women and the cow affixed to a turret at the north-west end of the eastern transept of Durham Cathedral. But, in all probability, the stone is rather emblematical of the riches of the Church than commemorative of any real occurrence.

> " And, after many wanderings past,
> He chose his lordly seat at last,
> Where his cathedral, huge and vast,
>     Looks down upon the Wear."

*Marmion, II.,* 14.

## Crow Hall.

"Far in a wilderness obscure,
   The lonely mansion lay,
A refuge to the neighb'ring poor,
   And strangers led astray."

*Goldsmith's Hermit.*

Crow Hall, in Newsham, was another place in which the Catholics, in times of persecution, met to hear mass. In the last century, it belonged to the Dickinsons, but how long it had been their residence does not appear. John, the son and heir, of Bartholomew Dickinson, of Crow Hall, and his wife, Anne, died here September 29, 1823, aged 59. His wife, Anne, a member of the old Catholic family of Corbishley of Thurnham, predeceased him on July 10, 1814, aged 49. Their son, Thomas Dickinson, succeeded to Crow Hall, and other estates in Haighton, Whittingham, Goosnargh, and Broughton, which the family had held since the 16th century. He married, August 14, 1815, Isabel, daughter of John Gillow, of Salwick Hall and Elswick Grange, and had two sons, John and Henry, and a daughter, Anne, wife of Rowland Savage, of the Rock Savage family, all of whom died *sine prole*. The husband of Thomas' sister, Margaret, after her death—their only child becoming a nun—was ordained priest at Ushaw College, and is now one of our most eminent and widely known doctors of divinity. On Sunday, August 17, 1712, Squire Tyldesley records: "Gave ye servants at Banister Hall 3s. ; left it about 7, and at Jump-lane-ends meet Mr. Gibson, recorder, Harson, and Mr. Benison ; they from Preston ; parted with them att Broughton ; I prayed at Crow Hall; stayed an hour at Lodge, and 2 att Natby; spent 6d. at Highgate; soe home." On a similar occasion, the diarist says, October 26, 1712: "Went with Mrs. to Bowers to prayers, but Sherdy did not pray for our master;" and to mark his disapprobation of the priest's not offering up public prayers for "King James III.," the diarist places a cross after " Sherdy " in the margin.   Two days later, October 28, he writes: " Went early in the morning to prayers at Hen. Madsley's; honest Mr. Gant being loyall."   Henry Mawdesley lived at Myrescough.   The Rev. James Gant, a member of an old Singleton family, descended from one of the retainers of John of Gaunt, lord of Singleton, is met with as saying Mass at The Dimples, the seat of the Plesingtons, in 1714, and in 1727 was stationed at Mowbreck Hall.   He also served Salwick Hall.   Again, on Sunday, December 27, 1713, the Jacobite squire enters in his diary that he went to Crow Hall, where he had reason to chide Mr. John Swarbrick for disloyalty.   In 1716, the Vicar of Preston, the Rev. Sam. Peploe, B.D., who was afterwards rewarded for his activity against the Catholics with the See of Chester, reported to the Commissioners for forfeited estates that Crow Hall, Newsham, in the chapelry of Goosnargh, was given to " superstitious uses."   One Edmund Fishwick left a sum of money to lease it, and ever since his death, which was then ten or eleven years ago, a priest had lived upon it, one Richardson, and then Mr. Swarbrick.   The estate went in William Shepherd's name, and the lease was supposed to be in his name in trust for the priests.   Jane Corwen, of Barton, Richard Clarkson, of Catforth Hall, steward to Sir Nicholas Sherborne, and Jennet Higgison, wife of Roger Higgison, of Barton, who lived by Crow Hall, might be proper persons to examine upon that account The Vicar further states that James Walton, a debt prisoner in Lancaster, lived on the estate seven or eight years, and that he, about two years before, being privy to the interests of the priests in the estate, compelled William Shepherd, the trustee, and a priest to compound with him for some benefit from it, otherwise he threatened to inform Mr. Read; and that North, gaoler of Lancaster, knew this.—*(P.R.O., Forfeited Estates, P.*134*.)*

## The Hough.

"Thy little kirk, both neat and white,
Attracts the wandering—busy sight."

*Thomas Billington—The Bridale.*

"Francis Kirk, gent., a reputed priest, of Newsham," appears
in the list of Popish recusants convicted at the Lancaster Sessions, January 15, 1716. *(Forfeited Estates,* P. 62.) He was a
secular priest, and resided at the Hough, in Newsham. Tyldesley alludes to him in his diary, Saturday, September 19, 1713:
"In the toun [Lancaster] al day; about 6, old Mr. Brookholls
and Mr. Kirke came to see me, and Mr. Brookholls stay⁴ 3 hou˖."
On Sunday, September 12, 1714, he says: "After dinᵣ, went with
Mrs. to Esqᵣ Brookholles. Over tuke Mr. Kirke." In the
*Forfeited Estates Papers,* P. 62, we read that William Wall, of
Preston, informs William Moore that one Mr. Kirk, of The
Hough, in the pᵗʰ of Goosnargh, is a priest. This William Moore,
a Preston attorney, begs that his name may not be made use of,
and expresses a hope that the Commissioners will indulge him
in this. Peploe informs the Commissioners in 1716 (134 P.) that
"a house and grounds, called The Hough, in Newsham, is a
tenement under one Mr. Hesketh. John Reynolds, and one Mr.
Kirk, a priest, live upon it. John Hesketh, of Newsham, and
John Hankinson, of the same, may be able to give some account
of it." The estate belonged to the Heskeths of Maynes Hall,
Little Singleton. John Hesketh, of Newsham, was a younger
son of William Hesketh, of Maynes Hall, Esq., by Perpetua,
daughter of Thomas Westby, of Mowbreck Hall, Esq. His
nephew, William Hesketh, married Mary, daughter of John
Brockholes, of Claughton Hall, Esq., and their sons, Thomas,
Joseph, and James Hesketh, succeeded their uncle, William
Brockholes, to the Claughton estates, and assumed the additional
name of Brockholes. When Shepherd was examined by the

Commissioners, he filed an information, in November of the same year, professing his discovery of his being a trustee for some estates in Newsham and Woodplumpton, called Crow Hall, near Broughton, four miles from Preston, granted to superstitous· uses, the rents of which were paid to Mr. Richardson, a priest (*P.R.O., Forfeited Estates, P. 62*) The Rev. Thomas Richardson a Douay priest, was a member of an ancient Catholic family which held considerable property in Myrescough for centuries, He was succeeded by the Rev. John Swarbreck, a priest ordained at the English College at Rome, who attended Crow Hall and Midge Hall till his death in 1731. In his will, he left instructions to his executors, the Rev. Henry Kendal, of Cottam, the Rev. Edward Melling, of Ladywell, Fernyhalgh, and the Rev. James Gant, of Salwick and Mowbreck Halls, to spend his effects in supporting a priest, if those deriving advantage from his services would erect a chapel at Midge Hall. He left £368 towards the project, and, at the eud of his will, says : " Blessed be those that forward these, my pious designs, and let those who offer to alter any part of them answer for it at the tribunal of Almighty God." His designs, however, were deviated from, and it was decided to erect a chapel, not at Midge Hall, but at Newhouse in Newsham, to which John Lund, of Midge Hall, was one of the principal contributors. The chapels attached to Crow Hall and Midge Hall were entered from the yard, "up-steps" as it was customary to build Catholic chapels in those troublesome times. At the former, Mass was occasionally said so late as the beginning of this century.

## 𝔑𝔢𝔴𝔥𝔬𝔲𝔰𝔢 𝔠𝔥𝔞𝔭𝔢𝔩.

" 'Twas the chapel were many a heavenly thought
   And many a contrite sigh
   Sweet peace to the youthful heart had brought,
   And joy that is born on high."

*F. C. Husenbeth.*

JOHN REYNOLDS, Reynold, or Wrennall, as the name was variously spelt, was the tenant of The Hough, Newsham, in which was the chapel. His descendant, William Wrennall, of Penwortham, married Ellen, daughter of Henry Finch, of Mawdesley, whose father, Thomas Finch, gent., married a sister and co-heiress of William Haydock, of Cottam, Esq. William Wrennall's son, Thomas Wrennall, of Newsham, married Elizabeth, daughter and co-heiress of James Newsham, of Bell Fold, in Newsham, who was half-brother to the Right Rev. Monsignor Charles Newsham, D.D., President of Ushaw College. The issue of this marriage was the Right Rev. Monsignor William Wrennall, D.D., late president of Ushaw College, now rector of the new church erected at the corner of Bloody-lane Ends, in Wesham leading to Mowbreck Hall; the Very Rev. Henry Canon Wrennall, of Stella; the Very Rev. Thomas Canon Wrennall, rector of St. Bede's College; and the late Rev. Joseph Wrennall, formerly prefect of studies at Ushaw College. The martyr Roger Wrennall, layman, who was executed at Lancaster, March 18th 1616, was no doubt an ancestor of this good family.

How long Mr. Kirk, a relative of the Kirks of Goosnargh, continued to officiate at The Hough does not appear, but after

Mr. Swarbreck's death, the mission was attended by the Rev. Roger Brockholes, who was serving Newhouse conjointly with Claughton in 1740. About this time a new chapel was erected on land purchased from the Hesketh or Brockholes family at Newhouse, which may be identical with The Hough estate. The chapel was small and ill-made, and it was dedicated to St. Lawrence. The Rev. John Carter, from the English College of Lisbon, was the first priest regularly stationed here. When Prince Charles Edward passed by in 1745, on his march to

NEWHOUSE CHAPEL.

Preston, Mr. Carter obtained an assurance from him, that his troops should not molest either his person or the mission property. In 1768, during the anti-Jacobite and No-Popery fermentation at Preston, Newhouse chapel narrowly escaped destruction. An infatuated mob, after destroying St. Mary's chapel, in Friargate, Preston, and burning that at Cottam, moved in the direction of Newhouse for the purpose of demolishing the chapel there.  But a neighbouring Protestant, named Hankinson, a descendant of the family of the man who betrayed George Haydock, the martyr, met the mob near Hollowforth Mill, and persuaded them not to touch the chapel.  He entreated them not to molest Mr. Carter, whom he highly praised.  He then provided them with food and drink, which appeased them, and thus they marched back to Preston.  Mr. Carter died Oct. 18th, 1789, but long before his death, about 1762, his nephew, James Carter, came to assist him in the mission.  He was the son of Richard Carter and his wife Elizabeth Mawdesley, who was probably a daughter or grand-daughter of old Henry Mawdesley of Myrescough, at whose house mass was occasionally said in the early part of the century.  Mr. Carter, in accordance with the general custom of priests, assumed his mother's maiden name, by which he was always known.  He remained at Newhouse for fifty-two years, and there died Feb. 4th, 1814, aged 78, a marble tablet within the chapel recording his memory. Towards the close of his life, he was assisted by his nephew, the Rev. Henry Carter, younger son of Robert Carter, and his wife Jane Cope, or Cooper.  Henry Carter was educated at the colleges of St. Omer and Douay, and came to Newhouse in 1805. Through his exertions the present chapel was erected in 1806, near the old site, and with a view to prevent any ill-feeling or difficulty with the Protestants, whose chapel at Barton, about a mile distant, was dedicated to St. Lawrence, the old patron of Newhouse was abandoned, and the new edifice dedicated to Our Lady.  In 1818 Mr. Carter retired in ill-health to Preston, where he died Nov. 24th, 1826, aged 65.  The Rev. Joseph Bryan Marsh succeeded to the mission, retired an invalid to a cottage in the neighbourhood in 1854, died in 1857, aged 73, and was buried at the north-east corner of the chapel.  It was he who erected the presbytery, adjoining the chapel, soon after his

appointment to the mission. He was succeeded in 1854 by the
Rev. Peter Holmes, son of William Holmes, of Preston and Newsham, and grandson of James Holmes, of Newsham, whose aunt
Margaret Holmes was the first wife of George Haydock, of The
Tagg. Mr. Holmes only remained a year, and was followed in
1855 by the Very Rev. Richard Canon Gillow, who had been
vice-rector of the English College at Rome, and twelve years
professor of theology at Ushaw College. He died at Newhouse,
Nov. 3rd, 1867, aged 73, and was buried under a handsome
stone, adjoining that to the memory of Mr. Marsh, erected by

NEWHOUSE PRESBYTERY.

his friend, Thomas Fitzherbert Brockholes, of Claughton, Esq.
Soon after he came to the mission, Canon Gillow erected the
schools, a short distance from the chapel. He was succeeded by
the Rev. W. H. Bradshaw; then came the Rev. Pierse Power

who cut down the fine old shrubs surrounding the house, and destroyed its beauty; next, in May, 1869, followed the Rev. Austin Powell, who re-decorated the chapel, and did much to improve the place; then in Sept., 1872, came the Rev. John Bilsborrow, a descendant of the donors of the Bilsborrow charity, of which the priest at Newsham should be a recipient; and, lastly, came the present incumbent, the Rev. Thomas Carroll.

After the Rev. Henry Carter· had erected the new chapel in 1806, he opened a burial ground, to the great ire of the parson of Goosnargh, the Rev. Joshua Southward, who demanded the interment fees, and began to assume a threatening attitude.

> "Hold ! I forgot—one said, a parson's dues
> Was the same thing with rhyming badge of Jews."
>
> *John Byrom*

At length, on Sept. 10th, 1810, he wrote the following letter to Mr. Carter:

"REVEREND SIR,—I hear not from you, nor what you mean to do, concerning sepultures in a piece of ground near to your chapel. You must know that you have no right to deposit bodies there, under a heavy penalty, and that at present, as minister here, I am cheated of the usual fees. Suppose your chapel was consecrated according to the Rites and Ceremonies of the Church of England, *corp's* (sic) could not then be interred in the consecrated ground adjoining, to the deprivation of our fees here. You probably may not be aware, by your improper conduct, what mischief you are doing to your body, and the Catholic cause, both here and in Ireland. The State has already been kind and indulgent to you, and you may still go on to look for more privileges, but you may depend upon this, that the higher powers will not remain long unacquainted with the undue advantage you at present take of the Established Church, and which must be a great check for anything more to be done for you. At present I have a correspondence with the Bishop of

Chester upon this business, and unless I soon to my satisfaction hear from you, I shall write to your Romish Bishop, Dr. Gibson, upon the subject—nor shall I cease from exerting my right in our Ecclesiastical Court.

"All I want is, primarily, the fees paid here, and then it is nothing to me how much you can get afterwards. I am, with all due deference and respect, etc., SOUTHWARD, minister of Goosnargh."

It was the burial of Mrs. Haydock, of Leach Hall, and of the Rev. James Haydock, of Lea, which excited the avarice of this characteristic follower of the loaves and fishes. It is to be hoped that these two tombstones will be restored to their original condition, and allowed to remain a memorial of the breaking down of intolerance. The inscription on one of these has been already given; that on the other may appropriately close the genealogical descent of the family.

### The last of the Haydocks.

"Now I am gone and have left you behind,
O, mortal folk, but we be very blind;
What we least fear full oft it is most nigh,
From you depart I first, for lo! now here I lie."

*Sir Thos. More.*

William Haydock, of The Tagg, the second son of George, through some unaccountable cause was brought up a Quaker His wife, Elizabeth, daughter of another Quaker, James Eccles, of Woodplumpton, was happily a staunch Catholic, for her mother, Anne, was a member of the good old Catholic family of Bilsborrow, which so materially helped to establish the mission of Cottam on an independent footing. She eventually succeeded to a moiety of the estate of her brother, Richard Eccles, who died without issue in 1762. Through her firmness her son George, and her daughter Anne, the wife of William Smith, of Elswick, gent., were thoroughly instructed in the faith and brought up most devout Catholics. The Eccles family was possessed of considerable landed property in various townships in the Fylde. The last of the family, Richard Eccles, offered his nephew, George Haydock, an estate called Crow Trees, then worth £300 per annum, if he would become a Quaker, but in vain. George was born in 1721, and was twice married. His first wife was Margaret Holmes, who died Aug. 21st, 1758, leaving a son, William, married to his second cousin, Mary, daughter of Oliver Hatch, of Hatch Mill (son of James Hatch, of the same, and his wife Mary, sister and co-heiress of Richard Eccles), by whom he had a daughter, Helen, wife of Mr. John Chapman. His second wife, whom he married Feb. 21st, 1760, was Anne, daughter of William Cottam, of Bilsborrow, and his wife Mary, daughter of Mr. Gregson, of Balderston, whose ancestor, the son of Gregory Normanton, of Normanton and Balderston, was called Greg's son, hence the name of Gregson in lieu of the ancient patronymic. Her sister, Alice Gregson, married James Heatley, of Samlesbury, mother of William Heatley, of Brindle Lodge, Esq., and dying May 1st, 1818, aged 94, was buried at Fernyhalgh; another sister became the wife of Thomas Caton, of the ancient Catholic family seated at Carr Hill, and was mother to the Rev. Thomas Caton, of Cottam, whose sister, Maria, was the mother of the Rev. Thomas Lupton, of Manchester. George Haydock died at The Tagg, Feb. 26th, 1783, aged 59. By his second wife he had six children— Elizabeth, who resided at The Tagg, and died there Sep. 12th, 1827, aged 66; Mary, born in 1763, who died Mar. 4th, 1772, aged 9; James, priest; Margaret, in religion Sister Stanislaus, O.S.A.; Thomas, the eminent Catholic printer and publisher, born 21st Feb., 1772; and George Leo, the biblical annotator. Mrs. Haydock eventually became heiress to her brothers, William and James Cottam, of Bilsborrow, who died unmarried

in 1804 and 1811, and thus Cuckoo Hall, which anciently belonged to the Haydocks, with other property once more returned
to the family.

> " In memory of the Rev. JAMES HAYDOCK of Lea,
> son of GEORGE and ANN HAYDOCK, of The Tagg,
> who departed this life, the 25th Apr., 1809,
> aged 45.
> Also of the above ANN HAYDOCK,
> who departed this life 17th Apr., 1822, aged 92 years.
> Also of ELIZABETH HAYDOCK,
> daughter of the above ANN,
> who departed this life on the 12th day of Sept., 1827,
> aged 67 years.

Having thus sketched the outline of the last generations of
the Haydocks of Cottam, we will proceed with the " Haydock
Papers."

> " Full many an object strange and new
> Have we beheld as on we flew."
> *C. A. Wheelwright's Comedies of Aristophanes.*
> *The Birds, Act IV. Sec. 1.*

## 𝔇ouay 𝔠ollege.

> " 'Tis gone, and for ever, the light we saw breaking,
> Like Heaven's first dawn o'er the sleep of the dead—
> When Man, from the slumber of ages awaking,
> Look'd upward, and bless'd the pure ray, ere it fled.
> 'Tis gone, and the gleams it has left of its burning,
> But deepen the long night of bondage and mourning."
> *Thomas Moore.*

The period at which these letters commence produced the
most disastrous events that ever agitated the civilised world.
The unhappy Louis XVI. had been seated but six years on the
throne of France, and the people, ground down by one of the

most heartless aristocracies that ever ruled a country, were
murmuring for a change. Revolution was rife throughout the
world. America was struggling to shake off her yoke; France,
Holland, and Spain, were assisting the United States; and, in
1780, a confederacy of the northern powers, styled the Armed
Neutrality, was formed against England.

It was in these portentous times that the Rev. Henry
Tichborne Blount resigned the presidency of Douay College, and
was succeeded in that honourable position by the Rev. William
Gibson, afterwards Vicar Apostolic of the Northern District.
This event occurred on May 31, 1781, two days previous to the
date of our first letter, written on the anniversary of James
Haydock's going to Douay. Born at The Tagg in 1764, he was
thus sixteen years of age. His parents had placed him at an
early age under the tuition of the Rev. Robert Banister at
Mowbreck Hall. This learned man had gained a high reputation during his twelve years' professorship of divinity at Douay.
He was an excellent classical scholar, and, in the judgment of
the venerable Alban Butler, possessed the Ciceronian style in a
degree equal, if not superior, to any of his age. In 1774 he
returned to England from Douay, and was placed at Mowbreck
Hall, a seat of the Westby family, where, besides his missionary
duties, he conducted a flourishing school to prepare boys for their
academical education. Thence James Haydock proceeded to
Douay.

The Rev. John Lund, alluded to in the letter, was the rural
dean of Amounderness, and priest at Cottam, where he was
placed in 1769. There he died, and was buried in his chapel,
where a tablet over the doorway bears this inscription :—

> "Sacred to the memory of the Rev. JOHN LUND,
> who having zealously discharged the missionary
> duties of this congregation for 43 years,
> departed this life, June 24th, 1812, in the 80th year
> of his age and 54th of his priesthood."

The Rev. Joseph Orrell, son of Humphrey Orrell, of Blackbrook, gent., was for many years priest at Singleton, until 1814,
when a new chapel was opened at Breck, near Poulton, and
Singleton Chapel was closed for a time.    He died at Blackbrook,
March 5th, 1820, aged 72.

Dom Henry Parker, O. S. B., born in or near Kirkham in 1752,
was probably a grandson of Alexander Parker, of Bradkirk Hall,
near Kirkham, Esq., by Dorothy, daughter of Thos. Westby, of
Mowbreck Hall, Esq., and he was a relative of Mrs. Haydock.
He was professed at St. Edmund's, Paris, in 1773, but was at St-
Gregory's Benedictine college at Douay at this period.    In 1786
he became sub-prior of St. Edmund's, and prior of that monastery
from 1789 to his death at Paris, July 8, 1817.    During the
revolution he was in prison.

" Douay College, *May* 29th, 1781.

" HONOURED FATHER AND MOTHER.

" As I cannot take a greater or a more pleasant delight in anything than to write to you, I now take the little leisure I have
to send you a few unregulated lines, which, nevertheless, I hope
will find an easy acceptance.    I certainly should not have written
to you so soon, our exam. now approaching, had I not been
pushed on by a favourable opportunity of having my letter
carried as far as Lancashire by one Mr. Laurenson.

" I received your kind and loving letter on the fourteenth of
this month, after the perusal of which, I understood that you
were all in a perfect state of health and happiness—thank God
for it.    On the same day I received a letter from my uncle,
William Cottam, by John Robinson, who came to see me,
together with Mister Henry Parker, before he set off again for
his journey's end.

" I shall never be able to make you satisfaction for the favourable kindnesses you have done me in procuring me a good
education, and recommending me to Mister Banister, there to
receive further instructions, and from thence to this College,
where I hope, by God's grace, to become His faithful servant.

I am now in the happiest state imaginable, but, nevertheless, I flatter myself with the hopes of repaying your kindness by praying for you, and procuring you all the happiness I am able.

" Take care of my two other little brothers, Thomas and George, and my sister Peggy; instruct and teach them how to be obedient in whatsoever state they employ themselves, and to be content with what God shall allot them; it is soon enough yet for them to think of coming into this country.

" I am very glad to hear that all my relations are in a perfect state of prosperity and health, which I pray God to continue them in. As for my sister Betty, she is grown old enough to help you in the house. Mr. Henry Parker is very glad to hear that she turns out to be a prudent young woman, and hopes she will so continue to the last period of life.

" I was a little shocked when I heard that Mister Lund was sick, but my uncle's last letter informed me that he was a little better.

" Thrice happy moments, indeed, when I was first appointed to come here. Pray inform Mister Banister that his prose is very true, to wit—the twenty-ninth of May surely was a happy day, when James Haydock was sent to Douay. Pray excuse the scrawl, since I am in a very great hurry. I will not mention anything now of the ways, manners, and customs of the college. I go to visit Mr. Henry Parker now and then, and the last time I saw him he was very well, and he bid me to remember him to you and my uncle and aunt Cottam—not passing over my respect to them both, and I will answer their letter the next opportunity. Pray give my most kind respect to Mr. Banister, Mr. Lund, and his housekeeper, Ellen, and to Mr. Orrell when you see him ; to all my other uncles and aunts, brothers, sisters, and relations ; to my brother William and his wife, and young Thomas—a few lines from him would find a very easy receptance, when an opportunity serves ; to my godmother, and tell her I am very happy in my situation. My compliments to John Williamson and his wife and children ; to your servant-men ; in a word, to all enquiring friends in Lancashire.

" Be pleased to send me a little money that I may buy books.

which will always be useful, whenever an opportunity serves. And begging your blessing, I remain your most dutiful and obedient son,                                    "JAMES HAYDOCK."

(Endorsed "To Mr. Haydock at The Tagg, to be left at Mr. Thos. Harrison's, Ginbow-entry, Preston, Lancashire.")

Under date April 2nd, 1783, he writes in grief to his mother, having received on the preceding 24th of March, the melancholy news of his father's death.

"But when I thought that it was the will of God, whose decrees are always good, just, and holy, I tried to stop them [his tears]. Blessed be the infinite goodness of God, who out of the abundance of his graces, vouchsafed to grant him full time to confess his sins and receive all the sacraments; that indeed afforded me great comfort. Indeed, I had had some thoughts of his death a few days before, tho' I never had heard the news of his being sick. . . . Comfort yourself, dear mother, with remembering that you have a son at Douay whose filial love for you shall never be wanting; think how happy I am here, separated from a deluding world, where there is nothing but sin and wickedness to be seen. Let it be your comfort to have the hopes of seeing me again. Come, come, dear mother, take courage; let not your heart be overwhelmed with grief and sorrow. Do not think his death will make me less vigorous in persevering in my studies. Come, I say, let us hope to see one another again ; let us hope to converse together face to face ; make but yourself happy, and I shall be happy. Was I to know that your grief is immoderate, it would give me more unhappiness than all the sorrow the death of my father has caused in me."

The next letter is the first letter written home by George Haydock (who took the name of Leo in confirmation), then eleven years of age, dated Douay College, Aug. 15, 1785, "I thank God I am very happy at the college, and I like it exceeding well." He next refers to the custom, still preserved at Ushaw, of new boys having two companions allotted them for three days' holiday, to instruct them in the routine of the college life and to wear off the rustiness of leaving home.

" I took for my play-fellows my brother and John Yates, who came not far from Preston, a great friend of my brother's. We had very good fun. We went to a house called Ecceshine (Esquerchin, the country house of the college, about three miles to the north-west of Douay), a house where the boys usually go to when they first come, or sometimes when there is a long vacancy from studies. Dear mother, we have got money-day every month, which in English money comes to about 15d., and that is to last a whole month. The gentleman that is to carry this letter is called Mr. Gillow. He is a particular friend of mine, and hears my confessions. He promises to come and see you. He, perhaps' on his return, may bring brother Tom along with him. If he does I shall be very glad to see him again, and if not, I shall make myself as happy as I can by endeavouring to grow daily in virtue, goodness, and piety."

His brother James appends a short note at the end of this letter. Both George and his older brother Tom received their preliminary education under the Rev. Robert Banister at Mowbreck Hall. Tom remained there longer than his brother, and was possessed of much greater natural ability. The next letter is his first from Douay College to his mother.

" Jan. 12. 1786.—I take up my pen to let you know that we are all well at Douay College, and I am very well content with this kind of life. I like the college very well, and I advance pretty well in my studies. . . . I am in the first school of underlow, and my brother is in the second. We had the Christmas vacancy very lately, and slept about an hour longer every morning, except once or twice, when there was confessions and communions. We have a good many play-days. On a play-day we sleep longer than commonly we do. The bearer of this letter is a young man coming over to England. His name is John Stapleton (of the Carlton family). He was in my school; he was in low-figures before, and came down to my school. We had skating very lately, but the frost has broke."

Then follows a letter from James Haydock on the same sheet with that of Thomas, in which he addresses a note to Mr. Lund (of Cottam), acknowledging a letter from him, and stating that he at present is in the school of philosophy, "*monstrum horrendum ingens*, we may justly compare logic to. Mr. Gillow's kind respects to you, who says he will most certainly visit his old friend Mr. Lund the very first occasion."

On Aug. 24, 1786, the three brothers again write long letters, as usual on the same sheet, to their mother at the Tagg. Thomas writes : "My brother James went to Louvain some time ago to see dear Peggy, but stayed not long and brings us the good news that my dear sister and all there are very well." His sister Margaret had joined the English Augustinians at the convent of St. Monica, Louvain, where she became a religious and took the name of Stanislaus. It will be remembered that Gilbert Haydock was chaplain there for many years, the nieces of Cardinal Allen, and other relatives of the Haydock family, having been members of this order, both at St. Monica's and its parent house dedicated to St. Ursula. Thomas Haydock then refers to his brother George being now in the same school with himself. " We go to bed at nine o'clock, and rise at five and a half. My cousin, Mr. Coghlan, and his wife, have been over very lately, and were very glad to see us." James Peter Coghlan was the principal Catholic printer and publisher of his day. His wife was the daughter of Richard Brown, of Clifton, near Preston, by his wife Helen Gradwell, aunt of Bishop Gradwell. Mrs. Coghlan was aunt to Dr. George Brown, the first bishop of Liverpool. It was apparently through the Browns that Mrs. Coghlan claimed relationship to the Haydocks. " I go to see Henry Parker frequently, and he is very kind to me and my brothers. Mr. Gillow, who conducted me hither, is my confessor, and is very well."

George, besides alluding to the Coghlans, says :—

"A young man, named Henry Bray, died very lately." He mentions the practice, still preserved at Ushaw, of allotting gardens to some of the younger boys. "I have got a little garden, and have had a good deal of lettuce out of it, which I eat along with oil and vinegar, which make it exceeding good . . . . Dear mother, you cannot conceive how regular we are taught to comply with our duties. We have one time for prayer, another for study, and a third for play."

James says :—

"This day Mr. Finch, who is a cousin of ours, returns back again to Louvain. He only came yesterday on purpose to see me and my brothers, along with another man who came much on ye same errand. He is a particular kind friend to sister Peggy. He assists her in all her difficulties, &c. He informs me that she improves very fast in ye French language, and is in very good health. She desires all that is kind to you, and dear sister, and Mr. Lund, and Ellen Kellet, and would be very glad to see sister Betty with her, were it God's will."

The Rev. James Finch was the grandson of Thomas Finch, of Mawdesley, gent., and Mary, his wife, daughter of William Haydock, of Cottam Hall, Esq., by Jane, daughter of Hugh Anderton of Euxton Hall, Esq. He became prior of a Carthusian monastery in Austria, and when it was dissolved during the troubles consequent on the French Revolution, he retired to England and resided at Ladywell, Fernyhalgh. He was buried in the graveyard attached to the new chapel at Fernyhalgh, and the following inscription is still to be seen on his tombstone:

" Sacred to the memory of the Reverend JAMES FINCH,
The last of the English Carthusian Monks.
He died March 3rd., 1821, aged 72.
Good Christian on this stone shed not a tear,
For virtue lies entom'd, enshrouded here ;
Religion, resignation, had combine
O'er these remains to raise a heavenly shrine."

Ellen Kellet was second cousin to the writers, being the

daughter of Robert Kellet, of Woodplumpton, and his wife
Elizabeth, daughter of Robert Haydock, of Leach Hall. Her
brother Richard became a priest, and for many years was the
chaplain to the nuns at Scorton. In this letter James again
alludes to Mr. Parker, "Henry Parker sends his kind respects to
you both ; he is going to quit Douay and go to Paris." We have
already seen that Fr. Parker was appointed sub-prior of St.
Edmund's, Paris, in this year.

Thomas writes to his mother :—

"*May* 3, *1787, Douay College.*—Would you think it proper
for me, who have been here almost a year and a half, not to
have writ to you at least thrice in ye time, to give you the
pleasure to know how I do, and improve, in learning and virtue,
as likewise to thank you for my education and especially for
sending me here, which certainly, dear mother, I shall thank you
for all my life. I am in low-figures with brother George, under
a very good master, and brother James is our pedagogue."

George begins :—

" It is with an intention to inform you of the good state of
my health, and how I improve in my studies, that I write to
you, as also to inform you that I have been here two years."

James says :—

"You see by ye two letters, which Tom and George have
wrote on the opposite sides, how much they have improved
in writing. They made them entirely themselves, so you may
be sure that what they there say is all their own. . . .
My defensions are approaching apace ; they will be over, I
hope, before ye beginning of July."

In the previous year he had defended with great *éclat* his *thesis
philosophiæ*. It was printed at Douay on a large sheet with a fine
engraving of the Holy Family after Bourdon—*Philosophia Ration-
alis. Prolegomena: ex logica viii., metaphysica vii. Præside
Reverendo Domino Joanne Gillow, philosophiæ professore. Tueri
conabitur in aula collegii Anglorum Duaceni. Jacobus Haydocke,*

*Die 23 Maii, 1786, à nonâ matutinâ ad undecimam.*   Dr. Gillow left Douay, where he had filled the chairs of philosophy and divinity for eleven years, on Oct. 3, 1791.   He was then stationed on the mission at York, where he built the chapel, and, on the death of the Rev. Thomas Eyre, president of Ushaw College, in 1810, he was appointed to succeed him.   He remained president till his death, Feb. 6, 1828 aged almost 75.

*Dec. 18, 1787.*   On this date the three brothers again write to their mother.   Thomas commences :—

"The love and duty I bear to you as a son would be comprised in too narrow bounds were they not to exceed the strait limits of Douay College.   Wherefore to remedy this I have embraced the departure of Nicholas Woodcock as a very favourable opportunity, as well to testify my affection for you and sister Elizabeth, as to let you know that all things are in a flourishing condition about us.   The reason for N. Woodcock's departure from amongst us you will be informed of on his arrival at Preston.   The consolation I experience in this situation of life is very great.   All our duties are performed with the greatest exactitude ; and these are the four constitutions generally made use of by the boys, *viz.,* pray hard, study hard, play hard, and eat hard—the two latter of which I fear I practise with too great diligence, but hope in a short time, punctually to perform them altogether, with the additional duty of obedience to superiors, in fulfilling which I find great delight.   From what I have said you may easily guess at my happiness."

The Woodcocks, who were related to the Haydocks, were descended from the Woodcocks of Woodcock Hall, in Cuerden, and at this period had just removed from Lemon House, in Walton-le-dale, to Preston, where they resided in a house and property which now forms the east side of Winckley-square.   Nicholas Woodcock was a younger son of William Woodcock, of Preston, who, by will dated Dec. 6, 1770, left his estates in Preston, Euxton, Billington, and Bartle in Wood-plumpton, to his eldest son and heir, Thomas Woodcock, of Preston, who sold his house and land in Preston, in 1807, to William Cross, of Redscar and Cottam Hall, Esq., for the form-ation of Winckley-square and Cross-street. Nicholas Woodcock returned to Douay College, which he left again on Oct. 31, 1792, and afterwards resided in Preston. He was then in his third year's theology. His older brother, John, then in his fourth year's divinity, escaped from the College on the same date, with three other students, the two Teebays of Preston, James and his brother Lawrence, in grammar and first-class rudiments respectively, and Patrick Flanagan, grammarian. John Woodcock was ordained priest at York, in Dec., 1792, and was stationed at Egton Bridge, Wycliffe, and lastly at Scorton, in Lancashire, from 1830 to 1837. Four months before his death, he retired from the mission, and went to reside with the Rev. J. B. Marsh at Newhouse Chapel, where he died Feb. 12, 1837, aged 70, and was buried in the chapel. He had two sisters, Miss J. Woodcock, of Preston, who died, Dec. 27, 1829, aged 74, and Miss Maria Woodcock, who died at Newsham in 1848. The latter gave £1000 for the establishment of a fund for ecclesiastical education at Ushaw College in 1842, and she left about £1300 for the same object by will dated Mar. 23, 1842, and codicil dated Apr. 10, 1845. Their ancestor, Richard Woodcock, of Walton, was the one who held Bank Hall, in 1641, whence the mission at Newsham derived. Fr. John Woodcock, O.S.F., who assumed his mother's name of Farington, and was martyred at Lancaster in 1646, was of this family.

George Haydock, in his letter, states that it was through ill-health that Nicholas Woodcock left Douay, and that he was ex-pected to return to the college about Easter.

There is nothing of general interest in James' letter.

Three letters from the brothers. Thomas addresses his mother and sister :—

" *Douay College,* 1789 (endorsed "autumn" by Geo. Leo Haydock). This favourable opportunity of the return of Mr. Gillow, the same who conducted me hither, and more especially the love and affection I bear you both, exact this letter from me, which my natural aversion to writing seems to forbid. But neither can you accuse me of neglect therein, conscious to yourself of the same backwardness. But to avoid apologies and give you, I am persuaded, a very sensible satisfaction, my health is vigorous and my hopes great, which are greatly increased from the expectation of once more seeing you in Lancashire, and from that constant correspondence in letters which must render happy our separation, which, when I think of it, gives me much more courage to go through my studies in which I have already spent three years and almost 10 months. Among 15 schoolfellows I generally get about the 5th place both in Latin and Greek."

After desiring to be remembered to a string of relations, including Mrs. Woodcock, he says :

" Inform Mr. Lund that as I have heard him say that he never despaired of me, it shall be always my study, that he may never have any reason to repent his prediction."

And showing that the sporting tastes of the family were still strong, he adds :

" Be pleased likewise, to give my kindest compliments and acknowledgements to my old and worthy friend, John Harrison [of Cottam], whom I have a particular affection for. I often think of our coursing together, and the much pleasure we took in that exercise, and, if you see him, tell him I have the gloves by me as yet which his son John left me when he was dying, and which I keep for his sake."

In George's letter is exhibited his early propensity for drawing.

" I imagine you received the little picture I sent you with some astonishment, not knowing that I could draw, and indeed I never learnt, but have made all the progress you see by my own application which I should have endeavoured to make better had I known that it was to be sent you. I shall now send you two more, one of which you may, if you please, give to sister Elizabeth, and if you desire any more I beseech you to send me word the first opportunity (since I can do one in 4 or 5 hours)."

He then alludes to two other drawings he is doing for his uncle William Cottam. On this letter is a memorandum, made by George Leo in later years, that "In Mr. Banister's letter dated 18th Sept. 1789, he says, Mr. Gillow called ye 4. If he were not so much for *alma* he would have embraced Garstang. Mr. B. thanks for our drawings." From this it would appear that the mission at Garstang was offered to Mr. Gillow at this time. The chapel was erected there in 1784, on the western side of the town, and was abandoned when the new church was opened at Bonds in 1858. Previous to this the priest of the mission seems to have generally resided at Scorton, though the Rev. William Foster is said to have lived at Garstang in 1771.

James writes :—

" I can easily conceive what comfort and joy it must give you to receive three letters at once from your three sons, of whom you form the greatest expectations of their being, if not three priests, at least three good Christians, and who, on their part, wish to convince you of every tender regard that duty and *religion* can inspire, under whose protection we most sincerely desire to put ourselves, persuaded that she will never fail to inspire us with filial sentiments towards so good a mother. Indeed, dear mother, we ought to show ourselves dutiful sons to our holy religion and to you; to our religion which teaches us to be grateful to our benefactors, and to you who have ever shown yourself a most tender and compassionate mother. Our behaviour being thus regulated towards God and our parents will not fail to draw down a blessing upon us. . . . . I have some hopes of seeing dear sister this next month, who expresses a great desire of seeing me. I heard from her a few days ago. She is perfectly well, and desires to be kindly remembered to you. . . . I have wrote by my good and great

friend Mr. Gillow to Mr. Lund, Mr. Banister, and dear uncle and
aunt Cottam at Mowbreck. Perhaps you may have the pleasure
of seeing him, as he means if possible to pay Mr. Lund a visit.
Henry Parker cannot prevail upon his superiors to give him
leave to visit his Lancashire friends. He wrote to me last
Sunday but one; was in perfect health, and desires to be remembered to you. If you see Mr. Gillow he will supply the
shortness of my letter, which you will scarce be able to read.
Indeed, I always write fast, which makes my letters generally
ill-wrote."

After apologising for a long silence, Thomas Haydock, in a
letter to his mother and sister at The Tagg, says :—

" *Douay College*, Feb. 7, 1791.—But I am of opinion that a
letter of great length would not give you great pleasure if it was
to be filled with news of this kingdom, which is at present in a
most deplorable condition. Remember me likewise to Mrs.
Woodcock, whose two sons are perfectly well."

George says :—

"Gratitude for all the care you have taken of me, and my
duty to you, have forced from me what faint-heartedness has
long kept me from performing. I am in very good health as
usual, thank God, and go on with a great deal more pleasure
than hitherto in my studies, for you must know that I have been
about half a year in poetry, so that now is the time, in a manner,
to begin all I have been through before, being only a preparation
to the schools which follow, *vis.*, rhetoric, philosophy, and
divinity. I have often got hard work to cobble up 10 or 12
verses for my theme, but I was in a better humour last night, so
that I have made about twenty-four or upwards. Excuse me,
dear mother, for always filling up my letters with the school
affairs."

In a long letter, James says :—

" I sent sister Peggy word that her pension and fortune would be paid to her convent at or about Candlemas, which will both content her superiors and afford her great satisfaction. She is perfectly well, and as I have often assured you, perfectly happy . . . . . I am as yet only sub-deacon ; my not advancing in holy orders is owing to the troubles of these countries. I expect that on Saturday before the second Sunday in Lent, I shall be advanced to deacon, which is the next dignity to priesthood. Pray for me on that day. Unless something extraordinary happens, I shall be priest, if not before, at farthest, next Christmas, and perhaps next year at this time shall be able to give a good guess when I shall have the happiness of seeing you. I tremble with the thought of the heavy charge which will be laid upon me when I come to England. I can only depend on the infinite goodness of Him, who, I hope, has chosen me for Himself, and I will perfect the good work which He has begun in me, and your good prayers for the worthily discharging my duty."

He was ordained priest at Arras in the beginning of 1792. Soon afterwards he came on the mission, and was appointed domestic chaplain to John Trafford, of Trafford House, near Manchester, Esq., the lineal descendant of Sir Edmund Trafford, the great persecutor of his ancestors. Previous to leaving Douay he had been some years prefect of the study-place, and taught catechism, in which branch of his duty, Dr. Kirk says, he excelled.

The letters from Douay now cease, and the better to understand the cause, and to fill up the gap, we will introduce an interesting narrative of the last days of the college, penned in 1852 and 1853 at the request of the late Very Rev. John Canon Walker, of St. Edward's College, Liverpool, by the last survivor of the *alumni* of Douay College, the Rev. John Penswick, who died at Garswood, Oct. 30, 1854, aged 86.

## The Beginning of the End.

Even now the devastation is begun,
And half the business of destruction done.
*Goldsmith's Deserted Village.*

The first uprising of that terrible moral earthquake, which
afterwards shook the world to its centre, had partially subsided
and a sullen calm, suspicious enough, had ensued, when the writer
of this narrative, John Penswick, who was three schools below
George Leo Haydock, arrived at the college. But the memory
of these occurrences was fresh, and the subject of frequent con-
versation amongst the students. What he was not an eye-
witness of, he heard from those who were, and they agreed in
their statements. Previous however, to entering upon the
description of the events that he has recounted, it is presumed
that those who may read his brief memoir have acquired a com-
petent knowledge of the horrors of the first French Revolution.
Without this preliminary knowledge, much of what he has written
would be almost unintelligible. It is from the outbreak of the
first revolution that his narrative commences.

"After the meeting of the *states-general*, the harbinger of all
the evils that followed, there were disturbances in every part of
France, fomented it was said by the influence and money of the
celebrated, perhaps we should say, the infamous Duke of Orleans,
Philippe Egalité. From these disturbances, accompanied with
terror and bloodshed, Douay was not exempt. Agitators and
agents for ill were sought, paid, and sent round in every direction,

first, to promote distrust in the constituted authorities, and afterwards to upset and destroy them.

"The nobility, clergy, and men of property, were arraigned before the public as joint accomplices in a plot to starve and destroy the people. It was first insinuated, surmised, and then proclaimed unblushingly, that the aristocrats had begun their operations; that they were attempting to enslave the people by starving them, and for that purpose were sending away boatloads of wheat and flour, necessary for the subsistence of the people, in order by these unjustifiable means to reduce them to absolute subjection. By such representations, groundless as they were, but confidently and impudently asserted and repeated, the passions of the populace were lashed into fury, and prepared for any measure of violence and guilt; and the soldiery, corrupted by beer and money, and instigated by the addresses of the remorseless Jacobin clubs, and the scurrilous, irreligious writings of the day, joined in these disturbances instead of quelling them.

"One instance, which occurred in Douay, will illustrate the extremities to which the populace was urged in its state of exasperated feeling.

"A tradesman in the town was accused, perhaps only suspected, of contravening the injunctions of the mob by despatching to the neighbouring towns certain quantities of wheat and flour. For this offence, real or supposed, he was arrested and instantly committed to prison, and one of the municipal guards was placed sentry over him with a drawn sword to prevent his escape. Intelligence of this arrest spread rapidly through the streets and alleys of the town, and as rapidly did the mob assemble, accompanied by bands of soldiery who had released themselves from all discipline and obedience to their officers, and goaded by the virulent harangues of the savage agitators and unprincipled tools of faction, they rushed with blind ferocity to the door of the prison to wreak their vengeance on a man, untried, unheard, and to whom was given neither time nor opportunity to prepare or plead in his own defence. One obstacle only was opposed to the instant execution of their bloody designs, and that was the firmness and resolution of the sentinel appointed to guard their intended victim. That man, being as conscientious as he was brave, and esteeming it his bounden duty to protect as well as to guard his prisoner, resisted strenuously for awhile, and with all his power, their mad attempts at murder. But what could a solitary individual do against an infuriated multitude? He was seized, disarmed, and hurried off to the market-place, and instantly run up to the fatal lamp-post, expiating by his death a great crime in their eyes, but in the judgment of all honest men, dying a species of martyr to the fulfilment of his own sacred duty. That man was Derbaix, the principal bookseller in the town, and printer to the English College. How preposterous was this frivolous pretence of scarcity appears from the fact that Douay is situated in the midst of a most fertile plain that produces abundantly more than is sufficient for the support of its inhabitants.

" Freed from restraint, and under the circumstances from the means of restraint, the undisciplined soldiery, and the more un-disciplined mob, perambulated the various streets, and visited in succession the houses of the principal citizens, and by their significant menaces, compelled them to join in their frantic cries of *vive la nation*, and then exacted beer and provisions as the price of their further forbearance.

"From these unpleasant visitations it might have been expected that the English secular college, consisting almost entirely of English students, would have been exempted. They were not their subjects ; they were not personally interested in their changes and revolutions ; they were not partizans of any of the factions which then ruled or attempted to rule ; they were mere strangers enjoying there an asylum and a refuge which had been denied them at home. What mattered it to them whether this desirable protection were extended to them under an absolute or a limited monarchy, which last seemed to be the expressed want and wish of the day ?   But no! a lawless rabble acts and does not argue.   The sovereign people were determined that their obstrusive aggressions should be made impartially.   In the plenitude of their assumed power they thundered at the College door requiring immediate admittance.   Some delay occurred, during which the superiors wisely instructed the younger students to receive the deluded multitude with some English cheers, such as boys know how to give, to propitiate them in somewise, and to prevent further violence.   Accordingly, after some further demur the mob forced an entrance into the College, and crossing the ambulacrum, rushed into the quadrangular court directly opposite, where, to their astonishment and apparent gratification, they were met by a laughing array of boys, who, throwing their hats up into the air, received them with loud huzzars, and vociferated at the top of their lungs the fashionable cry of the day, *vive la nation.*

"This cry, at that time, by no means denoted an acquiescence in the fatal measures which marked and disgraced the subsequent eras of the revolution.   It then imported merely the downfall and dismission of arbitrary power, not inherent originally in the French constitution, but assumed and usurped in the lapse of time, and arrogantly proclaimed when Louis XIV. had the audacity to announce *La France c'est moi.*

"The nation in its strength arose at last to depose this hateful absolute power, and, as it was said, with the concurrence in some measure of its present king.   This, at least, is certain, that the *states-general* were summoned by him to assemble and deliberate on the pressing emergencies that caused them to be convoked, and to apply a remedy to evils too deeply felt to be denied. Such a partial return to the paths of liberty and a participation in the government, was hailed with pleasure by the people of England, who watched with intense curiosity and interest the throes of a mighty nation bursting its trammels, and beginning to trample upon an odious despotism.

" The first acts of a nation striking in its own defence, and evin-
cing by the destruction of the infamous Bastille its determination
to be free, were highly popular in England. Great hopes were
excited ; great results were anticipated ; so that when these
uninvited strangers arrived in the College, it was not thought
inconsistent with any duty to welcome their arrival by joining
in the shouts of liberty and well-wishing to the nation. This
kind of reception, more favourable than they had anticipated,
had a magical effect upon the invaders. So far from resorting
to violence or personal ill-treatment, they subsided at once into
a sort of suavity of behaviour and comical amenity, and added
greatly to the amusement of the boys by their grimaces, antic
gestures and dances, which were mischievously applauded by
loud incessant peals of laughter ; and the mob accepting with the
modest assurance of Frenchmen these unmistakeable tokens of
merriment as a compliment paid to their own powers of pleasing,
were consequently highly gratified, and expressed in warm terms
their satisfaction at the mode of their reception. They then
departed, after partaking at their own request of the College
beer, taking with them some of the boys whose appearance or
behaviour had particularly attracted their attention.

" It was laughable to witness the motley and ludicrous appearance of these chosen companions of the military. Supported on
each side by the arms of the now friendly soldiers, they were
hugged and petted, and held up to the admiration of all good
citizens. They were then saddled with military accoutrements,
had cocked hats placed on their heads, and naked swords in
their hands, and in this quaint guise they were hailed and
applauded by the uproarious shouts of the surrounding multitude. Fortunately, laughter succeeded to preceding violence.
Even the insurgent bands bent on mischief, whom they occasionally met in their progress through the streets, stood still awhile,
contemplating with delight the unexpected display, and then
summoning all their energies joined heartily in the public merri-

G

ment, uniting at one time the grimaces and antics of the monkey with something of the ferocity of the bear dance. It was impossible for a bystander not to be gratified with the bearing of these students, their steadiness and self-possession, and at times with their radiant, honest faces beaming with fun and frolic. After the scenes of horror and violence which the town had witnessed without the power of repressing them, the burst of innocent and harmless mirth escaping from the lips of these boys was quite refreshing, and had a most composing effect; a gleam of sunshine streaming athwart a lurid sky.*

"At that time, when these unexpected uprisings took the world by surprise, the College was at the height of its fame and prosperity.

"Under the presidency of the Rev. William Gibson, who was afterwards bishop of the Northern District, and principally by his exertions, aided, of course, by the contributions of the nobility, gentry, and other friends, very considerable additions were made to the College buildings, and to college accommodation. Great taste was displayed in their erection, and they were as commodious as they were tasteful. Even the old part of the house was so ornamented and beautified as to stand in favourable competition with the new. The same style was held throughout, and it would have been difficult to have told that they had not both been built at the same time and on the same plan. The study-place, a noble room in the old wing, was remodelled and refitted, and furnished with elegant oaken desks capable of accommodating, easily and commodiously, a hundred students. This lofty and spacious room was crowded to overflowing, and was insufficient to contain the classes under poetry. The other public rooms, such as the libraries, the refectory, and the divines' school, in which at every competition the successful students received their premiums in the presence of the president and of all the

* It appears that these boys were borne in triumph the whole of the night through the streets of Douay (*Memorials of the Rev. Thomas Gillow*).

inmates of the College, were indeed noble apartments, such as are not usually found even in the houses of the first nobility. The apartments of the superiors were elegant and commodious, and such, in somewhat less degree, were those of the divines. The rooms for the students were also comfortable and sufficiently capacious to accommodate themselves and their pupils. For recreation, the seniors had their walled garden, laid out in extensive walks and stocked with choice fruit trees. The professors and divines had their garden, walled also on three sides, having vines affixed, and near them gravelled walks for exercise. On the fourth side their premises were separated from the grounds of the philosophers, rhetoricians, and poets, by a low wall surmounted by an elegant green palisade, which determined the boundaries of each without obstructing their view. To these latter classes were allotted grounds intersected by spacious gravel walks, over-arched by noble lime trees to protect them from the heat and glare of a too-often scorching sun. On the side, and at the end of a walk, were pleasant summer-houses, around which vines were thickly trained that they might admit an abundance of fresh air while they excluded the solar heat. The younger students had also their play-grounds, their ball places, their racket-corners, and all the appendages for pursuing the games accredited at the College. Apart from all these, and having as little as possible communication with them, were the apartments and lodgings of the servants and workmen necessary to do the menial offices and supply the various requirements of such an establishment. Such was the external œconomy of the College, and it is only fair to say that the duties attendant on it were performed with zealous regularity.

"Of the internal œconomy of the house, it was the opinion of the late Right Rev. Dr. Smith, formerly bishop of the Northern District, calmly and deliberately delivered, that neither within his own remembrance nor from any information that he could derive, was the College ever in better condition in all respects.

Never greater harmony prevailed among the superiors, never was greater zeal and ability displayed by the various professors, never was better conduct, greater attention to their studies, nor a more willing observance of the College discipline, than was found in the different grades of students at the time when these events occurred which have just been narrated.   In piety, in learning, in discipline, the College was at least equal to any other ; it certainly was surpassed by none.

" Moreover, there was a sort of prestige acting silently, but efficaciously, in the breasts of all the inmates when they reflected that their house had been the home of so many eminent men who had done honour to religion by their learned and voluminous writings ; that it had been the *alma mater* of at least one hundred and sixty pious and devoted priests who had laid down their lives in defence of religion ; and of a more numerous body still, who, having received their education at that College, abided the loss of lands and liberty sooner than forsake their religion. Surely this was a home to live in.   No one ever left it without reluctance; no one ever recollected it without delight.

" It was strange that the acme or accumulating point of the College's prosperity should have been a sort of signal of its decline ; that the riot of a day should have influenced beyond that day the welfare of such an establishment.   Yet so it was. It is said that within the tropics a small cloud sometimes appears on the horizon, at first scarcely perceptible to the eye, yet insensibly increasing in magnitude, and gathering strength from the deadly vapours that penetrate and surround it, till it expands suddenly over the whole face of the heavens, and, presenting to a trembling world a murky, baleful, malignant aspect, is portentous of storms, and tempests, and hurricanes.   Just so did these slight convulsions indicate the throes of that mighty volcano, which, already in active operation, and holding for a time a hidden but irresistible course, was soon to burst forth in all its might and in all its terrors, scattering ruin and desolation over the wide sur-

face subjected to its poisonous agency. These are trite com-
parisons, but no other occur to us that so vividly express the
horrors of the revolutionary days that succeeded to these preliminary outrages.

" It is not our intention to give even a succinct account of the
savage cruelties and unprincipled confiscations of the first
revolution. We will not attempt to delineate the uncouth
arch-demagogue Mirabeau thundering forth from the tribune his
seditious, felonious harangues, and vindicating atrociously the
rights of man to seize and appropriate the estates of faithful
subjects. We will not allude further to the massacre of thou-
sands of unoffending clergymen, nor the expulsion of the
remainder who preferred exile to apostasy. We need not recall
to remembrance the extreme injustice exercised against the
nobles who were forced, by every engine of terror, to fly for
safety to foreign lands, and then to hear that all their property
had been confiscated in consequence; neither is it necessary to
say that those who had the resolution to remain were as surely
incarcerated, or lost their lives unjustly under the red axe of the
guillotine, which never rested. An enumeration of all these cool
atrocities is foreign to our present purpose, excepting so far as
they contribute or tend to throw light upon the fallen fortunes
of Douay College.

" After this first onset on the quiet tenor of college life, nothing
occurred for a long time to disturb its peace, or to interfere with
the usual occupations. Compared with many other towns of
equal size, Douay suffered little from the harassing train of
agitations and authorised murders that disgraced the capital and
some of the principal cities of the south. It was a frontier town,
and in the prospect of an impending war with Prussia and the
Emperor of Germany, whose states were contiguous to, and
threatened its immediate vicinity, it might not be deemed prudent
or safe to introduce these extreme revolutionary measures, which
would have a tendency to sow disunion amongst the townsmen
and endanger the fortress.

"For the space of more than a year the inmates of the College dwelt in comparative security, and, if not encouraged, they were not molested.  Jealousies were, indeed, entertained of its supposed leanings toward regal authority, and once at least a direct complaint to that import was made by the municipal authorities to all the heads of houses in the town who owed allegiance to his Britannic Majesty.  This was an unexpected stroke, and if it expressed or insinuated actual or virtual interference in French interests was altogether unfounded.  But these were not times in which accusations of any kind could be safely despised or left unanswered.  Accordingly a joint exculpatory memorial in reply was drawn up and presented, expressing the great gratitude felt by all the houses for the kind shelter and protections afforded by the French nation for so long a time to the afflicted and persecuted Catholics of England and its dependencies.  In pursuance of these becoming sentiments, and influenced by every feeling of honour and respect, it was stated that it had been the declared and decided wish of all the colleges, accredited as that wish had been by long, uniform, and undeviating good conduct, to give satisfaction to the great and generous nation that had so long protected them.  Outlawed in their own native land for the bare profession of their religion, they had found safety and a quiet asylum in France.  They had never abused the confidence reposed in them, but had been most anxious to prove to all France that her favours had not been bestowed on unworthy recipients.  At all times they had carefully refrained from interference in the state in which they were permitted to dwell. They had neither sought, nor exercised, any authority, save only within the precincts of their respective colleges, and were even there only the acknowledged and permitted authority necessary to preserve peace, and uphold discipline ; beyond this point they had never gone, nor wished to go.

"This was the substance and purport of the justificatory memorial presented by the heads of establishments in Douay, but very lamely and inadequately reported here. The original was a copious, firm, and eloquent reply to the insinuations, rather than direct accusations, that had been made against us, and it was supported by proofs and arguments that would carry conviction home to every one who was not already predetermined not to be convinced. This memorial, it was said, was drawn up by Mr. Dillon, President of the Irish College, and subscribed by all the other heads of houses.

" The result of the meeting was, innocence was vindicated, but did not triumph. A sort of reluctant qualified admission of the justness of the arguments was made, but nothing friendly or refreshing. It was as plain that some secret agency was at work inimical to the interests of the memorialists ; and of those present, there perhaps was not one who did not consider himself in the situation so well described by the poet :—

> ' ———— *incedis per ignes*
> *Suppositos cineri doloso.'*
>
> *Horace, Od.* 2., *1. 8.*

" As stated above, no fresh attempts were made at coercion or restraint on liberty, yet the atmosphere darkened around, and its gloom appeared to have reached beyond the channel. What had occurred at the house, and elsewhere, had a decided and injurious effect upon the welfare of the college. It was impossible to combine lax principles, mob rule, and past outrages, with any fair prospect of future security. *Silens leges inter arma,* is an apothegm well appreciated and understood by more than parents, but when to this unenviable state was superadded in some dominant quarters the almost daily breach of all accredited laws, and no security for the observance of any that were inconvenient to present rulers, it was not surprising that parents should listen to timely and well founded fears, and be anxious to withdraw their children from scenes where there could be no reasonable assurance of even personal safety.

" The mainstay of order had been violently snapped asunder by the unprincipled expulsion of the clergy, a ruthless, insatiate attack upon property and man's best rights, rendering all others insecure. While religion prevailed and was respected, the grosser outrages upon life, liberty, and property, that were contemplated, could not be tolerated. Banish religion, and the teachers of religion, and ,the strongest barriers against vice are overthrown, disorder and murder by wholesale are rampant, and crime of every kind made easy. That this is no exaggerated view of the consequences resulting from the extinction of religious influence, subsequent events have too clearly shown. Some virtuous priests remained on their native soil, braving danger, and resolved at the risk of their lives to snatch some struggling individuals of their flocks from the awful consummation of dying without spiritual help ; but these were few in numbers, oftentimes in concealment, and consequently their good offices were much restricted.

"No wonder, then, that implicit trust was not reposed in a people who had tamely submitted to the destruction of all religious liberty ; who looked on with supineness, while daring and impious men were issuing their revolting decrees, that in France henceforward there should be no toleration for a non-juring clergyman, either to administer the sacraments, to offer sacrifice, or to exercise any of the sacred offices of religion. Liberty of worship was indeed ostentatiously proclaimed, but Catholic worship was construed to be pure fanaticism, a crime in their eyes deserving the severest punishment, even death itself.

"Can it surprise us that students were recalled by their anxious parents in shoals, or at least in quick succession ? The danger was becoming imminent ; the advantages of remaining were every day less ; and to those who were not designed for the ecclesiastical state, no object worth the expense of its attainment could be secured, which might not be provided more safely at home. Soon it almost ceased to be strange news, weekly, and almost daily to hear that some of the schoolfellows were summoned to repair to the town house, to be provided with the necessary passports for their journey homeward. How soon others of those who remained were to follow, could only be sur- mised. These partings, probably for life, were inexpressibly painful to those who were going, and to those who remained. The links which had united so many young persons in early friendships, in companionship, in studies, in play, and even in danger, could not be suddenly broken without a pang vibrating in many a heaving breast. But of this enough. It is sufficient to say that they went, and that they were greatly regretted.

" Deeper and deeper grew the gloom around, and darker and drearier the prospect into futurity. At first came what might be called petty annoyances. War having been proclaimed against the Emperor of Germany and the King of Prussia, the College was almost deafened with the constant roll of the drums regu- lating the drills of the recruits of the first requisition. Their mustering place was close under the study-place windows, and either the shouting of the word of command, or the noise of the drum, or the blast of some musical warlike instrument, was dinned in rapid succession into the ears, from break of morn until dewy eve, to the almost utter discomfiture of attempts at study.

" To this daily recurring plague were added other annoyances which tried the temper, if they did not improve it. A whole host of masons were sent into the house for the purpose of chiselling out and defacing the armorial bearings of the bene- factors, which had adorned almost every window in the interior of the College. These badges were represented to be too aristocratical, and too much opposed to their happy state of liberty and equality to be retained, a state which had been pro- claimed, but which did not exist. It was in vain that it was represented that those were the arms of English families only, and that having no reference to French politics, they ought to be taken out of the ban prohibiting armorial bearings. To those remonstrances no ear was given. Like St. Patrick's serpents such emblems could not, it seemed, co-exist with the safety of the Republic.

" The affairs of the College were so intimately interwoven with what was passing around, that it is difficult to describe its position without alluding to events which could not fail to have some influence favourable, or otherwise, upon its interests. Generally, in what fell under the scope of its inmates' observation, there was much to grieve them, and little to give them hope or confidence in the future. One enormity following another, ever growing but never diminished, showed them the bias of the men who ruled them, and that the tendency of most of the measures then decreed, were evil without alloy ; a sort of prelude and preparation of the dark tragedies soon to be enacted."

## 𝕿𝖍𝖊 𝕽𝖊𝖎𝖌𝖓 𝖔𝖋 𝕿𝖊𝖗𝖗𝖔𝖗.

" Oh, men ! ye must be ruled with scythes, not sceptres,
  And mow'd down like the grass, else all we reap
  Is rank abundance, and a rotten harvest
  Of discontent infecting the fair soil,
  Making a desert of fertility."

*Sardanapalus, Act I. 2.*

" EVEN in this preliminary stage of depravity, there were many outrages of which they were the unwilling witnesses ; much was done to shock all their best feelings, and much to fill the most thoughtless with horror. The churches, so long the spot to which the wearied spirit resorted to soothe its sorrows, represent its wants and renew its vigour at the altars at which its forefathers had worshipped and found life, and strength, and consolation, were now desecrated, and converted, some into unclean stables of the artillery horses, and some into shelters for the more unclean profane drivers. In the principal church at Douay, dedicated to the memory of St. Peter, where the altar of the living God had stood, there arose the mountain, a heap of piled earth, the emblem of the most bloody faction of the Jacobins. Here their pestilent orgies were held, and hence were issued their lists of proscriptions that consigned to the dungeons or the scaffold some of the most deserving men of the age. Merit of most kinds was obnoxious to them, and a strong recommendation to be included in their proscriptions. The other churches were principally made subservient to the wants of the army on their immediate frontier. They held its provisions and its supplies One that was filled to the roof with wheat in the straw took fire and was burned to the ground, and its profaned steeple toppled into the street. Gangs of yelling savages were employed to destroy the statues, images, and pictures of the saints, and with long ropes to pull down the crosses from their pedestals. It was a pleasure, however, to see that these degraded instruments of unprincipled infidels had few accomplices and few to applaud their almost infernal feats.

"Now another sad, harassing spectacle awaited them, the sight of the forcible ejection of the poor nuns from a neighbouring convent within their view, and even within their hearing. It was truly distressing to behold from the upper windows of the College the terror, the trouble, and confusion of those heartbroken religious, having no one to console them, no one to advise them; their anguish at departing, going for a few steps, then rapidly returning to take one more parting view of these scenes of their once happy and tranquil life, a lasting farewell of their beloved home, a home no longer to them; and at length thrust forth unmercifully into the wide public street to seek a resting-place they knew not where, and to find an asylum they knew not how. Whoever has seen a once peaceful hive suddenly disturbed or plundered, may have witnessed the consternation, the confusion, the helpless incertitude what to do or how to act, of this humble, laborious, and industrious insect; now fearful for the safety of its cells, fearful for its stores, and fearful even for its own very existence. Such a one may have some slight notion of the wretched outcast condition of these much-injured women, help-less as the bee, but without its sting. Their wailings and lamentations could never be obliterated from the memories of those who were the unwilling witnesses of this pitiable scene.

"Meanwhile, the condition of the College was not improved. There were many departures, but not one single recruit by way of reinforcement from England or elsewhere. It had the mis-fortune, moreover, to fall under the suspicion of the rulers, in common with every honest man who was not an abettor of the misdeeds at which humanity has now to blush. Its confidential servants were removed, and others substituted in their stead, on whom it could place no reliance. Even the few domestics that were permitted to remain became objects of distrust. Was there no secret understanding between them and the authorities, that they were retained when others were expelled? Had they not consented to become spies as well as servants? Such was the problem to be solved, but no sufficient data were given to facilitate or insure a solution. Its porter disappeared, and in his place three others were assigned, so that there was no reason to complain of a deficiency in numbers. Their business was to note and examine everything entering or going out of the College. Their assiduity in their new calling was so exemplary as to gain from the students the name of " the three spiders," a just compliment due to them for the zeal and agility they displayed at their unaccustomed post. Besides the main door, near which the spiders were posted, there were two other outlets from the College grounds ; both were now closed.

" By this arrangement it was vainly imagined that whatever the College possessed, or they coveted, was completely in their power. In this they reckoned without their host. Walls might be scaled, and they were scaled. Much valuable property, principally in plate, was conveyed beyond their reach by four of the philosophers, young men selected for that office from an opinion entertained of their prudence and daring. Their names were :— Richard Thompson, afterwards Vicar-General of the Lancashire District ; Thomas Penswick, the writer's brother, subsequently Bishop of Europum and V. A. of the Northern District ; John Clarkson, afterwards on the Mission at Ingatestone Hall in Essex ; and William Lucas, who eventually joined the army, and for some years resided in Birmingham. They certainly ran great risk at such a time and in such an undertaking ; but their courage never failed them, and they executed their task in a manner to ensure the full approbation of the superiors who employed them.[*]

[*] A few years before his death, the Very Rev. Vicar Thompson went over to France in company with some friends, and pointed out the places where

"The boa constrictor, it is said, does not usually destroy its victim at one fell grasp, but gradually encircles it, fold within fold, to secure its prey and prevent its escape. It then employs the lever of an irresistible muscular power by which it safely and securely effects its destruction. The College now began to feel the reptile tightening its cords around it. It foresaw danger, as who did not in those unhappy days? The proclamation of war against England, and the denunciation of death against all crowned heads did not mend the position. The Reign of Terror, as it was called, had then begun. Denunciation breathing blood and extermination was rife against everything that had hitherto been held sacred. Such menaces were ominous. The monsters of the Revolution did not deal in idle threats. The blow was often struck before the threat was issued. By the decided and atrocious measures of bold and unrelenting miscreants the public mind was paralysed with fear and sudden consternation. Even the best intentioned knew not how to act, or when to offer an available resistance. The axe which fell upon the neck of the French monarch fell with stunning effect upon the heads of all his subjects not actually involved in the guilt of this murder. Every man stood aghast, and, as it were, petrified on the first intelligence that a most foul act had been done, which would have been deemed and declared to be impossible if it had not been already effected. Men knew not what to think or what to

the treasure had been deposited. It was evident that some of the hiding places had been discovered, and a portion of the treasure, principally church plate, taken away. The remainder, from information furnished by Mr Thompson, and Mr. Penswick himself, who had accidentally witnessed the secretion through a key-hole, and had been soundly rated for his inquisitiveness, was afterwards recovered by the Right Rev. Mgr. Searle, who, in the spring of the year 1868, obtained permission from the Emperor Napoleon III. to search for it. These relics of the illustrious seminary, consisting principally of plate for the service of the refectory, were divided into three portions and distributed to the three Colleges, Ushaw, Old Hall Green, and Oscott. On many of the pieces are engraved the armorial bearings of the Duke of Norfolk, and of other old Catholic families.

expect. Human life had become cheap. It had been wrested from the chief and his much abused consort; why should it be respected in the subordinate? Henceforward, in each man's case, life hung on a contingency. Power alone conferred right; and woe to the wretched being who fell under the ban or displeasure of the powerful. An old grudge, a present pique, or even an inconvenient debt, might in the confusion of right and wrong instigate to a judicial murder. Arrests were multiplied and were accompanied by revolting circumstances. A municipal officer, girt with his sash of office, and attended by his followers and a train of musicians playing "Ça ira" or the Hymn of the Marseillais, usually at the close of the day, called at the house of him who had the misfortune to be suspected or denounced, placed seals on all his effects, claimed his victim, and forthwith escorted him to prison. Hope might wish him a safe deliverance, but in those days there was more of despondency than of hope.

"These scenes were so often repeated in various towns, and followed by so many executions in those days of terror, that men's hearts absolutely sank within them. They could have no enjoyment of to-day, who were in perpetual fear of what might occur on the morrow; or if they had enjoyment, it must have been of a very vague, faint, temperate kind, the poor satisfaction that they had been spared another day.

> ' Ille potens sui,
> Lætusque deget, cui licet in diem
> Dixisse, Vixi.'  Horace, Od. 3, 29, 42.

"Under such circumstances it may reasonably be asked, why confront and widen the danger when we had the power to withdraw from it? A reasonable question truly. Yet there was one most important consideration of weight to override and overrule, in the estimation of the superiors of the house, every undue attention to personal interests or personal safety. The prosperity and welfare of the largest establishment connected with the Catholic body in England had been entrusted to their prudence and active vigilance. Its very existence depended on their firmness. Had they withdrawn like many of the emigrants, who in the terror of the moment purchased safety by the sacrifice of the whole of their property, then indeed the most disastrous consequences would have ensued. The College with all its appurtenances being found untenanted, would have been treated as a derelict, and confiscated, and appropriation of it to national purposes would have been the immediate result. Such a consummation would have entailed, if not absolute ruin, at least a most serious and awful loss to the English Mission. They had then no other alternative. A crisis had arrived of absorbing interest, and on their decision might depend consequences that were absolutely immeasurable. To their honour be it said, they never faltered in their determination for a single moment. To one final resolve they arrived, and from it they never swerved— ' The College must be retained at all hazards.'

"To these pious and determined men, no other conclusion was admissible. On their firmness depended the welfare, not of the College alone, but of the English Mission, which had received its supply of priests principally from that establishment. If from their faint-heartedness or indecision it was unfortunately lost from what other source could the necessary supply of priests be obtained? The Society of Jesus had been abolished. The Franciscans and Dominicans were few, and perhaps declining in numbers and strength; the Benedictines were more numerous, but had no superfluity of disposable members; they had no more than were sufficient to supply the wants of their own monasteries and of the chapelries which they had founded, or which had been committed to their care. The secular establishments abroad did not supply collectively as many priests for the English Mission as the one effective college at Douay. It was then the hope and the main prop of the Catholics of England. It must therefore be retained at all hazards ; and none could be more vividly convinced of the importance of retaining such an establishment, nor more thoroughly impressed with the responsibility that rested upon themselves in such an emergency, irrespective of every selfish consideration, than the very anxious superiors to whose earnest care and unflinching energy its safety had been committed. Few in England can now have a conception of the many complicated and distressing difficulties with which the superiors were beset, nor the stern opposition they had to encounter and surmount. From the favour of the bloodthirsty government which then ruled France, they had absolutely nothing to hope, and little, if anything, from their scant sense of justice. Debarred from even the hope of aid from home, or from the assistance of friends on the Continent, with whom on account of the war they could hold no longer any communication, their sole reliance must henceforth be on Providence, and on their own earnest exertions. Several courses were open to them, but no plan of procedure could be devised which did not involve them in some painful dilemma They might in a body, like the Scotch and Irish, withdraw in safety beyond the frontier ; or, like the Benedictines, dismiss the main body of students, and only retain a small number of the superiors to hold possession of the College. Both of these expedients, particularly the first, appeared to be exceptionable, inasmuch as they exposed the College to the risk of confiscation. A last resource remained, viz., to confront danger in a body, and to await the result. But this resource, precarious as it was, had its serious inconveniences, of which we had been reminded by what had recently occurred at the English College of St. Omer.

" The superiors of that College had a short time previously been separated from their students and thrown into prison, upon the strength of a dropped letter, accidentally, as it was pretended, found in the streets ; and from this rigid confinement they were not delivered until after a long interval, during which the accusa-

H

tions made against them were proved to be futile or unfounded. In the interim, the College boys were committed to the care of certain clergymen who had taken the constitutional oath, and who came consequently under the ban of their rightful bishop. To such men, it may well be supposed, the students did not pay a ready or a willing obedience, and they often amused us in our common prison at Dourlens with the recital of the various pranks they played with their intended superiors. Yet, however good the conduct of the boys might have been, and was under the anomalous government to which they had been subjected, a recurrence of such a restraint upon conscience, and a like exposure to the schismatical contamination were greatly to be deprecated, and by every lawful means to be prevented. The boys of St. Omer's, from the great distance of that town from the frontier, had no available means of escaping from their state of thraldom and forced subjection to their present ill-suited and ill-suiting professors ; and if the incarceration of their own superiors had been greatly prolonged, it is impossible now to say what unpleasant consequences might have ensued.

"The episode about the St. Omerians demonstrated clearly enough the risks and inconveniences of the last-mentioned plan. But did not our own voluntary prolonged abode at Douay imply an equal risk? A risk certainly, but not an equal risk. The cases were not quite parallel. We stood on more favourable ground. Should it have pleased the sovereign people of France to subject us to a like degraded and degrading misrule, and removing our superiors from us to detain them prisoners in a distant stronghold, unless some very rigorous measures had been adopted against us (such as had never yet been dealt out to us, and such as we had no reason to apprehend), the day of their imprisonment would have been the date of our arrival in a compact body at Orchies, an imperial town, distant from Douay about twelve English miles. There we should have been sheltered from French insolence and French persecution. But a question may be raised—why not adopt this reasonable policy while the means of realizing it was within your reach? Your case was all but desperate; your prospects dark and dreary scarcely admitting the faintest ray of hope. Was it prudent to encounter evident and imminent danger when it was within your power easily to withdraw from it? Perhaps there was imprudence, and even great imprudence, of which the strong desire of retaining the College at all hazards can form the only fit excuse. Perhaps, also, there was a deficiency of energetic resolve in our very worthy president [the Rev. Jno. Daniel], who, having passed nearly the whole of his long life within the precincts of the College, from which he never had been absent for a whole continuous month— nor perhaps for a week—could not bear the idea of a separation from it. Great allowances must be made for his indecision in consideration of his strong attachments. Could he have surmised that the College had been lost through his own want of perseverance, that imagination, slender and groundless though it might be, would have been fatal to his peace, and perhaps to his life.

"There was another obstruction to the safe and smooth working of the last-mentioned plan, that had its weight in the scale of conflicting difficulties. Our treasury was low, and there was no way of replenishing it either from the funds in France which had been confiscated and withheld from us, or from payments from England, which from the time since the war was declared could by no possibility be conveyed to us. The payment of a cheque from an English bank by a banker in France would have been the death-warrant of the unfortunate and inconsiderate banker. Add to this the depreciation of paper assignats, amounting to more than four hundred per cent., and its consequence, a quadruple expenditure, and we may thence form an idea of the utter impossibility of providing every individual student with the slenderest means of arriving at his home. No alternative was left but casual charity on the road to

enable those who escaped to reach the English shore. So faint
a resource could afford no soothing satisfaction to the feelings of
our superiors, and we need not be surprised that, if they opposed
no great hindrance to the departure of those who deemed it
imprudent to remain, they gave it no great encouragement. It
was plain that the choice of expedients had become the
choice of evils, and it was difficult to determine which of
these in preference to the rest we were ultimately to select and
adopt.

"At length our deliberations were fated to have a sudden close
by the startling and unexpected intelligence that we were to be expelled from Douay as useless mouths in a town declared to be in
danger of siege. This was a final and fatal blow, upsetting and
dissipating the shadowy hopes that the most sanguine tempera-
ments alone could have entertained. In pursuance of the municipal
mandate of expulsion, we were ordered to name our place of refuge,
and Lens, a small town at the distance of a day's journey, was
selected ; and no exceptions being made to the place of our
choice, we received our passports to repair thither.

"Leaving Douay we stopped at Esquerchin, our country house,
distant about three miles, which was not greatly out of our own
way. There we remained unmolested during some months with
the knowledge and sufferance of the town's authorities, and I
almost imagine that it would not have broken the hearts of some
of those gentlemen if we had taken that favourable opportunity
of making our final escape. Had they no sympathy with the
inmates of a college, who, in succession at least, had been fellow-
citizens with them or theirs, not for years merely, but for ages?
If not, why did they tolerate our remaining so many months in
a spot not indicated in our passports, but whence escape was so
easy?

"We remained, as I have just stated, some months at
Esquerchin, and during our abode there we were very close
witnesses of the march of the French army to encounter the

Duke of York at the disastrous siege of Dunkirk. Some of the republican cavalry passed through our village. In the eyes of some of the upper officers of the French army with whom our superiors had an opportunity of conversing, the move of the Duke was opposed to every rule of military strategy, and in this opinion the Prince of Cobourg, who commanded the Imperialists, it was said, entirely coincided.

" The defeat of the English army freed Douay from the danger of an impending siege, but we were not recalled. Something worse than neglect seemed to be hanging over us. It could not be favourable to us, but from the temper of the times might and must be disastrous. It then became the firm conviction of those who thought at all, that our past patient endurance had been carried to the utmost extent warranted by common prudence and perhaps to a point beyond it, and that nothing was to be obtained favourable to our college interests by remaining a day longer. This conviction had its just weight with many most valuable men, such as the Revv. Messrs. Lancaster, Worswick, Peach, Bell, and others, who slipped away without leave-taking.

" Such, I strongly suspect, would have been the course of many who were left behind, if money, the great lever which is said to move nations and armies, had not been wanting. It might be in the power of the procurator to afford some small aid to the first applicants, but the whole contents of his exchequer would have been inadequate to supply even a trifling sum to each individual. There are some natures, indeed, in which it seems to be engrafted to hope against hope. The president was against the immediate flight, and with him of course were ranged the different professors who were unwilling to abandon him. Then there was a feeling that if the students departed, the inevitable consequence would be that the superiors would be thrown into prison in common with all the respectable ecclesiastics who were known to remain in France. This was an appeal to our feelings, which was almost irresistible. Even those who were thoroughly convinced of the futility of the president's hopes were content to abide the common risk with all its disheartening prospects, and to await the issue a little while longer.   When hope was almost, or rather quite extinguished, then did the tide of emigration set outwards.

" Gradually, but perceptibly, our numbers diminished, and the retirement of men in divinity and in the higher classes, who were well known not to be deficient in courage, was beginning to create a feeling of personal insecurity, or rather of impending danger to those who remained.   But before the conviction had full time to operate, we received an unexpected invitation from the municipal authorities to return to the town, and to resume possession of our College.   Such an invitation, preceded by no expression of feeling for the inconveniences and losses to which we had been subjected, the realization of no previous promise, but singularly dry and abrupt, seemed to some of us a very equivocal concession that boded us no good.   Over these just apprehensions, our orderly habits of obedience prevailed The order was given to us by the president to repair immediately to the town, contrary to the expressed opinion of some and the inward convictions of more.   Reluctantly enough some of us entered within the walls of the town, and were not greatly surprised to find that we had entered only to be entrapped."


## The Confiscation of the College.

" Good Heaven ! what sorrows gloom'd that parting day,
That call'd them from their native walks away ;
When the poor exiles, every pleasure past,
Hung round the bowers and fondly look'd their last."

*Goldsmith's Deserted Village.*

" Soon we were taught how mistaken our confidence had been. After a short delay, allowed probably to encourage those to enter who had been detained in forwarding our effects from Esquerchin, a municipal officer, having taken the previous precaution of surrounding the College and all its outlets with bands of armed men, entered the College about nine at night, when the superiors were at supper, and many of the boys, wearied with their labours and disquietude, had retired to rest, and announced to us his orders to remove us at once to the Scottish College, and into close confinement.

" On hearing this decree, the first idea that suggested itself to us was to escape from the premises in the dark, in the almost forlorn hope of finding some means of passing the town's gates on the morrow. This, at the first attempt, was discovered to be an impracticable measure. The next was to call up those who had retired to rest, and in conjunction with them to secure as much of our wardrobes, etc., public and private, as we could convey away unnoticed. The officer was very urgent that we should hasten our departure, without any solicitude about our clothing or other effects, giving us his assurance that all should be safely sent after us. To this notification, taking it for what it was worth, we paid no attention, but collected what we could in the very few moments allowed us for assembling. Some clothes, which were afterwards found to be eminently useful, were procured from the tailors' apartments, and a small amount of silver utensils, which, to avoid suspicion, had not been removed from daily use. When the patience of those appointed to escort us, which was by no means extraordinary, was exhausted, word was given to us to pass instantly into the streets, and thence, enclosed by two serried ranks of military, who were rigidly strict in the performance of their charge, we were marched quickly into the Scotch college, which having entered, our claims to our own establishment were declared to be extinct. In effect, it had been confiscated. From that fatal night we may date the final downfall of the noble English Secular College of Douay.

"Stripped of the support of all thy various aids of instruction and

everything that had hallowed thy previous existence, poor *alma
mater*, thine was a cruel and unmerited doom ; but thou hadst,
and deservedst to have, many sincere mourners. The end was
*qualis ab incepto.* Nursed and cradled in adversity and unremit-
ting suffering ; pursued throughout almost thy entire duration by
the merciless laws and refined barbarity of a merciless princess,
and harassed by the atrocious and insatiate hostility of succeeding
governments, who thought they did an agreeable thing to God
by hunting thy noblest sons to a cruel death ;—all those unnatural
but vain attempts to crush out thy very existence thou couldst
bear and didst bear. But when the sanguinary laws that had
been created against thee had at length been cancelled, or greatly
modified, then in almost the first moments of thy peaceful rest,
in the very dawn of thy hopes, in the midst of thy aspirations
after labour untrammelled by fears of prison or death, a storm
arose from an unexpected quarter in which thou hadst hitherto
been kindly fostered, cherished, and protected. Not France,
once the soul of honour and unbending integrity, dealt thee thy
death-blow, but the most worthless of her sons, profiting by the
explosion of a sanguinary revolution, rose like the Seine to the
surface, and wresting the reins of government from feeble hands,
rioted then in every excess that can degrade the name of man
Their envenomed darts were ever aimed at a noble quarry, and
thou, in common with the best, sankest under them. Thy virtues
were the occasion of thy fall. Never stain nor spot has tarnished
thy unblemished escutcheon. Farewell, then, kind *alma mater* ;
farewell, a long farewell.

   " Here my task is ended. What followed has been recorded by
one who kept a regular journal of events.* As far as I recollect,
it is meagre in details, as might be expected from one who had
so little communication with externals. The boys, if they had

   * Narrative of the seizure of Donay College, and of the deportation of the
seniors, professors, and students, to Douriens. By the Rev. Joseph Hodgson,
V.G.L.D., in a letter to a friend. *Catholic Magazine, vol.* I., 1831.

chosen, could have supplied him with more abundant particulars, but the opportunity has now passed, and his must continue to be the only register of these events.   Some more last words, I find, are expected from me, at least in explanation ; be it so, provided they be short.

' Sicut.

Parvula, nam exemplo est, magni formica laboris
Ore trahit quodcumque potest atque addit acervo.'

" It has been asked, were there no grounds for accusation, real or insufficient, for the expostulation of the town's officers, to which the memorial of Mr. Dillon was the authorised reply ?   The only grounds, known to the students at least, were certain letters addressed by Dr. Coombes to the editor of one of the royalist newspapers that had a considerable circulation throughout France.   In them he expresses the strong indignation felt by every Englishman at certain acts of the first Assembly, and their deplorable consequences, and exhibits himself as sufficiently authorised by the general feeling to convey these sentiments to the public.   These letters, I believe, were forcibly written, and described in no measured terms the author's aversion from the violent proceedings of the Assembly.   Dr. Coombes was then a very young màn, an accomplished scholar, and an excellent linguist ; but he was indiscreet, and had not much tact.   When it became known to the superiors that he wàs in communication with the newspapers, he was ordered immediately to desist. Although by his obedience he might make his peace with his superiors, he was less happy with the powers that then ruled. The question was often put to us by persons in authority, ' Is Crombs ' (for so they called him) ' still with you ? ' and on our replying no, that he was in England, for he was one of those who escaped on the road to Arras when our guards were regaling themselves in the canteen, the invariable remark was ' It is well for him,' intimating, as we understood them, that he would have paid for his imprudence with the forfeiture of his head.　I know no other ground on which the accusation made against us could rest, unless it were on our known hostility to the vice and irreligion that then prevailed.

"I may relate an anecdote about which I think the writer of the journal is silent, because it was personal, and reflected honour upon himself.　During those awful times there was no unconstitutional priest known to be in the vicinity of Dourlens. A gentleman in the neighbourhood, lying on his sick-bed in imminent danger of death, was extremely anxious for the services of a priest.　Fixing upon some dragoons in our garrison as best able to assist him, he prevailed upon them to bring one out of the citadel, in the disguise of their uniform, when one of their company was stationed as guard at the outer gate.　Mr. Hodgson was the person selected, and while the soldiers were attiring him in the gallery, into which our room door opened, he dispersed all the boys in various quarters, upon some pretence or other, the better to conceal his departure.　Unfortunately I returned, having forgotten something, to the displeasure of Mr. Hodgson, who was rather cross, ordering me to say nothing of what I saw, but not to the discomfiture of at least one of the soldiers, who knew that I had been privy to some of his escapades of the same sort, and to secure my silence had offered to take me out in the same disguise whenever I chose.　This offer I declined, and he was content with my assurance that I would not betray him.　In revenge for my being scolded, I will say that I never saw an uglier dragoon than Mr. Hodgson, nor a more awkward recruit.　But although he figured indifferently as a soldier, he was at home in his duties, which happily for the sick man and for himself he completed, escaping detection.　An alarm indeed was given during the procedure that the commander was coming, but it appeared that he only called to see his sick friend, and during his stay Mr. Hodgson was concealed under a bed in the garret, not knowing meanwhile whether he was not personally indebted for this gracious call.

"I may record an incident in the edifying life of the late Right Rev. Bishop Poynter, which, as far as I know, has not been noticed elsewhere. When our restrictions in matters of space and recreation ground, which had been imposed on account of the escape of so many of our companions, and to prevent the flight of more, had been somewhat relaxed and a wider circuit had been conceded for air and exercise, Mr. Poynter, profiting by this indulgence, ascended the walled ramparts which separated the two citadels, and, in full view of both, calmly, quietly, and composedly recited there for a time, almost daily, the divine office. His purpose appeared to us to be two-fold, viz., to testify by this noble demonstration his obedience to God in almost the worst times, his adherence to his own personal duties irrespective of consequences to himself, and to console and reanimate the faltering courage of so many French captives, to whom hope had become almost an entire stranger. If such were his object he succeeded. When better times followed they often expressed to us their great admiration of his noble conduct, and their grateful thanks for the well-timed edification he had given them. Does not his behaviour show that the spirit that animated the pious originators of our noble College, founded at the expense of so many personal sacrifices, which supported their admirable successors under the terrors of imprisonment and death, had not deserted its own house at its close? May the same divine spirit continue to shed its blessings on the affiliation of that once favoured home.

"It may be objected that the shadowing I have delineated of the excesses and horrors of the first revolution are too dark, and have been unduly exaggerated. I am persuaded, on the contrary, that the description I have given is lenient and understated. It is one thing to hear of tyrannical proceedings, and another to smart under their infliction.

'Segnius irritant animos demissa per aurem,
Quam quæ sunt oculis subjecta fidelibus, et quid
Ipse sibi tradit spectator.'

" With this observation I beg leave to make my bow and retire,
repeating as we were wont—

'Laus Deo Semper.'"

I loved thee in my youth's sweet dream
Of fresh and pure delight,
When basking in life's morning beam,
Where all around was bright ;
And there came across the gleam
No cloud to chill my sight.

And when that dream was faded far,
That dear delusion o'er,
No change, no time thy form could mar,
I only loved thee more !
And I watched thy waning star
More fondly than before.

F. C. Husenbeth.

# The Flight from Douay.

"That quiet land where, peril past,
The weary win a long repose,
The bruised spirit finds, at last,
A balm for all its woes."                    *T. K. Hervey.*

*London, Aug.* 14, 1793. "Dear Mother—We send before these few lines to diminish the surprise you possibly might receive from ye sudden and unforeseen arrival of your two most dutiful and loving children. You will hear ye reasons of our departure from Douay College, and receive ye satisfaction you could desire, when we are come to our beloved home, where we shall lay before you ye pressing urgencies which have forced us to cross the seas (very much against our will) and to return to Lancashire. We set out on our journey ye 5th of August, and arrived amidst ye congratulations of all our friends who were informed of our circumstances at London, Aug. 14th, from whence I have the pleasure to address this letter to you, most dear mother. Be pleased to make yourself, and other our friends and relatives, as easy as possible on our regard, for 'tis not on account of some silly whim or misdemeanour that we propose to make you this visit, but for causes which have not only prevailed on several before us to leave this troublesome habitation, but likewise have engaged one of ye professors (masters), called William Davies, a person of a very good character and advanced to ye order of deaconship, to undertake ye same journey in our company. But, dear mother, let this suffice for ye present, until we come in person to give you a more exact detail of this adventure. In

ye meantime we remain as before, and for ever, your ever
dutiful and obedient sons—George Haydocke and Thomas
Haydocke. P.S. We shall come down as soon as possible. We
write this from ye apartment of J. P. Coghlan, who sends his
kindest compliments (together with his wife's) to you and all
friends."

In a correspondence with the late Very Rev. John Gillow,
D.D., vice-president of Ushaw College, George Leo Haydock,
dating from Penrith, Oct. 6, 1849, gives some details of his flight
from Douay. He says that previous to his escape "five others
tried and were taken to prison at Lisle for a fortnight, and then
joined the rest of the college at Esquerchin till sent to Dourlens.
Three of them set out before us and were stopt at the citadel for
want of passports, and returning, put us on our guard ; so we
went behind and pretended to be fishing. Two more joined
them, and proved unsuccessful. One of these was Francis
Canning, of Foxcote, my schoolfellow. Another was John
Rickaby, who was ordained deacon and priest with me in Lent,
1797, and Sept. 22, 1798, and died in the asylum at Manchester,
Feb. 5, 1821, after being priest at Garstang and Nunnington
awhile. W. Davies, deacon, left us at London, and went to
Wales. We walked by Orchies, Tournay, then took the coach
to Bruges, where the nuns [English canonesses of St. Augustine]
entertained us two days, and lent us, I think, £5, to be repaid in
London, as it was by me. We had no difficulties to encounter,
only the English consul at Ostend would not believe but we
were French, and when I told him my brother and I were born
three miles from Preston, N. W., at the Tagg, he said he knew
Preston but had not heard of that house, which I observed was
not surprising. We found afterwards this General Haynes had
carried a pack ! He would not grant us a passport, so we ventured without one, and were never asked for one. Arriving at
Dover we proceeded by coach to London, where we were entertained kindly for a week by J. P. Coghlan and his wife Elizabeth,

formerly Brown, a relation of ours from Clifton, where the present
Bishop George Brown was born—and was my scholar along
with Bishop W. Hogarth, from 1798 till 1803, during which I
was master of all under poetry, and general prefect at Crook
Hall. Towards the end of Aug., 1793, we visited our brother,
James Haydock, lately fixed at Trafford House, and then walked
home with him thirty miles. I remained at Tagg House till the
end of November, when I was ordered to go with Thomas
Penswick to Old Hall Green, where we arrived about the 3rd
Dec. My brother Thomas seemed undecided, but afterwards
went to Lisbon, and returned in the summer of 1795. I had
left the College Nov. 3, 1794."

In a letter dated Oct. 10, 1849, in answer to some further
queries by Dr. Gillow, Mr. Haydock says—" Richard Broderick, just entering with me in high-philosophy under Bishop
Smith or Rev. W. Wilds (still alive at London), Louis Havard, a
Welshman, in low-philosophy, a year younger than I, and
another student, were stopped at the citadel of Douai, at 11
o'clock, and sent to inform us, and we advised them to try
another road and join us at Tournay or Orchies, nine miles off.
We went by the canal at the back of the citadel of Douai at 1
p.m., conducted well by a countryman who came to supply the
College with faggots. He went a moderate distance before us,
with his coat over his shoulder, till he came to a rising ground,
when he crossed the high road and we put up our fishing rod and
followed him through woods, seeing the guard for the last time,
and presently coming among the Germans, expecting a battle
shortly. We called upon the good old curate of Orchies, who
had just returned to his house and feasted his friends. It was
so late that I wondered how he could read his office. We wrote
by our trusty guide to some at the College advising them to employ him. Soon after we left, it seems, John Rickaby, a *patriarch*,
as we called him (about low-philosophy), and Francis Canning,
my schoolfellow of the same age, in whose green coat I escaped,

as he had grown out of it, joined the three [mentioned above], and they had got within a mile of being out of the French dominions, when unluckily they had to pass through a village, and some soldiers drinking, demanded their passports, and took them to Lisle. I was informed that they were skulking behind a hedge, instead of going boldly, in separate twos or threes. I had no merit in planning our escape, but engaged in it very reluctantly, being in bad order for walking, as I was growing rather too fast at 19. My brother Thomas insisted on my going with him, and had money, etc. We left at the college about 50. Nearly 100 had escaped before, and of the 50, one half contrived to slip away on the road, or from Dourlens, a state prison where the students of Douai and St. Omer's were confined in October, till after the execution of Robespierre, when they were permitted to come with their goods to England. I lost nearly 200 vols., and only saved an *Imitatio Christi* (left me by my pupil Th. Murphy) and Boileau, which I have yet, and perhaps the fishing rod at Tagg House. . . . . I must observe the nuns who were so kind to us at Bruges (where Mr. Davies had been lately ordained deacon) were Augustinians, and Mrs. Moore, a relative perhaps of the celebrated Sir Thomas More, was the reverend mother. I had a sister, Margaret Stanislaus, a nun at Louvain, of the same order, who is still alive, aged 82, at Spetisbury House, whom I visited thrice at Hammersmith in 1794 and never since."

In another letter to Dr. Gillow he says—" I never heard my brother James tell any of his adventures. I suppose he got a passport just in time. Mr. Peach [Rev. Edw.] also was too intent upon his studies to communicate what happened to him 4th Aug. Of the little boys who went the same day to St. Omer's. Thomas Murphy was my pupil, and had left me his rich furniture, which I had just put with my books and pictures, in the best order when my brother Thomas was so urgent for me to flee. I went to confession to Rev. Joseph Hodgson, and know not whether it would not have been better for me to have remained. I should have saved, besides my catalogue since 3985, most of the Fathers, etc., nearly 200 vols., which at 19 I had scraped together with my little pocket money, and should have got more, probably, if my schoolfellows had not wasted a good deal in little theatrical attempts at scenery, in which once I was to act as parson, while one was to be hanged, and really was in some danger. Such things were, moreover, forbidden. I remember Rev. B. Rayment, prefect-general, seeing something of the kind going on, dashed his hand through a pane of glass to lay hold of an actor on guard in the philosophers' school. It was here, about this time, that Mr. Wilds called upon me to defend on so easy a subject as the existence of God, and I was almost dumb! for we had heard the Jacobins were in the next house, and had threatened to break in and murder us all as aristocrats. I think our good master was as much under the Reign of Terror as myself."

The following is a catalogue of the last inmates of Douay College, drawn up by Dr. Gillow and sent to Mr. Haydock for revision, to which additions are made.

CATALOGUE FROM THE DOUAY DIARY FOR OCT. 1st., 1792, OF THE LAST 103 MEMBERS OF DOUAY COLLEGE, WITH THE ASCERTAINED HISTORY OF EACH.

### SENIOR PROFESSORS.

1. Rev. John Daniel, president, born at Durton, near Fernyhalgh, Lancashire, in 1745; liberated from prison, Feb. 25, 1795; installed president of the new College at Crook Hall, June 30, 1795, resigned within the octave to watch over the interests of the dissolved College, and died at Paris, Oct. 3, 1823, aged 77.

2. Rev. Joseph Hodgson, S.T.P., vice-president, and professor

I

of Divinity, born in the diocese of London, Aug. 14, 1756; liberated Feb. 25, 1795; served the missions of St George's-in-the Fields (now Southwark Cathedral), Castle-street, London, V. G. London District, and the Ladies' School at Brook Green, Hammersmith, where he died Nov. 30, 1821, aged 65.

3. Right Rev. Wm. Poynter, S.T.P., prefect of studies, born at Petersfield, Hampshire, May 20, 1726; liberated Feb. 25, 1795; V.P. of Old Hall Green College, president in 1801, coadjutor bishop of London District, 1803, to which vicariate he succeeded in 1812; died Nov. 26, 1827, aged 66.

4. Rev. Thomas Smith, professor of natural philosophy, born at The Brooms near Ushaw College, Durham, Mar. 21, 1763; liberated Feb. 25, 1795; missionary in Durham, coadjutor bishop of Northern District, 1807, to which vicariate he succeeded in 1821; died at Ushaw College, May 30, 1831, aged 68.

5. Rev. Benedict Rayment, professor of moral philosophy, born at Worcester Jan. 7, 1764; withdrew Feb. 10, 1793; chaplain at Lartington Hall, missionary at York, V.G. Northern District, died at York, Mar. 23, 1842, aged 78.

6. Rev. Joseph Beaumont, *alias* Hunt, procurator, born at Stone Easton, Somerset, May 22. 1762; liberated Feb. 25, 1795; missionary at Usk, and Shortwood, retired in March, and died at Clifton, Dec. 1, 1838, aged 76.

7. Rev. Thomas Stout, prefect general; liberated Feb. 25, 1795; missionary at Southwark, Callaly, 1796, and 1797 Thropton, Northumberland, till death, July 26, 1828, aged 61.

8. Rev. James Newsham, professor of rudiments, born at Lytham, Lancashire, in 1774; left before Oct. 1, 1793; chaplain at St. Monica's convent, Louvain, O.S.A.; at Crook Hall as a convictor, died at Hammersmith, June 11, 1825, aged 51.

### MINOR PROFESSORS.

9. Rev. William Wilds, professor of poetry, born 1768; liberated Feb. 25, 1795; chaplain to the Bavarian Embassy at

London, missionary at Warwick-street; died in Upper John St., Golden Square, Jan. 18, 1834, aged 87.

10. Rev. James Haydock, professor of grammar, born at The Tagg, Lancashire, 1746; withdrew Feb. 11, 1793; chaplain at Trafford, and missionary at Lea, where he died Apr. 25, 1809, aged 43.

11. Rev. William Henry Coombes, D.D., professor of rhetoric, born at Meadgate, Somerset, May 8, 1767; escaped Oct. 16, 1793; professor of divinity at Old Hall Green, and afterwards V.P., degree D.D. 1801, missionary at Shepton Mallett for 39 years, retired to Downside, in 1849, where he died Nov. 15, 1850, aged 84.

12. Rev. James Lancaster, deacon, professor of music, born in Lancashire, in 1765; escaped Oct. 12, 1793; ordained priest at York in Dec., 1793; missionary at Chester, had his leg amputated, went to Blackbrook, 1820-3, and died at Chester, Oct. 8, 1827, aged 62.

13. Rev. John Lee, deacon professor of syntax; escaped Oct. 12, 1793; ordained priest at Old Hall Green; missionary at Warwick-street, London; died July 13, 1839, aged 71.

14. George Simpson, layman, writing master; left Aug. 4, 1793, yet his name appears in the list of prisoners at Dourlens.

#### SCHOOL OF DIVINITY.

15. Rev. Wm. Davies, 4th year, deacon, born at Usk, in Wales; left Aug. 5th, 1793; ordained priest in England; missionary at Chepstow till 1805, Dartmouth till 1814, and died at Chepstow, Dec. 30, 1814.

16. Rev. Wm. Croskell, 3rd year, deacon, born at Bulk, Lancashire; liberated Feb. 25, 1795; ordained priest at York, Apr. 18, 1795; missionary at Linton, chaplain at The Bar Convent, York, again on the mission at Linton, and Durham, where he died, Feb. 19, 1838, aged 70. V.G. Northern District.

17. Rev. Thomas Berry, 3rd year, sub-deacon, native of

Lancashire; liberated Feb. 25, 1795; ordained priest at Crook Hall, Apr. 1, 1797; missionary at Culcheth, Ince Blundell, Cottam, 1826 till 1845, and Great Crosby, where he died in 1851.

18. Rev. Robert Blacow, 3rd year, sub-deacon, native of Mowbreck, Lancashire; escaped Nov. 24, 1793; taught in Rev. Arthur Storey's School at Tudhoe; ordained priest at Crook Hall, Dec. 23, 1794; taught in the school at Scholes Hall; missionary at Fernyhalgh from 1811 till death, Oct. 18, 1823, aged 56.

19. Rev. John Woodcock, alumnus 4th year, born at Preston; left Oct. 31, 1792; ordained priest at York in Dec. 1792; missionary at Egton Bridge and Wycliff, Yorkshire, and Scorton, Lancashire, from whence he retired four months before his death at Newhouse, Feb. 12, 1837, aged 71.

20. Mr. George Taylor, alumnus 4th year, layman; left before Oct. 1, 1793; died at Bath about Christmas, 1813.

21. Rev. James Delaney, cler, 3rd year; liberated Feb. 25, 1795; ordained priest at Old Hall Green; missionary for 19 years after the Rev. T. White at Winchester; died Nov. 24, 1847.

22. Rev. John Bell, alumnus 2nd year, born at Snaith, Yorkshire; left, Nov. 8, 1792; tutor to the young Silvertops at Minster Acres, then prefect-general at Crook Hall, where he was ordained priest, Dec. 23, 1794, and was professor of rhetoric and poetry there till 1817; missionary at Samlesbury, Lancashire, till 1828, and after that at Kippax Park, Yorkshire, whence he retired and died at Selby, May 31, 1854, aged 87.

23. Mr. John Baines, alumnus 3rd year, native of Lancashire; left Nov. 8. 1792; said to have married in France; died in or near Liverpool.

24. Rev. Wm. Beacham, alumnus 3rd year; left Feb. 11, 1793; ordained priest at Old Hall Green; chaplain in Kent, where he died, Dec. 1812.

25. Mr. Nicholas Woodcock, alum. 3rd year, layman, born at Preston; left Oct. 31, 1792; tradesman in Preston, where he died.

26. Rev. James Worswick, alum. 3rd year, born at Lancaster; escaped Oct 12, 1793; ordained priest at York, April 18, 1795; missionary at Newcastle-upon-Tyne, where he died May 6, 1843, aged 72.

27. Mr. Charles Thompson, cler., 3rd year, layman; escaped Jan. 15, 1794.

28. Mr. Robert Freemont, alum. 2nd year, layman; native of London; left Aug. 4, 1793; pursued his studies at Old Hall Green.

29. Mr. John Dowling, alum. 2nd year, layman; liberated Feb. 25, 1795.

30. Rev. John Law, alum. 2nd year; date of leaving not ascertained; ordained priest at Old Hall Green; missionary at Ingateston, Essex, where died, Sep. 6, 1832, aged 65.

31. Rev. John Lingard, alum. 1st year, born at Winchester Feb. 5, 1771; left Feb. 21, 1793; tutor to William, Lord Stourton; professor and vice-president at Tudhoe, Crook Hall, and Ushaw College; ordained priest at York, May 6, 1795; left Ushaw College for the mission at Hornby in Sept. 1811; D.D., 1821; the historian of England; died at Hornby, May, 17, 1851, aged 80.

32. Rev. Fris. Bowland, alum. 2nd year; left in Mar., 1793; ordained priest at Old Hall; missionary at Reading, Berks, Eastbourne, and Petworth, Sussex.

33. Mr. Christopher Dalin, alum. 2nd year, layman; left Feb. 18. 1793.

34. Rev. Edward Peach, alum. 1st year, native of Gloucestershire; left Aug. 4, 1793; ordained priest at Old Hall Green; chaplain to Fortescue Turvill, of Bosworth, Leicestershire, Esq., for ten years, missioner at Birmingham from 1807 till his death, Sept. 8, 1839, aged 69.

35. Rev. John Devereux, alum. 1st year; escaped Oct. 16, 1793; ordained priest at Old Hall Green; missioner at White-street and Moorfields, London, and died at Paris, Apr. 10, 1838.

36. Rev. Charles Saul, alum. 1st year, native of Yorkshire ; escaped Oct. 12 1793 ; pursued his studies at Old Hall Green and Crook Hall ; ordained priest at Crook Hall, where he was prefect-general, and master of all under poetry ; missioner at Carlisle from 1798 till Christmas, 1800, and Bishop Thornton till death, June 5, 1813, aged 46.

### NATURAL PHILOSOPHY.

37. Rev. Richard Thompson, born at Wigan in 1772 ; escaped Nov. 24, 1793 ; pursued his studies at Old Hall Green and Crook Hall ; ordained priest at Crook Hall, Apr. 1, 1797 ; missioner at Manchester, and Weld Bank, near Chorley, where he died Dec. 30, 1841, aged 69 ; V.G. of the Lancashire district.

38. Rev. John Clarkson, born at Grimsargh, Lancashire ; escaped Nov. 24, 1793 ; ordained priest at Old Hall Green ; missioner at Ingatestone, Essex ; died Feb. 13, 1823.

39. Rev. Thomas Gillow, born at Singleton, Lancashire, in 1769 ; escaped Oct. 12, 1793 ; pursued his studies at Old Hall Green and Crook Hall ; ordained priest at the latter college, Apr. 1, 1797 ; professor at Crook Hall ; chaplain to the Claverings at Callaly Castle, Northumberland ; missioner at North Shields from 1821 till death, Mar. 19, 1857, aged 87.

40. Thomas Haydock, layman, born at The Tagg, Lancashire, Feb. 21, 1772 ; left Aug. 5, 1793 ; pursued his studies at the English College at Lisbon and at Crook Hall ; eminent printer and publisher at Manchester and Dublin : died at Preston, Aug. 25, 1859, aged 87.

41. Thomas Cook, layman ; left before Oct. 1, 1793 ; pursued his studies at Old Hall Green ; kept a shop at London awhile.

42. Edward Monk, layman, a native of Lancashire ; escaped Oct. 16, 1793 ; pursued his studies at Old Hall Green and Crook Hall ; living in 1859.

43. Joseph Montgomery, layman ; left Oct. 20, 1792.

44. Timothy Duggan, layman; left Jan. 21, 1793.
45. John Hall, a Protestant, layman, left Feb. 11, 1793.
46. Joachim Oliveira, layman, left Feb. 21, 1793.

### MORAL PHILOSOPHY.

47. Rev. Richard Broderick, a native of London; liberated Feb. 25, 1795; ordained priest at Old Hall Green in 1799; missioner at Lincoln's-inn-fields above thirty years, and died Oct. 29, 1831.

48. James Harrison, layman, born at Garstang, Lancashire; liberated Feb. 25, 1795.

49. Right Rev. Thomas Penswick, born at the Manor-House, Ashton-in-Makerfield, in 1772; escaped Oct. 12, 1793; pursued his studies at Old Hall Green and Crook Hall, at the latter of which he was ordained priest, Apr. 1, 1797; missioner at Chester in 1797, and afterwards in Liverpool; consecrated, in 1824, at Ushaw College, bishop of Europum, coadjutor to Dr. Smith, V.A. of the Northern District, to which he succeeded in 1831; died at the house of his brother, Randal Penswick, Jan. 28, 1836, aged 63, and was buried at Windleshaw.

50. Rev. George Leo Haydock, born at The Tagg, Lancashire, Apr. 11, 1774; left Aug. 5, 1783; pursued his studies at Old Hall Green and Crook Hall, at the latter of which he was ordained priest, Sept. 22, 1798, and was prefect-general and professor of all under poetry for four years and a half; went to the mission at Ugthorpe in 1803, Whitby in 1816, Westby in 1830; withdrew to The Tagg, Cottam, for eight years and a quarter; missioner at Penrith from 1839 till death, Nov. 29, 1849, aged 75, exactly seven days after he had revised this catalogue.

51. John Canning, layman; born at Foxcote, Warwickshire, in 1775; escaped Jan. 16, 1794; died in the East Indies in 1824.

52. William Lucas, layman; escaped Nov. 24, 1793; pursued his studies at Old Hall Green; entered the army, and settled in Birmingham.

RHETORIC.

53. Rev. Lewis Havard, born at Devynock, Co. Brecon, Apr. 12, 1774; liberated Feb. 25, 1795; ordained priest at Old Hall Green in 1800; missioner at St. Mary's, Westminster, till his retirement to Brecon, where he died at his nephew's, the Rev. Lewis Havard, junior, Apr. 2, 1858, aged 84.

54. Rev. John Rickaby, born near Wycliffe in Yorkshire; escaped Oct. 17, 1793; pursued his studies at Tudhoe and Crook Hall, at the latter of which he was ordained, Sep. 22, 1798; missioner at Garstang, Lancashire, Nunnington, Yorks, and died in the asylum at Manchester, Feb. 5, 1821.

55. Andrew O'Callaghan, layman, a native of Chester; left Oct. 21, 1792.

56. Wm. Barry, layman; left Feb. 18, 1793.

57. Charles Sims, layman; liberated Feb. 25, 1795.

58. Maurice O'Connell, layman, born at Carhen, Ireland, in 1776; came from St. Omer's College in 1792; left Jan. 21, 1793; entered the British army, and died on the expedition to St. Domingo.

59. Daniel O'Connell, the Liberator, born at Carhen, Ireland, Aug. 6, 1775; left Jan. 21, 1793; died at Genoa, May 15, 1847, aged 71.

POETRY.

60. Arthur Clifford, layman, born in 1777; liberated Feb. 25, 795, died at Winchester in 1830.

61. Rev. Joseph Swinburne, a native of Northumberland; liberated Feb. 25, 1795; ordained priest at Crook Hall, Apr. 3, 1800; missioner at Hedon, Yorkshire; retired and died at Hull, Dec. 7, 1865, aged 71.

62. Wm. Stourton, 17th Baron Stourton, born at Allerton Park, Yorks, June 6, 1776; left Feb. 21, 1793; died Dec. 4, 1846, aged 80

63. Nicholas Kirwan, layman ; left Jan. 21, 1793.

64. Thomas Pitchford, a native of Norwich; left Jan. 21, 1793; ordained at Old Hall Green ; missioner at Snaith and York, chaplain to Miles Stapleton, Esq. ; died at York, July 30, 1808.

65. Stephen Phillips, layman ; escaped Jan. 15, 1794; tutor at the 10th Baron Petre's ; married his daughter, Apr. 30, 1805, against the wishes of the family, and both had to work for a living.

66. Richard Davies, layman ; liberated Feb. 25, 1795.

67. Rev. Thomas Lupton, born at Poulton-le-Fylde, Lancashire ; escaped Jan. 16, 1794; pursued his studies at Tudhoe and Crook Hall ; ordained priest at the latter, Apr. 3, 1800 ; missioner at Manchester, Newhall, and Garswood; died Apr. 29, 1843.

68. Lewis Clifford, layman ; liberated Feb. 25, 1795.

69. John Bates, layman ; escaped Jan. 16, 1794.

70. John Eldridge, layman ; escaped Jan. 16, 1794 ; pursued his studies at Old Hall Green ; schoolmaster at Birmingham till death, June 13, 1831, aged 59.

71. George Aylmer, layman ; left Nov. 20, 1792.

72. John Frankland, layman ; left in Jan., 1793.

73. Edward Beck, layman; left Oct. 31, 1792.

74. Francis Hay, native of Brittany ; went to Paris Nov. 16 1793 ; ordained priest and on the mission in Brittany in 1817.

### SYNTAX.

75. Rev. Thomas Dawson, native of Yorkshire ; escaped Jan. 16 1794; pursued his studies at Tudhoe and Crook Hall ; ordained priest at Durham from Crook Hall, Dec. 17, 1803 ; took charge of the mission at Lytham in 1804, went to Croston in 1829, and died at Mawdesley, Lancashire, Dec. 6, 1832.

76. Vincent Eyre, layman ; born in Derbyshire in 1774 ; left Oct. 20, 1792 ; high sheriff of Derbyshire ; died in 1851.

77. John Smith, layman: left Feb. 11, 1793.

78. Robert Dale, layman; left Jan. 8, 1793.

79. Rev. John Bradley, native of Lancashire; escaped Jan. 16, 1794; pursued his studies at Tudhoe and Crook Hall; ordained priest at the latter, Dec. 4, 1802; missioner at Yarm, where he died Oct. 24, 1852.

80. Rev. Thomas Storey, native of Yorkshire; escaped Jan. 16, 1794; pursued his studies at Tudhoe and Crook Hall; ordained priest at the latter, Dec. 4, 1802; succeeded Geo. Leo Haydock as prefect-general and professor at the college; missioner at Stockton, where he died, Sep. 13, 1822.

Mr. Haydock has preserved some lines written by one of the students " On the ordination of the Revv. John Bradley, Thomas Cock, Thomas Storey, and Robert Gradwell," Dec. 4, 1802. Though meriting little praise as a poem, they may serve as an illustration of the apostolic spirit which animated the collegians. Appealing to his genius the youth commences :—

> " The grief Britannia felt, O Muse resound,
> When persecution stained her hallowed ground,
> When irreligion held its ruthless sway,
> And errors led her faithful sons astray."

After full vent has been given to the struggling tempest of Britannia's breast, an angel is sent from Heaven to soothe her with tidings of Emancipation and the Restoration of Religion :—

> " When this bless'd Isle once more, thy chiefest care,
> Shall all thy bounties, all thy glories share,
> When error bound in adamantine chains
> No more shall blast thy ever blissful plains."

and addresses the young missioners with the peroration :—

> " O ! hail ye four design'd at Heaven's command
> To be the saviours of your native land,
> Your fame shall flourish in eternal day
> And round your temples endless glories play."

to which some wag has appended :—

> " Bradley as first, in stature so in fame,
> And Cock th' immortal, no ignoble name,
> Storey, thy deeds posterity shall tell,   '
> And Gradwell, feared by all the powers of Hell ! "

## GRAMMAR.

81. Rev. John Penswick, born at the Manor-house, Ashton-in-Makerfield ; liberated Feb. 25, 1795 ; ordained at Durham from Crook Hall, Dec 17, 1803 ; missioner at Birchley, Lancashire, Jan., 1804, till Mar., 1849, when he retired to Garswood, and died Oct. 30, 1864, aged 86, the last survivor of the Douay collegians.

82. Thomas Bray, layman ; remained at the college, sick, and died there Oct. 30, 1794.

83. Wm. Veal, layman ; escaped Jan. 16, 1764.

84. Rev. Thomas Cock, born in Lancashire in Jan., 1774; escaped Jan. 16, 1794 ; pursued his studies at Tudhoe and Crook Hall; ordained priest at the latter, Dec. 4, 1802 ; chaplain at Cheesburn Grange, and Burn Hall ; accidentally drowned at the latter, Aug. 1, 1854, aged 80.

85. Matthew Forster, layman, native of Northumberland ; liberated, Feb. 25, 1795 ; pursued his studies at Crook Hall ; died in Northumberland.

86. Peter Flanaghan, layman ; native of Ireland ; left Oct. 31, 1792.

87. Henri Boithamon, layman ; native of Brittany ; being a Frenchman went to Paris with his brother Albert, no. 96, and Fran. Hay, no. 74, Oct. 16, 1793.

88. James Teebay, layman ; native of Preston, left Oct. 31, 1792 ; steward and land agent ; died at Ingol Cottage, near Preston, Jan. 24, 1854.

### FIRST CLASS RUDIMENTS.

89. Lawrence Teebay, layman ; native of Preston ; left Oct. 31, 1792 ; shopkeeper at Preston, where he died.

90. Vincent Oliveira, layman ; left Feb. 21, 1793.

91. John Bulbeck, layman ; native of Havant, Southampton ; liberated, Feb. 25, 1795 ; died at Havant.

92. Thomas Brennan, layman ; native of London ; liberated Feb. 25, 1795.

93. James Arkwright, layman ; liberated Feb. 25, 1795.

### SECOND CLASS RUDIMENTS.

94. Edmund Costello, layman ; left Aug. 4, and died at St. Omer's College, Aug. 24, 1793.

95. Rt. Rev. Robert Gradwell, born at Clifton, Lancashire, Jan. 26, 1777 ; liberated Feb. 25, 1795; being ill of fever, 9th Aug. 1793, he was allowed to remain in the college when the rest were sent to Esquerchin, and thus was enabled to save the college diary, which he carried with him when he rejoined the collegians ; ordained priest at Crook Hall, Dec. 4, 1802, and remained as professor of poetry and rhetoric for seven years ; missioner at Claughton, Lancashire, from 1809 till 1817 ; degree of D.D. in 1820 ; rector of the English College, Rome, till 1828 ; consecrated bishop of Lydda, June 24, 1828, and appointed co-adjutor in the London District ; died at Golden-Square, London, Mar. 15, 1833, aged 56.

96. Albert Boithamon, layman ; native of Brittany ; went to Paris, Oct. 16, 1793.

97. Joseph Lopez, layman ; left for St. Omer's College, Aug, 4, 1793.

98. Christopher Galway, layman ; left Feb. 18, 1793.

99. Augustin Amarigo, layman ; went to St. Omer's College, Aug. 4, 1793.

100. George Strickland, layman; born at Sizergh Castle, West-moreland, Oct. 23, 1780; left Jan. 8, 1793; died near London in 1843.

101. Thomas Murphy, layman; born at Cadiz or London; went to St. Omer's College, Aug. 4, 1793.

102. Michael Langton, layman; went to St. Omer's College, Aug. 4, 1793.

### THIRD CLASS RUDIMENTS.

103. Joseph Fountain, layman; liberated Feb. 25, 1795.

The students were allowed by the revolutionists to bring their private property to England, but that of the college was lost. The indemnity paid by the French government to the English government, in 1815, was retained by the latter on account of its being Catholic property devoted to "super-stitious purposes." The money was expended in paying off the debt in-curred in the building and finishing of the Pavilion at Brighton for George IV. when he was Prince of Wales.

## St. Omer's College.

"The shade of youthful hope is there;
That lingered long, and latest died.
Ambition all dissolved to air,
With phantom honours at her side."

*Wm. Robt. Spencer.*

In 1849, Dr. Gillow was engaged with his history of "The Foundation of the colleges at Crook Hall and Old Hall Green by the refugees from the English secular colleges at Douay and St. Omer's respectively," and in answer to queries on this subject Mr. Haydock wrote that he had no means of knowing what passed at St. Omer's. He had heard that the Rev. Richard Brettargh, a deacon only, died at Doulens—the only collegian who died in prison; "he was a great friend of my brother James, who found his brother long steward at Trafford House." In order to trace the continuity of Old Hall, we shall here introduce an account of the expulsion of the professors and students from the English College at St. Omer   and their imprisonment at Arras and Doulens, written anonymously by one of the community.

It was originally founded by Fr. Persons, in 1593, as a Jesuit college.  In 1762, the Parliament of Paris determined on the expulsion of the Jesuits from France, and the English members of the Society were doomed with their French brethren.  The college authorities, having information of this design, resolved to transport their establishment bodily beyond the parliament's reach, across the frontier of France, and the city of Bruges was selected for their asylum.  There they removed in August of that year, and in 1764 the college buildings were handed over to the English clergy.  Thus the secular college at St. Omer was practically a new establishment.  The revolution nipped it in the bud before it arrived at maturity ; indeed, it never prospered, although it possessed eminent men for its presidents.

The first president of the new college was the Hon. and Rev. Thomas Joseph Talbot, D.D., who only held the office from 1764 to the time of his appointment as co-adjutor-bishop to Dr. John Hornyold, V.A., of the Midland District, in the beginning of 1766.  The venerable author of " The Lives of the Saints," the Rev. Alban Butler, succeeded him, and died at St. Omer,  May 15, 1773.  The Rev. William Wilkinson then became the third   : president, and at his resignation in 1787, the Rev. Gregory Stapleton was appointed to the office, which he retained till the suppression of the college.

The following narrative is from a manuscript possessed by the late Charles F. Corney, Esq., of London, who kindly gave permission for its publication.

" The confinement of the different English families, at this time resident in St. Omer   was looked for with anxious expectation by certain malicious republicans, and every species of artifice was consulted for its execution. This, however, was attended with certain important difficulties. Some specious pretext was to be formed to conceal its injustice, and inspire the nation with abhorrence for these generous and benevolent strangers, whose benificence it had so long experienced. All Europe was to be deluded by some artful and ingenious contrivance which might palliate this open violation of the rights of hospitality, and this was the plan they had determined to pursue:

" A certain printed letter was entrusted to a well-known republican which contained a long list of English who had engaged in a plot against the town. This was to be dropped in a public part of the town, where some person might find and pick it up, or, most probably, some person had been appointed for that purpose, for it was not every one that would have disclosed its contents; an aristocrat would have concealed them. Be that as it may, the commission was performed with the greatest punctuality ; the letter was immediately dispatched to the municipality, the conspirator denounced, and measures accordingly pursued. Among the persons in the letter, our chief professors were ranged the first, and then came the names of the principal individuals in town. Information was sent to Paris, and a decree pronounced, to confine all the British resident in France. No sooner was this decree received at St. Omer  than a troop of between two and three hundred soldiers was  dispatched to the British houses in town.  Mr. Cornthwaite, * our procurator, had

* The Rev. Richard Cornthwaite, a native of Lancashire, born about 1736, studied, and was ordained priest, at Douay, where he took the college oath, Dec. 27, 1760, at the age of 24.  He succeeded the Rev. Thomas Talbot (afterwards bishop) at Brockhampton, near Havant, in Sussex, when that gentleman was elected president of St. Omer's College, in 1764. About 1779, he was appointed chaplain at Sedgley Park School, and after the death, at Finchley, Sept. 28, 1782, of Mr. William Mumford, the procurator of St. Omer's College, succeeded to the office, and was of great service to the college in that capacity.  After his escape to England, he settled at Harvington Hall, Worcestershire, where he died, Sept. 11, 1803 aged 67.

escaped some time before, and two hours after his departure from Calais, the marchaussée arrived there to confine him.

" Throughout St. Omer, where the first arrests were executed, the greatest silence and consternation universally prevailed. The people were ignorant of the motive of all these sudden transactions, and waited for the result in astonishment and suspense, when on a sudden they descried an English gentleman taken out of his house by some of the soldiers, and escorted to the town prison. In the meantime a large troop of about 200 entered our college and were sent with the greatest order to their respective stations. The principal officers very politely went up and arrested the masters ; the boys were forbidden to stir from their seats, and the motive of these proceedings was still involved in the same obscurity. I, with a number of other boys, was at that time in the ciphering school ; our professor was taken out, and two or three sentinels stationed at the door. Some of our boys attempted to run out, but the soldiers immediately told us they would put the first person to the bayonet who should venture to stir beyond a certain line. And now the soldiers had performed their duty, the professors were arrested, seals fixed on all their doors, and the boys were ordered to the study-place. The masters were immediately conducted, some to the French college, others to the town prison, where they spent all the night in a miserable and dreary confinement with the greatest solicitude as the mystery was as yet undisclosed. The boys after the space of about two hours were allowed to move out into the garden, and began their recreation as usual. Football was at that time the ruling game, and the boys and soldiers played promiscuously together. The rest of the day was spent according to custom till bed-time. The next morning a number of the guards were removed, but some were still detained to guard our college ; two cannons were placed at each door, and all walks out prohibited. The masters were escorted from the town prison where they spent the night to the

French college. Here each one was confined in a separate room. All this happened in the parching heat of summer ; the rooms were about three yards long and a yard and three quarters broad. In these little cabins they were enclosed for fifteen days, secluded from all correspondence, broiled by the scorching heat and not allowed even once to stir out. The windows were exceedingly small, and the guards ordered to fire at them if they ventured to look out. Their repasts were brought round every day, and I believe that bread and water was their only allowance. Be that as it may, their friends used to contrive, I think, to send them something. After a short time Mr. Fletcher * found means to discover the reasons for their confinement by means of a newspaper, which another person, Mr. Brown, had procured, who gave him the clearest information of every thing through a hole in the wall. They were arrested, I believe, some time in July [1793]. After the close of those fifteen days, three commissaries from the national convention arrived at·St. Omer. Amongst them was the famous Bellaud Varennes, who became afterwards so conspicuous, and hauled down the despotic Robespierre from his tribune to the guillotine. He was attended by citizen Neon, as secretary (at present the commissioned agent for the care and superintendence of the French prisoners), and ordered to search into this mock conspiracy and examine our professors. The municipal officers conducted him to the prison, and the masters were brought before him in their turns and interrogated. Moral and political subjects were principally regarded. They were asked what mode of education they generally pursued, what sort of instructions they delivered on religion and politics, what sort of principles they wished to infuse, were they attached

---

* The Rev. John Fletcher, subsequently D.D., was educated at Douay and St. Gregory's, Paris. When the latter seminary was dissolved, he went to St. Omer's college, where his great-uncle, William Wilkinson, had been president for some time. Here Mr. Fletcher was a professor during the whole time of the imprisonment of the collegians at Arras and Doulens, and returned to England with them, when they obtained their release in 1795.

K

to Mr. Pitt, and would they defend the town in case of danger?
To these different questions they replied with all their prudence
and ingenuity, and their answers were taken down in writing.
After this examination they were allowed a little more liberty—
viz., to dine together, to walk about two hours a day in the
gardens, and different other little liberties. After two months
or so, five of our masters (for they were eleven in all) were permitted to return to us, and we received them with the most
cordial satisfaction. Till this time, since the first arrestation
took place, we had been subjected to the tuition of five French
masters. This was the reason why they did not confine the
masters and boys in one common prison, and it is well known,
because they supposed that if a separation took place we might
easily be perverted and gained over to their interest. But in
this they were grossly mistaken, and our own professors observed
that the boys never behaved better than at this very period.

"That same day the French masters entered the house, bustle
and tumult began to break forth. Their behaviour was exceedingly obliging, but the French and English characters constitute
a distinction which can never be combined, never act in concurrence. We had agreed when they were first introduced to
study regularly two hours every school-day, but in those two
hours very little was done; some ran out of the study-place,
others remained idle; all was bustle and confusion. On recreation days the boys used to form into different parties and run
all over the house; when the masters were at one end of a
gallery, run to the other, and abuse them in the most insulting
and contemptuous language. Whenever a bustle became serious
the sentinels were immediately called forth (for they had remained all this time in our college), and the fear of incurring
their displeasure deterred us from hurting the professors. One
morning they were determined to punish us and deprive us of
our breakfasts, but all their endeavours would have proved in-
effectual had not the guards come forward to their assistance,

and driven us from the refectory, who repented afterwards for
their interference, and assured us that they would never come
forward again on a similar occasion. We found afterwards from
experience that they kept their word. As soon as we were expelled the refectory we ran all together into the garden and
formed into two ranks. The master was parading before us quite
pale with fury ; the Marseillais Hymn was struck up, and those
parts where liberty came in, such as ' Liberté, Liberté, chèrie,'
were sung in the most extravagant and exulting strain. Whenever the master turned his head he was kindly saluted with a
stone or two, while the guards were well acquainted with all that
passed. At last the boys thought proper to break up.

"When our masters in the French college were allowed to walk
in the garden, we spoke to them over the wall that separated the
two colleges, and Mr. Stapleton* exhorted us to continue these
tumults, and encouraged us in our insubordination. Two or
three of the boys were allowed to visit their own masters when
their confinement was at this time alleviated, and one of these
boys happened one day to engage in a dispute with a French
professor of ours who happened to be in the garden at the time.
This was reported to the municipality, and all further correspon-

* Gregory Stapleton, son of Nicolas Stapleton, of Carlton, Esq., studied
at Douay, where he was procurator for many years. In 1785 he left to travel
with young Mr. Stonor, of Stonor, and when Mr. Wilkinson resigned the
presidency of St. Omer's College, in 1787, Mr. Stapleton, on his return from
Italy, was chosen to succeed him. When the collegians were liberated,
in 1795, President Stapleton took them to Old Hall Green, and was installed
the first president of that establishment upon its erection into St. Edmund's
College. In that office he remained till he was appointed vicar-apostolic of
the Midland District, and was consecrated bishop, Mar. 8, 1801. This appointment was made, said Mr. M'Pherson, the Scotch agent at Rome, "as
a stop-gap, and to prevent the appointment of another person, whose appointment had long been solicited by the Irish bishops, some in England,
and by Sir John Cox Hippesley." In the following year he set out for Paris
to attempt the recovery of the lost property of the English colleges and convents. At St. Omer he was seized with a fatal illness, and expired in the
inn called St. Catherine's, May 23, 1802, aged 54. He was buried in the
cemetery attached to the ancient church of St. Martin, St. Omer.

dence was instantaneously prohibited. We were asked one Sunday if we would hear mass. A priest was proposed who had taken the French oath, but we refused it without the least hesitation, and they never once thought of offering us a priest a second time. In short, the two months or six weeks we spent without any mass, though the boys said their prayers very regularly, while the French masters walked up and down the church with the philosophers.

"At last the famous day arrived when a few of our masters returned after their long separation. What they called the college council, such as the president and some of the most distinguished professors, were still detained in their former confinement. The night before they came (for they arrived so late as one in the morning) some of the principal municipal members were introduced into the refectory, summoned all the boys, reproached us for our misconduct to the masters, and closed their harangue by giving out these severe orders, that two of the most seditious should be sent to the dungeon. This was no sooner heard than all was silence and consternation. At last, however, they were induced to pardon them after the most urgent entreaties. As our professors were to be soon after introduced into the college, they wished, I suppose, to prevent all misconduct towards the French professors before their departure, and these Frenchmen sneaked off as soon as ours were admitted. All the time that we were under their jurisdiction, scarce a day passed without some new scene of disorder, and this did not agree with the schemes of perversion which I before mentioned, so that the municipality was obliged to dismiss them and return us some of ours, whom we received after we had heard their voices with the loudest expressions of satisfaction. These few were restored to us about two months after their first imprisonment. From that time till we were all united in the French college, one whole month intervened, which we spent in the greatest quiet and subordination, so great was the change occasioned by the difference of masters and dispositions. I have forgotten to state that on the 10th of August, that celebrated procession day, our masters were nearly massacred ; so great was the ardour of the populace for their execution that they could hardly be restrained from entering the college. This is really true without the least exaggeration."

## The Beginning of the General Imprisonment.

" Enjoy thy bondage, make thy prison know
Thou hast a liberty, thou canst not owe
To those base punishments ; keep entire, since
Nothing but guilt shackles the conscience."

*Zouch Towncley.*

"About the 6th or 7th of October [1793], in the midst of our nightly repose, we were awakened on a sudden and ordered to get up. What is this for? Why this bustle? What is their reason for calling us up at this early hour? was the general cry. The boys, however, rose with the greatest expedition. When all were up and assembled in the dormitory, we received immediate orders to proceed to the refectory. But mark! we were no sooner conducted to the refectory than four or five guards appeared, who had been commissioned to detain us there till further orders. What was become of our masters, no one individual could tell. But a troop of soldiers had been sent to conduct them to the parlour, and there they were all enclosed. Their papers were examined, and after an hour or so we were sent to bed, but our masters, I believe, stayed up. The next morning a report was spread that we were all going to be sent to the French college. As yet, however, all was in a state of uncertainty. The boys were disclosing their respective wishes. Some were desirous of remaining, others of being reunited to the

president, and the rest of the professors, who had been left behind in the French college when these five that I mentioned
were returned.   All was bustle, solicitude, and perplexity.   Both
boys and masters were, however, employed in packing up their
little baggage, but nothing could be taken out of the church,
and the chalices and silver plate were seized.   At last our final
orders were received, and the matter immediately decided.   The
students and all were sent off, bag and baggage, to the French
college, there to remain till they were conveyed to the prison of
Arras.   Our present imprisonment was scarcely perceived, as the
garden we played in was as spacious as our own at the college.
The deprivation of a walk out was an inconvenience that attended our confinement, but which, however, we hardly felt.
The gaoler was exceedingly good-natured in this respect.   In
the midst of the greatest severities of the frost, though he was
unable to skate himself, he sometimes took them out, and left
them to skip about and enjoy their little liberties, whilst he
stood shivering in the cold, or at least was provided with a very
small fire which the boys had lit up with a few scattered sticks
and a scanty pile of turf.   During all this time we continued our
studies and prayers as usual, but were deprived of the pleasure
of hearing mass.

" We had now been confined about eleven weeks in the French
college, when a commissary, called Duquesne, arrived at St.
Omer, about a week before our departure for Arras.   He was
entrusted by the convention with the management of different
affairs.   At last a day was appointed for the determination of
our fate, and if our pretensions to liberty were justly grounded
we were to be gratified with that important privilege.   But when
they had at last adopted this happy resolution a member of the
municipality named Damart rose up and interposed.   The
measure was consequently dropped, and hence we may date the
first origin of our calamities.   His reason for acting in so strange
and ungenerous a manner was this.   A certain English friend of

his had been deprived of his freedom by a similar interposition. This little hump-backed dwarf, about four feet and three or four inches tall, was affronted, and determined to gratify his resentment. No sooner, then, was our enfranchisement proposed, than he rose up with the greatest precipitation, and exclaimed : " No, my citizens, either all must be liberated or none at all ; " at least he made use of nearly the same expression. That moment the deliberation was presented, those that had been liberated were again confined, and one man's resentment blasted all our expectations.

" This little niggardly fellow had made a very serious commotion on a former occasion. There stood two very high towers in the French college, which commanded a distant prospect on every side. These some of the boys were desirous of ascending, and ventured as far as the top, where they looked about and examined the different views. Some people of the town happened by chance to perceive them, and it reached this little insignificant coxcomb's ears. As a member of the municipality he thought it highly becoming his dignity to take notice of an affair of such importance, and came to the French college with all the pomp of a magistrate, accused us of being spies, and sent the guards immediately to the towers to seize everyone they could find. Some of them escaped, others were arrested, and brought before him. After he had harangued and reproached them, he gave orders to send them to the dungeons, but after the most pressing solicitations was persuaded to let them off. This fellow was one of our greatest enemies and opponents.

" A short time after our confinement was determined upon, even on the very day of its determination, a report was spread that we were to proceed to Arras. For the space of about four days we were kept in perfect suspense. The news at last arrived, and the boys were flushed with the most gratifying expectation. Our baggage was prepared, carts put in requisition, an escort of horsemen assembled, and on Sunday we set off.

Very few were allowed to take their beds ; I, with most others, left mine behind. The day was spent in travelling ; towards the close of the evening we arrived at the place of our destination, which was the Orphelines prison. That night about a hundred, consisting of the collegians and some English families, men and women, were placed in a large garret without any straw to lie upon. I slept in my blanket on the bare floor. A supply was allowed the next day, to each a single truss, which lasted about six weeks. For nearly three days we received no provisions. A large jar of our butter had been stolen, but still we were pretty well supplied with that essential article, and some bread which we brought with us, otherwise we must have inevitably starved. The national allowance was a loaf a day. With what little money the college was supplied, they contrived to procure something else. For the whole month, however, that we lived in that prison, our allowance was exceedingly scanty. A small piece of bread and a little cup of milk was our morning repast. For dinner we could sometimes procure a little scrap of meat, but seldom above three mouthfuls. I remember myself eating all my meat allowance at a mouthful. A little soup was generally made, and brought up with our meat, but very little was to be got. For three weeks together our dinner's provision consisted of a salt herring, some bread, and a few potatoes, but we were often obliged to remain without a herring. For the two or three first days after our arrival at Arras we lived exceedingly contented with a slice of bread and butter. Our supper meal was the same as that we had for breakfast, a little bread and milk. Had we been allowed a spacious place for recreation these different inconveniences would have been much less regarded, but we were all confined to one little court (where the gaoler kept his poultry, and a great number of the *gens* suspects used to walk about and refresh themselves), and a little garden somewhat bigger than ours at Isleworth.* In the court it was impossible

* Perhaps this remark may afford a clue to the name of the writer of the MS.

to play without offending the different people that were walking about and occupied the greatest part of the space (for about 150 persons, French and English, were confined here), and the little garden, which was also pretty well crowded, afforded very little room for any sort of exercise or amusement. But, notwithstanding all these disadvantages, our vocal concerts, which afterwards became pretty frequent, and our little jovial entertainments kept up our spirits and banished all solicitude. Those alone were depressed by cares and apprehensions who were capable of forming a just conception of their unfortunate situation and the dangers that surrounded them; and our masters were very sensible of their misfortune.

" Desmaux, the commissary who came to visit our prison, behaved with the greatest asperity, and always addressed us with an air of haughtiness which was at that period the general tone of republicanism. For those were the most honoured that behaved with the fiercest brutality. The gaoler, apprehensive of suspicion, affected an air of superiority, but discovered on all occasions a very great fund of humanity. For every convenience, even the smallest articles that were admitted into the prisons of Arras, the person to whom they belonged was obliged to pay his toll to the gaolers, and this obligation they took care to make use of to the best advantage, and committed a number of extortions.

" Such was the curious life we led in that prison. At last, after repeated solicitations and wishes, orders were received for our emigration into another prison, after about four weeks' imprisonment in this. We set off immediately, bag and baggage, for our place of destination. It was called the Hôtel Dieu. This prison was even worse than the former. In one respect, however, it was preferable. The garrets were more extensive, and afforded us a good deal more room, and the shouts of the people round the guillotine could no longer be heard as from our last prison. But these advantages were almost counterbalanced by superior disadvantages. Our want of a proper place for recreation was still more restricted. The places allowed us were a pretty long narrow court, exactly like a street, where the different English families that were confined in the same prison used to fill up the space, so far at least as to deprive us of our romping amusements, and a small church where it was impossible to run about without exposing yourself to the disagreeable necessity of mangling the bodies of the dead (for we sometimes found scattered lumps of flesh), or of contracting some infectious distemper by the noxious vapours that might arise. Such were the places allotted for our recreation, and who could conceive it? The horrid Frenchmen proposed to appoint a dormitory for the boys in that very church where all these inconveniences were so much to be feared! In this prison we began to renew our studies, which had been so long intermitted, and employed our time to the best advantage. Our victuals in this prison were nearly the same as in the last, with a little improvement. One day, however, all the boys, except some of the little ones who happened to procure a little bread, were obliged to fast till six in the evening without the least refreshment, and numbers were dropping on their beds in a state of languor and debility. At last their dinners arrived, which consisted of nothing else but some hot bread that was very unwholesome, and some light watery French soup, which very few ventured to take, and with a little cheese, I believe, and perhaps a scrap of meat.

"It was in this prison, and the next, which I am going to mention, that our masters felt particular apprehensions, and not without reason. For one night, so we were informed, whilst we were all asleep, a captain with a troop of soldiers was sent to the prison to massacre all the prisoners, on a report that a conspiracy had been detected. This person was very punctual in performing his orders. He went accordingly to the prison and inquired of the gaoler whether he had heard of any seditious disturbance. "No," said he, and the captain immediately returned.

That very night, had not the gaoler, who was a hearty sort of a fellow, attested our tranquillity, we should all have been assassinated in our beds ; and this he himself related.

"After a five weeks' confinement or so in this prison, without any prospect of deliverance, and an endurance of nearly the same hardships as in the last, we were ordered to get ready for an- other emigration. Accordingly, we set off with the commissary Gilles, bag and baggage, in the afternoon, and arrived at this new temple of misery. It was called La Maison des Capucins, because it had been a convent belonging to that religious order. Here we were allowed the full enjoyment of a large kitchen garden, though we were sometimes confined to different parts by the caprice of an imperious committee, which was composed of the most distinguished English amongst us, who were charged with the superintendence and care of the boys. This committee was appointed by the votes of all the rest of the English except our boys, and a president was always selected. They supposed that if the boys were allowed to vote they would naturally choose their own president, and consequently preclude them from all participation in this affair. The boys insisted upon their privilege, but the president ordered them to be quiet, and they complied. The best rooms were allotted to the English that had accompanied us into this prison, and they lived very comfortably during this confinement. The boys were no longer enclosed in a garret, but occupied the rooms below. Here after the second night, we were provided with another truss and a half of straw, after sleeping upon two, or one and a half, which we re- ceived at our first prison for about nine weeks.

"In all these prisons it happened of course that if one advan- tage was enjoyed, it must necessarily be counterbalanced by some proportional disadvantage. And in this prison our repasts were even worse than in the others. Bread and milk at morn- ing and night as usual, but for dinner liver and old cow's udder, bread and treacle, water soup—in short, a most miserable allow-

ance, and yet cow's udder was considered as a treat when meat
was so very rare. Our studies were also continued, our spirits as
vigorous as ever, and vocal concerts still more common than before,
although all music had been nearly forgotten in our last prison.
As we were singing ' Braves Soldats,' and parading through the
cloisters, the gaoler came up and stopped us, and gave orders
never to sing it any more. We remonstrated, and replied that
the words were democratical. 'The words are democratical,'
said he, 'but the tune is aristocratical, and I forbid you to sing
it any longer. Sing what you please provided you don't sing
that.'

" A little time before we left this place for Doulens, a curious
affair took place, that inspires a very just conception of the base
and niggardly dispositions of the republicans. The gaolers who
had been apprised of our future departure proposed a deep con-
certed scheme for dividing the gardens among the English.
Each one was to pay six livres in ready money for his separate
allotment for three months. All was agreed to, the money was
paid, and a few days after we were sent to Doulens, and the
Frenchmen enjoyed the sweet fruits of this perfidy ; another
instance of national generosity.

" The day before we set off, the Frenchmen very liberally proposed to furnish our dinner at the national expense. Dinner
was accordingly served up. The soup was brought upon the
table, tasted, and sent off. Then came up a mixture of livers,
lights, and I don't know what, all jumbled and hashed together
in such a slop that no one would eat them, notwithstanding all
their hunger and distress, but left everything but their bread,
which all enjoyed. We wished and wished again for no more
national dinners, and our wishes were fulfilled, for the next day
we were sent in waggons to Doulens, after a month's confinement here, and about three months and a half at Arras, that
ever memorable seat of our sufferings, for as long as we remained
there our lives were in continual danger.

"The day we set off for Doulens, which, however, I by no means desired, as I conceived that our prison was preferable to any other we might possibly meet with, fifteen people were ordered to the guillotine. Another instance of French kindness ; Le Bon, the governor of Arras, ordered the waggons to be conducted round the guillotine, at the moment the executions were to have taken place, in order to daunt our courage, to give us some faint idea of the operations of that wonderful machine, and to leave us this last legacy of his kindness and affection. The master of the horse rode up with great fury to hasten our departure, confined us all within our ranks, and conducted us from our door round the market-place, but very fortunately these miserable victims had been executed a moment before, and we returned, after taking the tour and viewing this surprising machine, to the very door from which we had set off. We then began to proceed on our journey, accompanied by a small escort of cavalry. We arrived at Doulens about eleven o'clock at night, and advanced immediately to the capital, where the Douay collegians were imprisoned. This citadel stands in a very conspicuous situation, and commands a most delightful prospect. Here, there were sufficient rooms for every sort of recreation, as the platform is very spacious. When we came here we found no room, no place whatsoever prepared for our reception ; the house where the Douay collegians were confined was shut up on every side, and each of us began to think of sleeping on the ground. I myself was excessively cold and fatigued and cared very little where I slept. At last the Douatians were awakened, informed who we were, and opened their door to us with the greatest hospitality. But all their hospitality was incapable of providing us with better lodgings than a garret about as long as the length of this house,* but not near so broad.

* This refers to the house in which the writer of the narrative was residing at the time of writing. The collegians arrived at Doulens in May, 1794.

In this little place fifty boys were jumbled together, and obliged for that night to wrap themselves in their blankets on the bare floor. This garret was preferable, however, in some respects to the others we had been confined in. The windows were more numerous in proportion, as there were five in this garret, and only five in our first garret at Arras, where about one hundred people were lodged, and about three in the second, where between thirty and forty were confined. Here, then, we were left unprovided with straw for the first night. The next day we received a very good supply about a truss-and-a-half a piece. Our meals were far better provided, and the bread was exceedingly good in general, though for three weeks it was quite purple and unhealthy, and many suffered very severely from *pulssian.* The milk was remarkably good, but we seldom got sufficient for breakfast and supper. At dinner the meat that was served up was also very good, and always enough for myself, though numbers of others were not so soon contented.

## The Release.

"Tymes go by turnes, and chaunces change by course,
From foule to fayre, from better happ to worse."

*Fr. Robt. Southwell.*

"The garret at Dourlens made the place excessively disagreeable. It was always the custom to separate our apartments by hanging curtains from the beams that spread across the room. These in the scorching heat of summer rendered the place rather more offensive than it would otherwise have been, and the parching rays of the sun, which were all day beating against the roof, warmed it very nearly as much as the hottest stove. But this was one of our smallest inconveniences. If you happened to awake in the night it was almost impossible to recover your sleep, so tortured you were with fleas. My shirt, which I used to change now and then (I don't recollect how often), was after two nights spotted all over with blood. In this citadel, and in this garret, we remained for three months. One of our professors * died with a putrid fever, and the boy that I slept next to was infected with the same distemper, which, however, I was so fortunate as to escape.

"About two months after our present confinement, we sent a

---

* The Rev. Richard Brettargh, was a son of Mr. Richard Brettargh, of Ince, co. Lancaster, the representative of the junior branch of the Brettarghs of Brettargh Holt, in Little Woolton, near Liverpool. He was born at Ince, June 21, 1765, and after a preliminary education, in all probability at the Rev. Simon George Bordley's school at Aughton, was sent to St. Omer's College, where he was ordained deacon and appointed a professor. He died on June 24, 1794, and his body was buried in the public cemetery outside Doulens, none of his friends being permitted to accompany it to the grave.

petition to Robespierre, which was composed by one of the boys and entreated for release; but all to no purpose, for we never received an answer. Not long after we were informed of his death, which delivered us in a great measure from our anxieties and apprehensions. Indeed, it was generally supposed that all would have perished within a week, if the death of this tyrant had not occurred to cheer up our languishing spirits and animate our hopes.

"A short time after his death, having remained about three months in this citadel, we were sent off to the other, where we were all more comfortably situated, as the soldiers' barracks had been prepared for our habitation. But no new provision of straw was allowed, and for half a year I was obliged to be content with two trusses, which became as hard almost as the floor itself. My rough sharp pointed books, shirts, and other little baggage, served as a pillow. Every morning we were called out to the roll, as usual in the last citadel, and we found this upper citadel in many respects more pleasant than the lower. Our rooms were more comfortable, and the play-ground more extensive, but the prospect rather more confined. Whenever any English prisoners arrived, all communication was prohibited, though this privilege was allowed in the beginning.

"At last, after three months' confinement in this citadel, that made our total imprisonment at Doulens amount to six entire months, we were gratified with the pleasant and unexpected news of our return to St. Omer, which was at last to terminate our memorable imprisonment, We set out from St. Omer about the beginning of January, and returned about the latter end or beginning of October [1794].

"After the death of the tyrannical Robespierre, the commissioners and magistrates in all the departments were succeeded by persons of more moderate dispositions. Bertier was appointed governor of that country which included the town and territory of St. Omer. To him we addressed a petition for our return, and he was so kind as to comply with our request. A wealthy farmer, who lived in the suburbs of St. Omer, was so kind as to provide us with waggons for our return, and on that happy day we bid the most gratifying farewell of our lives to this last of prisons after our professors had embraced the commander of the town, who had formerly been a pedlar, and treated them with this familiarity because he had been put in possession of all the pots, pans, and rusty goods, which we had left behind.

"When we came to St. Omer we returned to the French college, for ours had been converted into a military hospital. After sleeping here for two nights on the bare floor, the district supplied us with books, beds, and every convenience of that description, and we lived very comfortably. At last our president set off to Paris, and obtained a decree for our return to England after we had remained about a week in suspense and expectation. As soon as the wished-for news arrived, all was singing and exultation. Everybody received a new suit of clothes, for in prison we were covered with rags, and universal happiness prevailed. When our president returned to St. Omer we set off immediately (so great were our apprehensions lest the decree might be retracted), and arrived at Dover after a ten hours' fatiguing passage."

*Fecit anonymus.*

* When the collegians returned to St. Omer in the latter part of October, 1794, they were sixty-four in number. The president, Mr Stapleton, watched every opportunity to avail himself of favourable circumstances, and at last obtained a passport with leave to go to Paris with a petition signed by every individual of his College, of Douay College, and of the English Benedictine College at Douay, for permission to return to England, which was granted. On St. Chad's Day, Mar. 2, 1795, he, with the gentlemen and scholars of St. Omer's, President Daniel, with the gentlemen and students of Douay College, and Dom James Jerome Sharrock, Prior of St. Gregory's, Douay, with his community, arrived at Dover. The president with a number of the St. Omerians went to Old Hall Green; the Douay

L

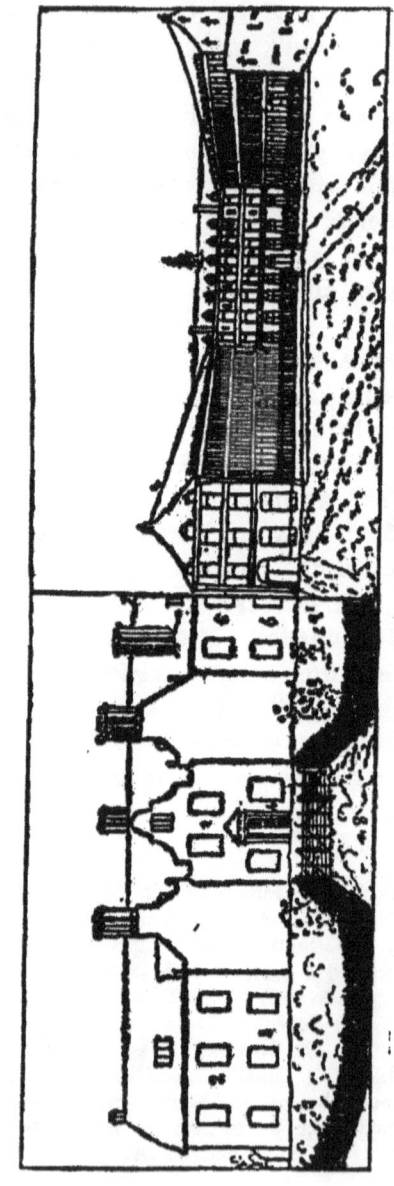

OLD HALL AND DOUAY COLLEGE, 1793.

1. Fire-School. 2. Dormitory. 3. Study-place. 4. Hall. 5. Boys' Dormitory. 6. Kitchen. 7. Chapel. 8. Highway. 9. Douay College.

## Olv Hall Green.

" Within this cloister'd calm retreat,
Where sacred science loves to fix her seat,
How did their moments tranquil wing their flight
In elegant delight ! "

*Anon.*

In a letter to his brother James, at Trafford House, near Manchester, dated Old Hall Green, Wednesday, Dec. 19, 1793, George Leo Haydock writes—"I departed from ye Tagg Nov. 28th, in company with our servant Richard, and arrived about 1 o'clock at ye house of Mr. Penswick, who lives near Garswood, 26 miles from our habitation.* We set off about 6 o'clock on horseback, and came in quite *à propos* for dinner, which was served up with great magnificence, and at 4 Richard returned homewards. No particulars worth notice occurred in our journey. I was exceedingly well treated during my stay at Garswood, so that after 3 or 4 days I was almost as much grieved to quit as to leave ye Tagg; almost, I say, for one circumstance gave me occasion of a short sorrow which I will

collegians were scattered amongst their homes, Crook Hall, and Old Hall Green ; and the Benedictine College settled at Acton Burnell, Salop, the seat of Sir Edward Smythe, Bart.

* Thomas Penswick was agent to the Gerard family of Bryn, in which office he was succeeded by his eldest son Randal. His second son, Thomas, became V. A. of the Northern District, and John, the third son, was the last survivor of the Douay collegians. They were descended from Thomas Penswick, of Great Eccleston, in the Fylde, who, by his wife Ellen, had a son William. The latter, by Grace his wife, a member of the old Catholic family of Johnson of Lea, was the father of the Rev. Thomas Penswick, ordained priest at the English College, Rome, who was chaplain at Hardwicke, near Hartlepool, the seat of the Maire family, when the mansion was attacked by a no-popery mob in 1746. His younger brother, Randal Penswick, was father to Thomas Penswick, the agent to the Gerards, who resided at the manor-house in Ashton-in-Makerfield.

now explain to you. We had proposed to repair to Old Hall Green, according to ye commands of ye Rt. Rev. Bp. Gibson, in a post-chaise, provided some other of ye Douay refugees would join us. Ye person we at first expected was Thomas Gillow, but receiving information from Mr. Jo. Orrel that he did not propose setting off before he had received orders from ye Bp., Thomas Penswick rode that afternoon to see if he could prevail with Mr. Monk to bear us company, but not finding him within, he left word for him to come if he thought proper ye day following. Accordingly he arrived towards ye evening of Sunday ye 1st. of Advent, quite prepared, yet he had not received orders from the Bp., so that Mr. Penswick advised him by no means to proceed. He returned therefore about eight o'clock without taking anything for supper, and ye day following came again with a request on Mr. Penswick to defray ye expenses of his journey, and he should be shortly repaid, which he refused to do lest ye blame should be laid upon him if Bp. Gibson designed him for some other place. Upon this second disappointment he seemed little pleased, and being pressed to sit down to dinner, absolutely excused himself." . . . Unfortunately a portion of the letter is here torn off. It continues under an original sketch, by the writer, of Old Hall and Douay College.

" The regulations we here observe are not quite settled on a firm foundation, so that I can only inform you of some particulars. We rise at 6 o'clock, go to church at ye half hour, and meditate out of Bp. Challoner in ye same manner as during ye retreat at Douay. At 7 study divinity, till 8, when we all repair to hear prayers, or Mass, with the boys, who do not bear us company in ye aforesaid meditation. At a quarter to 9, breakfast, of milk and bread (tea on fasting days), study till 1, when a dinner equal to what we had at Douay *saltim* is served up. I had forgot that at half-past 11 we are to repair to school after ye Epiphany—Mr. Coombs, our master, who only came

down with the bishop last Monday, having a desire to go as far
as Bath to see his relations. This day, he and Bp. Douglas
examined us all on ye gospel of St. Matthew, but in fact rather
answered himself than asked us questions. He is a person of
a most amiable character, and seems to deserve ye love of
every one. He informed us that Mr. Potier (a man as good and
agreeable as himself) was to be our head superior, and Mr.
Coombs ye second in authority and respect. After dinner we
play till 3, go to school at 5, till 6, then common prayers for
half-an hour, supper at 8, music for half-an-hour to prepare for
ye church, where we have sung ye offices and masses since our
arrival here, to ye great satisfaction of ye auditors. At 10 we
go to bed in ye dormitory, for we have no better accommodations,
and, indeed, we may think well to have so good, when we consider ye sufferings our friends undergo at Doulens, where they
have only a little straw to sleep on, and are forced to cover
themselves with their old tattered coats, which now scarce
defend them from ye injuries of ye weather. This description
we have received from Mr. Blacow, who effected his escape by
means of a rope, down a high wall of about 38 feet, together with
Mr. Thomson of Wigan, Clarkson and Lucas, who remained at
Louvain. What had become of us had we remained till now, or
according to your designed advice gone to Louvain ? Though
I know not whether in effect it had not been better, for my
sister seems to think that she could procure us some college in
those parts, by means of Mr. Catrow, for what we can easily
give. I received her kind letter two days before I left Tagg, as
likewise one from Mr Varley in answer to one we had sent him
to settle matters. The sum we had to pay was £24 10s. 0d.
with ye pensions included. The reason I set off from home so
suddenly was because I heard from Mr. Orrel (whom I saw at
Mr Banister's) that Penswick intended setting off to Old Hall
Green, Thursday, ye 28 of Nov, unless I came, or sent a
letter, which at that time I thought not proper to do as not

knowing ye resolutions of parents, friends, and especially Mr.
Lund, whose advice I asked ye day before I set off, and upon
his answer took my measures accordingly, viz., to make a stay
at Old-Hall Green till such times as I could procure a place at
Lisbon or Valladolid, or, which seems more to coincide with my
ideas, at Rome. Whithersoever I intend going at present
is not so firmly resolved upon but that your advice may
alter ye scales, or if Old-Hall Green be more agreeable and convenient at Spring, here I may perhaps take up my abode.
'Ne puisje ici fixer ma course vagabonde, et connu de vous
seul ignorer tout monde.' The pension I have here to pay is as
yet unknown to me, but I suppose it will not be as much as at
Douay, considering that we have no pocket money or clothes
allowed us. But I intend before long to get information of ye
truth in this particular. I heard Mr. Banister's letter from Bp.
Gibson in which were contained questions whether I and
Thomas intended to proceed to Old-Hall Green and whether we
were in a condition to pay one whole pension betwixt us, if so
he promised himself to pay ye other till such time as he had
received an answer from ye Pope. Upon which Mr. Banister
wrote him word that he believed I intended going forward, but
with regard to Thomas he had taken another way. Soon after
his lordship sent to Mr. Thomas Penswick a congratulary letter
with orders for him and Mr. Geo. Haydock to repair as soon as
possible to ye place aforesaid, from which I gather that he will
make up for all deficiencies. This is ye opinion of Messrs. Banister and Orrel. I must now draw to a conclusion, being fully
persuaded and conscious of performing my utmost for your
satisfaction. We are 12 divines in number, 10 from Douay, 1
from Lisbon, and another from Rome. He goes under ye name
of Mr. Freen, and has informed me of several particulars relating
to ye English college in those parts, which tho' they receive not
my entire approbation, yet they appear not in those horrid
colours in which it has always been painted. Ye greatest defect

is a too great satiety, or rather surfeit, of study, and a small
diminution of ye Douay liberties, which if my vocation remains
firm and secure I can easily bear up with. But of this I shall
inform you more in a short time. I have written to my mother,
as likewise to Mr. Coghlan, for whose service I shall perhaps
have occasion to procure a razor, &c., which I stand in need of,
for ye barber is here so exorbitant as to require 3d. only for
shaving, which will not long keep my purse in temper. Mr.
Potier is a painter of ye same turn as myself (I mean has learnt
without a master), and was exceedingly well pleased to see my
picture of Douay College. He offered me very kindly ye use of
his paints, &c., but if I think proper to proceed in this art, I
intend purchasing a box, &c. *Sed finis sit.* Compliments,
respects, and duty, you will give out as is most convenient, and
remember that I stand now in equal need of prayers as you pretended to do at Douay. I therefore beg and beseech you to
show your mercy and compassion on me as you do I make no
doubt on so many others ; pour into my wounded soul ye oil
and wine of ye good Samaritan, that at ye last day you may be
found instrumental in ye charitable office of procuring ye
salvation of a—dutiful, loving, and affectionate brother—George
Leo Haydocke.—*P.S.* You'll excuse all inaccuracies and
defects in this letter, considering that I am forced to write in ye
hurry and confusion of a rumgumtious fire-school ; and since I
had till this present moment forgot to mention ye *petite* larcenies
I have committed on your properties, I now ask your pardon,
and humbly entreat you to mark down all such things for which
I am indebted to you, or for which I may have occasion to ask
you in future times, if perchance I should remain any while in
these parts. Amongst other things I desire you would set down
ye price of your breeches and ye great riding-coat I have made
bold to take along with me, which indeed I should not have done
had time sufficient been allowed me. A library is not as yet
quite collected to serve our purposes, however, our master is

hard employed about it ; for which reason if I should stand in need of any book which may not be absolutely necessary for you, I make no doubt but you will favour me with it. I send for nothing at present, for things being in a fickle and uncertain condition, I am uncertain what to call for. I am just going to write to sister Stanislaus, so you'll pardon me if I leave you with a fraternal *adieu*. Thursday : This morning a votive mass was sung for our suffering friends at Doulens, *Amen."*

Mr. Varley, to whom Mr. Haydock refers, was ordained priest at Douay, and for many years was agent for the college in London, in which capacity he was highly serviceable. In 1776 he was elected a capitular, and dean of the English Chapter on the resignation of Mr. Lindow. He was greatly respected by his brethren, and died Nov. 27, 1806. His letter to " Mr. Geo Haydock, with Mr. Banister, Mowbrick, near Kirkham, Lanca-shire," dated London, Nov. ye 13th, 1793, is as follows :—" Dear Sir,—This morning I received your letter without date. I suppose you have made your calculation right. I find marked in Douay book, ye 19th of August, £10 10s. 0d. paid you by me, and £2 3s. 6d. for Mrs. Moor's account at Banker Wright's, total £12 13s. 6d., which with your pensions makes the sum you are to pay Mr. Banister for me, £24 10s. 0d. So that you will find 2 pence difference betwixt your account and mine. I was very glad to see you arrive safe from Douay. The latter end of last month arrived Messrs. Monk, Rickaby, Penswick, Gillow, Devereux, Lancaster, Lee, Saul, Law, Worswick, and Coombs. Mr. Coombs stayed at Louvain, but is safe. They left behind them 43, all of which were arrested and sent to prison at Doulens in Piccardy. Pray God preserve them. Mr. Daniel had too much faith in the French about him; he has now time to repent for not sending all away. I wish my nephew Stout had bore you company. I beg you will say all that's kind from me to Mr. Banister. I remain, dear Sir, your obedient, humble servant Thomas Varley.'

Before proceeding with the description of the school at Old Hall Green we will give a brief sketch of its history, including that of its antecedent at Twyford :—

> " A litel schole of Cristen folk ther stood
> Down at the ferther ende, in which ther were
> Children an hepe y-comen of Cristen blood
> That lered in that scolè yer by yere,
> Such maner doctrine as men used there ;
> That is to say ; to syngen and to rede,
> As smale children doon in her childbede."
>
> *Chaucer, The Prioress's Tale.*

In the reign of James II., a school was founded at Silksteed, near Winchester, of which the Rev. William Husband, *alias* Bernard, was the master in 1692. Subsequently it was removed to Twyford, near Winchester, where, in 1696, it was conducted by the Rev. John Banister, *alias* Taverner. It was in this year that Pope was sent to the school, and remained over twelve months under this learned master. It is said the poet was dismissed in consequence of writing a lampoon on his tutor, and was transferred to a Catholic school situated close by Hyde Park Corner, kept by another priest, where he nearly lost all that he had gained under Mr. Banister. Some of Pope's verses were still to be seen scratched on the windows at Twyford in Dr. Kirk's time. The Rev. James Brown assisted in the school early in the eighteenth century. About 1726 the Rev. Fris. (*alias* Ino. Walter) Fleetwood took charge of the establishment, under whose *régime* it was most successful. A curious pamphlet published in 1733, entitled "The Present State of Popery in England," represents Twyford as containing upwards of a hundred scholars at the time when the author wrote, and says it was "chiefly under the care of one Father Fleetwood." It was in 1732 that Mr. Fleetwood resigned his charge in order to become a Jesuit. He probably carried with him to the Society the interest he had with the scholars at Twyford and their parents, which caused the school to decline, and made it difficult, says Bishop Stonor, to supply his place. His assistant master, the Rev. Joseph Gildon, a priest educated at the English College at Lisbon, then taught the school not only to his own credit, but to the great advantage of his pupils. His death is thus recorded by Mr. Thomas Berington, Dean of the Chapter: " We have lately had a great loss. Good Mr. Joseph Gildon, master of the school at Twyford, dyed on July 26th, 1736." A priest named Taverner appears to have succeeded Mr. Gildon as assistant master, who ultimately retired to Warkworth Castle, the seat of Mr. Holman, where he died in 1745. On the retirement of Mr. Fleetwood the head mastership or management of the school seems to have devolved on the Rev. John Philip Betts, for it was he who applied to the Dean of the Chapter for help, and received an advance of £200, for which he gave a b'll of sale on his household goods and chattels, dated Feb. 15th, 1734, n.s., to Mr. John Shepherd, the treasurer. Besides this debt, the house was mortgaged to Mr. Holman, of Warkworth, who possessed property near Winchester. The pecuniary difficulties with which Mr. Betts had to contend, added to the loss sustained by Mr. Fleetwood's retirement, caused the school to languish, so that it is no wonder that the no-popery cry, raised after the Stuart rising of 1745, occasioned the close of the establishment. Mr. Betts then retired to Gray's Inn, London, where he had the care of the clergy library, and died March 28th, 1770.

Shortly after the death of the last Lord Aston, his residence called Standon Lordship, in the county of Herts, was rented for the purpose of re-establishing Twyford School. The Rev. Richard Kendal, a native of Fulwood, near Preston, who defended universally at Douay with Gilbert Haydock, to the great admiration of all present, was appointed chief master or president of the new school. It was established on the same plan as Twyford, and like it was principally intended for the sons of the Catholic nobility and gentry in their tender age.

Soon after the marriages of the Aston heiresses, Standon Lordship was sold, and in 1767, the school was transferred for a short
period to Hare Street, not far from Braughin in the same county.
Here the accommodation proved extremely inadequate to the
wants of the school, and the Right Rev. Bishop James Talbot
first rented and soon after purchased the ancient manor-house
and farm known as Old Hall Green, about two miles from
Puckeridge. After making many improvements, and adding
considerably to the building, he opened it as a school in Oct.
1769, under the superintendence of the Rev. James Willacy,
who presided over this growing establishment until about the
year 1791.

In Mr. William Mawhood's diary, late in the possession of
his descendant, C. F. Corney, Esq., of London, we find the
following references to Old Hall Green.—"Sat. 9 July, 1769,
called on Bishop Talbot, settled at £22 per annum for my boys,
got his letter to ye master. Monday, 9 Oct., 1769, called on Mr.
Talbot, who says Mr. Willacy will be in town this day, and
return Friday or Saturday next. . . . Monday, 16 Oct., 1769, set
out for Old Hall Green with Mr. Palmer; dined with Mr.
Willacy; left ye two boys; went from thence to Baldock. . . . .
Wed., 8 Nov., 1769, Mr. Willacy of Old Hall Green called; our
boys very well. Thurs., 9 Nov., 1769, Mr. Willacy dined with
us at Finchley; went with him in ye even to shew him the way.
Tues., 5 Dec., 1769, our two boys' went to Mr. Willacy, Old Hall
Green, on Monday, 16 Oct., 1769. Wed., 9 May, 1770, paid Mr.
Willacy in full for my two boys' schooling half a year, due ye
16 April last. Wm. £12 13s. 1½d., Charles, £12 16s. 9½d., total
£25 9s. 11d."

The two bishops Talbot, their brother the Earl of Shrewsbury,
the Earl of Fingal, and the chief of the Catholic nobility and
gentry, who were not at the colleges abroad, received the first
part of their education at Twyford. Now, at Old Hall, we meet
with the names of Arundell, Clifford, Petre, Howard, Bedingfeld,

Jerningham, Stonor, Dormer, Blount, Wright, Barret, and the northern names of Charlton, Salvin, Clifton, Riddell, Haggerston, besides the two Irish families of Butler and Power.  Of its habits and studies we may gather some idea from a copy of the rules of Standon Lordship, which would doubtless be framed on the model of Twyford, where Dr. Talbot had made his own first studies.  It was he who guided the establishment founded by himself and Bishop Challoner at Old Hall Green. Rules 4 and 5 enjoin on all school days a lesson in some catechism suitable to the age and capacity of the students ; as 1st age, *Douay Abstract* with Mr. Gother's *Instructions for Children ;* 2nd, *Fleury's Historical Catechism ;* 3rd, Turberville's *Abridgment of Christian Doctrine*, with the chief master's approbation. Another rule tells us that after the catechism lesson is said, each scholar is to have his task set in English, Latin, or Greek, about which he is to be employed till 12 o'clock.  The masters were evidently not all laymen, for another rule says that as soon as the morning-prayers are ended, one of the priests shall begin mass, so that there were other priests besides the principal. At six o'clock the bell was to be rung for evening prayers, consisting of the Litany of the Saints, the Rosary or Bona Mors, with the night exercise and reflection or meditation for the following day ; " all which are to be read leisurely and distinctly by ye ablest readers among the scholars in their turns."  Here we have an insight into the devotional exercises of the times.

The president, Mr. Willacy, was a native of Catforth, Lancashire, and was probably a relative of the late president of Standon Lordship, Richard Kendal.  Like him he received his preliminary education at Dame Alice's famous school at Fernyhalgh, and was afterwards sent to Douay College, where he took the college oath at the age of nineteen, June 29, 1757.  There he taught poetry and rhetoric, and was esteemed a good classical scholar.  He continued as president of Old Hall Green till about 1791, at any rate his name appears as such in the *Laity's*

*Directory* for that year. He died at Canford House, Sept. 25, 1805, aged 67.

The next president was the Rev. John Potier, another Douay priest, born in the diocese of London, Sept. 22, 1758. It is said that he came to Old Hall, probably as assistant-master, about 1785. The school continued to flourish, without any material alteration in the mode of instruction, or in the management of the temporal concerns of the house, until the year 1793.

In the previous year the Bishops of the London and Northern districts, Dr. Douglass and Dr. William Gibson, were looking around for a suitable house to receive the refugees from Douay College in case of necessity. After the seizure of the college, it was decided that Bishopric (Durham) was the most preferable situation, but owing to various disappointments in obtaining suitable premises, Bishop Douglass, with the consent of Dr. Gibson, directed the refugees to repair to Old Hall Green as a temporary shelter. It was not then intended to interfere with Mr. Potier's lay-school.

We will now let Mr. Haydock describe the school as he found it, and the accommodation provided for the Douay collegians. It is an extract from a letter to Dr. Gillow, dated Penrith, Oct. 10, 1849. After describing a playful escapade of the divines, he adds: "This simple college trick had very important consequences. It displeased, as it well might, the Rev. Mr. Potier, solicitous for his school, and the Bishop at London; both exceedingly good to us all. Only once we had to complain a supper of some meat stinking, and we went to bed. We had to much indulgence and liberty. I was quite content; some, however, concocted a letter and Mr. Penswick came and persuaded me to sign it. I think it would have been better if we had all from Douay been together, whether in ye north, as we supposed Bishop Gibson wished, or at Old Hall Green, where there was land ready, given I believe by Bishop Talbot. Since we left there were too few for the church, and gents' and shop-keepers' sons proved rebellious often. Probably now they may do better at both colleges. Old Hall Green was a House which would accommodate about 40 boys, and perhaps 15 of us, sleeping in a dormitory at first, and afterwards in a detached house, used before as ye school infirmary, perhaps 100 yards from ye great Hall, and nearly as far from a wooden building intended for us till such times as a college could be made ready in ye splendid gardens, where, not long after, one was erected. I was told ye other night by Sir Edw. Doughty (who gave me 10s. for our church) that Mr. Wilds was professor. He or Mr. Bowland, or Dr. Lingard, might probably inform you of more, if you cannot receive instructions on ye subject from your intelligent uncle at North Shields (the Rev. Thomas Gillow) who I understand was born in 1770, and was once appointed a bishop. Mr. Cock, of Cheesburn Grange, is 4 months older than I am, and was at Douai, once leading me to scale a wall for apples; and Mr. Th. Wilkinson, my master in rhetorie, may remember as much."

In another communication to Dr. Gillow, who asked him if he left Old Hall in consequence of a memorial, or round robin, sent by the northern students to Bishop Gibson, Mr. Haydock replied, "I left in consequence of ye letter signed by Thomas Gillow, Charles Saul, Richard Thompson, Thomas Penswick, and George Haydock. 1 then seldom signed Leo, a name taken at confirmation, 22nd September, 1784, as born 11th April, 1774. I do not remember ye date of this famous letter, which Thomas Penswick, engaged me to sign, and which I have since regretted, as Bishop Douglas earnestly wished to have all united, and said Bishop W. Gibson had agreed. When, therefore, Thomas Gillow, Thomas Penswick, and I, went to London, hearing about September that we were to remove to ye north, his lordship called upon Mr. Gillow and me, and persuaded us to return. Mr. Penswick had gone with my great coat home, and lost it at ye inn in Manchester, and about Dec. went to Crook Hall. When at last about that time ye students from ye north removed thither, I stayed at Tagg House, reading ye vulgate, etc., till

things were more settled. On ye 13 Jan., 1796, ye late Bishop
Robert Gradwell, my pupil at Douai, accompianed Thomas
Haydock and myself in a post chaise through Brough and Tudhoe to Crook Hall, where we found a few, 17th Jan., and I gave
£20 to Mr. Eyre, who said he had not received so much before,
at which I rather wondered. Edward Monk was not ordered by
ye Bishop to go to Old Hall Green ; he came to borrow money
of Mr. Penswick's father, who refused, but he followed us soon,
and got to be sub-deacon at Crook Hall. He found himself
comfortable, and would not sign ye letter. Neither did Thomas
Pitchford of Norwich. He was not from ye north, and of course
had not to remove, and was not in divinity. Being at ye fireside
with us, Mr. Saul jokingly talked about cats, that one could pull a
man through a pond. Thomas would bet none could do so with
him, so there was a trial, and with a little foul play ye cat was
victor. This rough college trick made Mr. Potier fear his little
school would be hurt, and he complained to ye bishop, who,
next time he came, did not visit ye divines as usual. He said,
' I am affronted. It was beneath ye dignity of ye lowest Lancashire man.' Unlucky expression, as we were five from that
county, who along with Charles Saul from Yorkshire removed
as some were hurt also at their beds being taken for ye school
children and worse given, as I remember was done thrice to
Mr. Penswick and myself. We were also placed in a house which
had been used for an infirmary, and for those in ye itch, etc.,
etc." In his letter of Oct. 10, 1849. he describes the trick above
alluded to—"A cat with a rope fastened round ye middle of
Thomas Pitchford, who had Clarkson for a friend, giving him a
pinch of snuff on one side of ye shallow pond, while ye rest were
holding ye cat on a blanket, and I was ye whipper-in on ye other
side, actually, with some of their help, drew him through, while
he cried out 'I was not ready,' and for some time did not seem to
find out ye trick. Poor Thomas often took long walks to Bishop
Stotford and Hartford with me, and we got some chocolate, etc."
In the same letter he continues, "I could not tell you in my last

at what time precisely ye letter to Bishop Gibson was written, nor to whom he sent his orders. I think they were communicated by Rev. John Lingard to Mr. Saul, who probably received a letter before from Rev. John Bell (still alive but off ye mission) about September, intimating that we were soon to be removed, so Mr. Penswick immediately, with your uncle and myself, set off as I told you. The former got home ; we returned for other six weeks, till ye bishops could come to some determination, and then, in ye beginning of Nov. I think, having been 11 months in Hartfordshire, I returned home till Jan. 1796."

In Mr. Haydock's first letter from Old Hall, he refers to the Rev. Wm. Hen. Coombes, afterwards D.D., being placed over the Douay refugees. He was professor of rhetoric at Douay, and when the collegians were being conveyed in waggons to be imprisoned in the citadel of Doulens, he succeeded in effecting his escape, Oct. 16, 1793. He was one of the ten refugees whom Dr. Douglass conducted to Old Hall on the feast of St. Edmund, Archbishop of Canterbury, Nov. 16, and it was this circumstance, connected with the peculiar character of the saint as a model of a virtuous scholar and zealous ecclesiastic, which afterwards in-duced the bishops to adopt St. Edmund as the patron of the establishment when it was erected into a college. Writing to Dr. Gillow, Mr. Haydock says, "I am sorry to hear Dr. Coombes is almost blind, and forced to retire to Downside. Even while our professor of divinity he seemed shortsighted, but contrived to call up Peach and me almost every day to answer, while he passed by Monk, etc., at which I rather wondered. He told me I should be a doctor, and they hoped soon to obtain leave ' to grant degrees.' However, unless they be quick they will be too late for me!"

Thus Mr. Potier and his staff and Mr. Coombes and his students worked on until the members of the two colleges of Douay and St. Omer were released from their confinement at Doulens. In the meantime, says a MS. account, "as Old Hall Green was prepared merely for a temporary shelter, it was not thought expedient to lay out in providing additional accommodation a greater expenditure than the apostolical spirit of the times deemed necessary. As a testimony of the self-sacrificing zeal of these great men it is only just to record what they deemed sufficient to satisfy their necessities. A single room, and that of no great dimensions, besides a portion of the attic, was the only part of the house that could be spared for their use. The former served for their refectory, class-room, and for the hours of relaxation ; the latter provided a few with cells for the hours of private study and repose. To accommodate the remainder a wooden barn, almost attached to the Hall, was partitioned off into cells, which the young men in their humour designated their coffins. To this asylum flocked such of the late students of Douay college as had been fortunate enough to effect their escape before their friends were incarcerated in the strong citadel of Doulens, and whose spirits were yet sufficiently steadfast to allow them to persevere in the purpose for which they had endured so much. Here they assembled to the number of twenty."

The landing of the two imprisoned communities of Douay and St. Omer, March 2, 1795, sent some more of the Douay students to Old Hall Green. At this time there remained of the Douay refugees, sheltered by Mr. Potier at Old Hall under Mr. Coombes, John Lee, William Beecham, John Law, Fris. Rowland, Edward Peach, John Devereux, John Clarkson, and Thomas Pitchford, nearly all of whom were studying theology. Dr. Gregory Stapleton, the late president of St. Omer, together with one of his professors and about twelve students, and also James Delaney, Richard Broderick, and Lewis Havard, students from Douay, repaired to Old Hall. The establishment was now removed from the charge of Mr. Potier, and placed under the government of the late president of St. Omer's college. Mr. Potier removed to Puckeridge, about two miles distant, where he opened a preparatory school as before. In 1812, he transferred his school to Shefford, in Bedfordshire, where he continued it till his death, Mar. 31, 1823.

M

"It was still," continues the M S., "the intention of Bishop Douglass and the southern clergy to unite with Bishop Gibson in establishing a large college in the north as the filiation of or substitute to Douay college. For this purpose, according to the Rev. Thomas Eyre's narrative, ' on the 20th March, Sir John Lawson, in company with the Rev. Gregory Stapleton (appointed head at Old Hall Green) and the Rev. Thomas Smith, lately liberated from prison, took a view of Thorp-Arch, near Wetherby, Yorkshire. This house, built as an inn for that watering-place, was considered by them well calculated to receive all the students heretofore at Douay.' It is consistent with this to suppose that Dr. Stapleton purposed to carry on Old Hall Green as the filiation of the college at St. Omer, of which he had been the president, and from which the considerable majority of his present subjects had been derived. This supposition is confirmed by Mr. Daniel's assuming and then formally resigning to Mr. Eyre the presidentship of Crook Hall, by which he continued the line of the presidents of Douay in that establishment. Again, ' Apr. 28, Messrs. Daniel, Poynter, and Wilds arrived at York. They and Bishop Gibson went to reconnoitre that residence (Thorp-Arch) of which they had already received such favourable reports as if it had been erected for the particular purpose of a college. All seemed disposed to accede to the idea of purchasing it, if two or three preliminary articles be agreed to, which it seems will be easily settled with the explanations given by them.' However, subsequently, more difficulty was found in determining the preliminary articles, as well as the amount of purchase money, than was at first expected. Accordingly the design of establishing two colleges began to be entertained. The understanding upon which this was carried into effect is indicated by the following transaction.

" We are informed by Dr. Lingard that on the 29th of June, the feast of St. Peter and Paul, Mr. Daniel, the late president of Douay, who had been liberated from prison, came to Crook Hall. He was in law proprietor of all the monies in England belonging to Douay college. He came with Dr. Gibson ; on the following day, Mr. Eyre resigned, Mr. Daniel was installed president, and Mr. Eyre vice-president. By this means the line of Douay presidents was continued in the college at Crook Hall which was exclusively founded by the late members of Douay college.

" Before the end of the octave, Dr. Stapleton, then appointed over Old Hall, arrived. After long conferences, Mr. Daniel resigned the presidentship to Mr. Eyre, and went away with Dr. Stapleton. According to the testimony of the Rev. Thomas Gillow, of North Shields, he was induced to resign the presidentship of Crook in the hope that in the event of the return of better times he might claim by the title of President of Douay College any compensation that the French Government might make for the seizure of that property. He accordingly retained that title till his death with a view to availing himself of any favourable opportunity. As soon as he was able to return to France, he took up his residence in the house of the late English college at Paris, where he resided till his death, Oct. 3, 1823. He yearly paid to Mr. Eyre all the dividends belonging to the Northern District, the capitals of which were in his hands.

" The negotiations for the purchase of Thorp-Arch had now been discontinued, and a determination come to of establishing an ecclesiastical college in the south of England. This was finally carried into effect on the 15th of Aug. 1795, when Dr. Stapleton was formally installed by Dr. Douglass president of Old Hall Green college, and on that day the work of the college began. Four days later the foundation stone was laid of the present new college at Old Hall Green.

> " A bishop by the altar stood,
>   A noble lord of Douglas blood."
>             *Scott, Marmion, Canto VI.*

" As Dr. Stapleton had been educated at Douay and removed to St. Omer, he modified, in drawing up the rules for his new college, the constitutions of both of those colleges according as he judged most adapted to his altered circumstances. He held the presidentship till his nomination to the Midland Vicariate under the title of Bishop of Hiero-Cæsaria. He was consecrated on March 8, 1801. He was succeeded in the presidentship of Old Hall Green College by Dr. Poynter, the vice-president, who governed till his nomination to the London Vicariate as Bishop of Usula, in 1803.

" The assignment of so early a date, Aug. 15th, 1795, for the organization of the college at Old Hall Green may seem irreconcilable with the advertisement that appeared in the Laity's Directory for 1796. That advertisement was as follows, ' Old Hall Green Academy, near Puckeridge, Hertfordshire, 26 miles from London, in a pleasant and healthy situation, is now under the special intendance of the president of the late English college at St. Omer, assisted by professors of every science capable of adorning the scholar, the gentleman, or the man of business.' It is true that in the above notice the education of ecclesiastics seems not to have been contemplated, but it must be remembered that the directory was, in those times, made up for the following year early in the month of June, at which time it was in contemplation to purchase Thorp-Arch for an ecclesiastical college for the whole of England, and to continue Old Hall Green as a lay academy. In the directory of 1797, the advertisement of Old Hall appeared according to its new organization as a college.

" In this manner were established the two first secular colleges in England, the one exclusively by the president and members of the college at Douay, the other by the president of St. Omer's College together with a number of the Douay refugees. Thus was transferred to the retreat at Crook in the day of her own distress that great college, which for so many years had preserved the remnants of the faith amidst the general persecution, and adorned the church with so many martyrs ; while the college at St. Omer was perpetuated in the asylum at Old Hall Green."

## St. Monica's Priory, Loubain.

" Convent sisters then departed
Forth to mingle with the crowd ;
Forc'd by tyrants, iron-hearted,
From their holy solitude."

*Sidney Johnson.*

This convent of canonesses of St. Augustine was begun on the 10th of Feb., 1609, by Mrs. Mary Wiseman and several other English ladies, who had been professed in the priory of St. Ursula in the same town. With the approbation of the arch-bishop of the diocese, they purchased a building, and converted it into a monastery in honour of the Immaculate Conception of our Blessed Lady and of St. Michael, under the title of St. Monica's. They received young ladies for education, which was the chief means of their subsistence. Their chaplains were singularly learned and pious men, of whom Gilbert Haydock was not the least distinguished. Thus they continued till the disastrous period of the French Revolution, when the Low Countries were invaded, in the year 1794. With this brief introduction, mainly taken from the Hon. Edw. Petre's notice, we will now give Sister Stanislaus Haydock's account of the flight of the nuns to London.

*Sept.* 8, 1794. "My dearest Sister—I am ashamed of myself for my past negligence in not writing to you or dear mother before this. It has not, I do assure you, proceeded from want of affection, for that would be an unpardonable piece of ingratitude, which I hope never to be guilty of. You desired to know the particulars of our journey; to comply with your request I will inform you as well as I can. We left dear Louvain that lamentable day, ye 28th of June. We were forced to quit our beloved convent, 47 (sic) in number ; 21 nuns, 4 priests, 12 lay-sisters, 4 pensioners, 3 servants, and a young lady.   We had 4 wagons to be crushed into, so you may imagine we were finely crowded. We came through Holland, and continued in our wagons till we arrived at Breda, where we stayed one night and were very civilly treated.   From thence we went in a barge to Rotterdam. I think our misery in the barge exceeded that of the wagons. At Rotterdam we stayed a week, very uncomfortable indeed ; thence we took shipping, which was going from one misery to another still greater.   We were not far advanced when, in a dangerous spot, the captain got in two Dutch pilots who ran us aground, where we were obliged to remain near a day and a night with the ship very much sunk on one side, so that we could not stand without holding by something to support ourselves.  We had contrary winds almost all the way, which prolonged us near eight days on sea ; the miseries and distresses which we suffered there from sickness, &c., were greater than I can describe.   We landed at Gravesend, where we rested ourselves one night, being, as you may imagine, most heartily tired.   The day after we set off again by water for Hammersmith, where we arrived all safe, but wearied out of our lives.   We are here very different indeed to what we were at Louvain.   We are obliged to be three or four in a room, very much pinched for place, and many other inconveniences.   However, we must resign ourselves to the will of God ; I doubt not but He will support us under the pressure of our afflictions.   It is the greatest cross He could have sent us excepting being under the French.   My dear, I am infinitely obliged to you for your kind favour.   I am afraid it will distress you ; it was, indeed, particularly acceptable to me in our present circumstances, for which I return you my most grateful thanks.   Mrs. Pendrill, Mrs. Dillon, Mrs. Woods, and Mrs. Taylor desire their compliments to you and would be very glad to see you.   But what, my dear, do you think would be my joy if such a thing was to happen.   According to inclination nothing would give me so great pleasure as once more to see you and dear mother, my uncles and aunts, friends and acquaintances. But that's out of the question, therefore, I must make a sacrifice of that satisfaction. You will be very much surprised to receive this letter from the hand of my dearly beloved George. We have great reason to be content with him; indeed, I must say he has behaved most affectionately to me . . . . At Hammersmith we wear our habit and keep our order as well as circumstances will permit, tho' not quite as we have been accustomed to at dear Louvain. We don't rise at midnight, but at 5 o'clock in the morning, which I find much harder as you know I always loved my bed and do so still. Poor Sister Miller takes the death of her father very edifyingly; it was a great affliction to her. Adieu to my nun, Miss Walton; my love to her if she lives anywhere near you. I took your offer of anything I want very kind . . . . I thought, perhaps, you might have some thoughts of coming to see me, and tho', I do assure you, it would be a true and sincere pleasure to me, yet I do not wish it at present, because I could have very little enjoyment of you; it is not now with us as it was at Louvain. There we could entertain our friends comfortably with lodging and board, but not so now. . . . I remain, my dear sister, your loving and beloved—Stanislaus Haydocke."

Across this letter George Haydock wrote the following short note to his sister;—" Coghlan, London, Sep. 12, 1794. Dear Sister Eliza,—your surprise will, no doubt, be very great to find this letter come to you by ye post after what I told you a few day ago concerning my purposed journey to Lancashire. But, alas! that pleasure was unfortunately snatched from me just as I was on ye point of setting off, for his lordship, Bishop Douglass, calling upon me, gave me notice of his determined purpose to keep us still at Old Hall Green, notwithstanding ye four several letters from ye north which alarmed us during ye space of two days with ye news of a speedy removal. He advised me, if I

pleased, to return. In compliance with his desires I dismissed
ye thoughts of paying you a visit and went to forbid my passage
in ye coach, but it was too late, so that I was forced entirely to
lose a guinea which I had given, and so content myself to repair
again to ye barn of Old Hall, which is to be our future lodging.
You may think I am not well pleased, but yet 'tis better than if
I had come down in vain. Excuse my liberty of writing in my
sister's letter.—Compliments, &c., G. Haydock."

## The Convent at Hammersmith.

"Such soothing influence reigned around,
    I felt as if on holy ground."

*Edw. Wilcock, Occasional Verses.*

The house in which the Augustinian nuns found a refuge was
known as the ladies' school, established in the days of Bishop
Challoner, and under his immediate patronage. For many
years it was attended by the bishop's chaplain, the Rev. Joseph
Bolton, a native of the neighbourhood of Preston, who, after Dr.
Challoner's death, was appointed vicar-general to his successor,
Bishop Talbot. Mr. Bolton was a great friend to the establishment, and was the author of a small pamphlet addressed to Mrs.
Bayley, the superioress of the school, entitled "A Sentimental
Letter from a Gentleman to a Lady." Mr. Bolton died Dec.
16, 1783. Brook Green House, Hammersmith, was advertised
in the Laity's Directory in Mrs. Bayley's name, from 1791 to
1818. Eliza Haydock was at school here in the years 1783 and
1784. The Augustinians remained at Hammersmith till the

year 1800, when they removed to Amesbury, in Wiltshire, to a house built upon part of the site of the ancient Benedictine convent, but in the following year they settled at Spetisbury House, near Blandford, in Dorsetshire.

## Spetisbury House.

" These Sisters, like our priesthood, with a firm enlightened zeal,
Devote their generous minds to God and human weal."
*Edw. Wilcock, Occasional Verses.*

Sister Stanislaus Haydock has furnished us with a very rough sketch of the convent as it appeared in the early part of the century. For some time the Catholics in the neighbouring town of Blandford attended the little chapel attached to the convent. Afterwards a small chapel was fitted up in Blandford by Mr. Towsey, which was served for nine years by Dr. Pierre Moulins, and on his retirement, in 1814, by the Rev. Joseph Lee. On Sep. 8, 1830, the nuns opened a new chapel, designed by Mr. Peniston, in connection with their convent. Reference to this is made in a letter to her brother George by Sister Stanislaus Haydock

*Dec. 27, 1828.* "Rev. mother's respects, and desires me to tell you that she does not wish to distress you by contributing anything towards our chapel, as she knows priests have many calls for their money. . . . We have had a sad advent. A good lay-sister has received the last sacraments, but, thank God, is at present better. . . . She is one that is very useful. We are a very distressed community, plenty in number, but not many to do much for one reason or another. . . . Adieu, my dear brother. I hope we shall meet in a happy eternity, if not in this world. I should be sorry to put you to the expense of the journey to Spetisbury. Mrs. Preston, our superioress, sends her respects."

Written across this letter is one from Sister Catharine Berington. "Allow me to thank you (which I do most sincerely) for your good will to assist us towards our chapel, and, in the present case, I must request you will let the will stand for the deed, as I know a good missionary has many calls for his money. I never wished your good little sister to mention our building to you, but she could not be satisfied without doing so. Allow me, dear Rev. sir, also to observe that the community has never been wanting in our gratitude to any member of your respectable family for past donations. The names of your two uncles and dear mother and sister, with their several benefactions, are on record. Yours also will, in due time, be added to them, without your contributing anything to our chapel. So your little sister need not be uneasy on that head."

In another letter, dated Spetisbury House, Jan. 24, 1831, Sister Stanislaus says to her brother, "I have selected the enclosed little emblem from amongst my treasures, which I feel much pleasure in begging your acceptance of, only requesting you will put it in your breviary, that it may occasionally remind you to pray for your affectionately attached sister." This was the picture of St. Monica which she had brought with her from Louvain. "I was much pleased to tell our dear Sister Mary Joseph Cowban that you had been drinking tea with her brother (Mr. James Cowban of Westby, who died May 29, 1838, aged 62). She is, I assure you, a most valuable and worthy member, much liked by us all; the cloth is indeed good, and if you have any in your congregation like her, we shall make them truly welcome. Should you see the Rev. Mr. Berry, of Cottam, you can tell him that Mary Crook appears to be going on very well and happy, with my best respects. Mr. (Rev. Joseph) Lee requests his kind regards; also Rev. mother and community unite in respectful compliments. I thought your seal very *a propos*, and liked it much." She then refers to the illness of Sister M. Frances and Sister Monica, and concludes her letter with the following postscript: "I cannot omit just telling you that we have had some little share of alarm from the mob having been very near us, when they did a great deal of mischief. But all seems quiet now, and we only suffered from fright. I trust it is useless to beg you to say mass for me on the 2nd, our holy profession day. Adieu, Adieu."

For some time Sister Stanny, as she was generally called, had complained of her eyesight, which was now very bad. On Apr. 2, 1839, she commissioned Sister Mary Paul to write to her brother: "We have had a most splendid Holy Week; all the ceremonies in grand style, such as she has not seen since she left Louvain. Poor Mr. Lee, tho' much better than he was, cannot perform any of his duties—nay, can scarcely help himself at all (he died at the convent, Jan. 20, 1840, aged 75). Dr. Gentili has been with us since the beginning of advent. He is a very clever, pious, and zealous man—quite a saint—and I am sure it will be our own faults should we not become saints too. During our retreat, he preached to us every day." Appended to this letter are a few lines from Sister Stanislaus—"I have thanked Sister Mary Paul for her charity in writing this letter for me. . . . We had most grand doings this Easter. Dr. Gentili, all solemnity, and most respectful in the church; he is a good preacher, in fine, he is everything that is good and holy. Pray for us that we may become such. Adieu, my dear brother."

*June* 28, 1840. Sister Stanislaus writes to her brother;— "Now about our dear cousin Sister Philomina Lupton; she died May 23rd the death of the saints, regretted by her whole community. They doubt not but that she is in heaven, dear creature. She sent me two pictures, one of which I send you, begging you to keep it as a relic for her sake ; the other, a beautiful one, the death of St. Stanislaus, which I shall not part with. Her father and sister were at Stape Hill a little while before she departed this life. . . . A letter to-day informs us that Dr. Weedall is gone to Rome to get off ye heavy burthen of a bishop's charge, so your supposed superior may perhaps fail, tho' I don't think he will gain his point. They say he is a very clever man, tho' little, like you, and timid. . . . We have sung a *Te Deum* for thanks for the Providential preservation of the life of our young queen. Adieu, my dear George."

*Feb.* 2, 1841. Sister M. Paul writes to Mr. Haydock for Sister Stanny, who scribbles a few lines on the letter, though nearly blind. "This 2nd of Feb., you know *sans doute* is her profession day, and she was looking wofully about to find a charitable sister to write to you, when I, not having a better present to offer, offered her my pen for the occasion, and the more willingly as I find you have not forgotten M. Paul. I hope you have proved to their cash that (W)right's bank was the wrong one. We (tho' happily, thank God, not very considerable sufferers) have been inconvenienced by the failure, and ready money this Xmas has been a very pleasant sight (in allusion to Mr. Haydock s remittance, and the failure of the Catholic bankers). . . . She thinks you will not be able to collect enough to build a new chapel (at Penrith), so thinks you must make the old one do a while longer. But I shrewdly suspect that as you are on such intimate terms with the *great*, you will besiege their hearts and pockets to the benefit of your poor flock. I wish you success. . . . Rev. mother and Mr. Calderbank present their compliments ; they and the community are well. We have a stove now in the chapel, which makes it very comfortable. Mr. Hardman of Birmingham made us a present of it. . . . How do you like your new bishop? Bishop Waring paid us a visit soon after his consecration ; he has a niece who is a nun here."

*Spetisbury, Dec.* 28, 1843. A letter to Thomas Haydock, Liverpool, from Sister Stanislaus, written by a scribe for she cannot write herself on account of her eyes, with four lines endorsed—" In my own hand-writing, but am obliged to trouble others to help me. 2nd Feb. my profession day, the 6th after my jubilee. Pray, for I always do for you."

*July,* 9, 1844. "My dear George, I suppose you have accused me of *neglect*, but don't judge from what seems like it. I wished to entertain you with some account of our good bishop, Dr. Baggs. He is nothing tremendous as to the exterior appearance, but very amiable in his manner of conversing. Rev· mother told him I was the oldest in the house, so he made me sit by him in our recreation room, and said 'you are my grand-daughter.' He is low of stature, not handsome, all the beauty is within. Mr. Calderbank is gone to Bath with him to bring some of the bishop's relations to board here. The bishop is only 38 ; he may bury me in time. I find old age comes on apace—often tired with doing nothing. I am glad you have given the Tagg the pleasure of a visit. I suspected you would about the time you did. . . . Have you yet fixed the spot for your intended chapel [at Penrith]? Does Mr. Howard continue his former kindness towards you ? . . . I have said my matins since pente-cost, which is a great comfort to me. I renew *our* engagement frequently. Do you the same, the 17th of this month, the 50th year of our arrival in our native kingdom of old England and our jubilee. Alas ! I am the only nun left professed at dear Louvain. . . Have you heard of the wonderful conversion of Captain Trafford ? I suppose one of ye sons that poor James had to do with of that family. It's better late than never. . . . I do not write to any one but yourself. . . The superior of Stape Hill is dead ; pray for her and me. Adieu, Stanislaus Haydock." [Capt. Trafford was of the Norfolk family].

*Sep.* 12, 1845. M. E. Smith writes to Mr. Haydock :—" Sister Stanny thinks it high time that you should know that she is still in the land of the living, and that she is ' as well as she ever shall be till she dies.' She seems to me quite as well as she was before she was last taken ill, and goes about just as ever. . . . We have been celebrating the jubilee of one of our nuns, Sister Magdalen Howell. She is, I assure you, quite a brisk old lady, younger than Sister Stanny, who remembered her a scholar. . . . Probably you have heard that our bishop had a paralytic attack in the very same chapel at Bristol that our late bishop had the

same unfortunate *memento mori.* Dr. Baggs is, I believe in a
very poor way, but at present somewhat better than he has
been. . . . Sister Stanny sends a large quantity of love to be
disposed of as you think proper, and if you keep it all to yourself, it will be quite right, for ' George cannot do wrong in her
eyes.' "

Sister Stanislaus Haydock outlived her brother, George Leo.
She died at Spetisbury House, April 11, 1854, aged 87, religious
profession, 65, the last survivor of St. Monica's convent
Louvain.

> " Here she lies, whose spotless fame
> Invites a stone to learn her name."
>
> *Francis Beaumont.*

## Crook Hall.

> " Crook Duacensi positum colono
> Sit meæ sedes utinam senectæ,
> Sit modus lasso maris et viarum
> Militiæque."
>
> *Lingard, Imitation of Horace.*

On Jan. 16, 1794, eleven of the Douay students escaped over
the walls of their prison at Doulens. They arrived in London
on the 31st., and saw Dr. Douglass, but as the bishop could offer
them no refuge, they repaired to their homes. Five of them
belonged to the north, and Bishop Gibson very soon after their
arrival directed them to proceed to a lay-school kept by the
Rev. Arthur Storey at Tudhoe, near Durham. Mr. Thomas
Cock arrived there on Mar. 10, and was shortly afterwards joined
by Messrs. John Rickaby, Thos. Dawson, Thos. Lupton, and
Thos. Storey. Three of these had been taught by Dr. Lingard
at Douay College. Accordingly when he heard of their being
assembled at Tudhoe School, he obtained permission from
Lord Stourton (by whom he was engaged as tutor to his
son) to join his former scholars, and he was formally appointed their teacher by Bishop Gibson. We learn from the
Rev. Henry Gillow's historical introduction to " The Chapels

CROOK HALL.

at Ushaw," that meanwhile the bishops were searching for a suitable place to establish a college to receive the Douay refugees, and on the 5th of May, Bishop Gibson, in company with the Rev. Thos. Eyre and Mr. John Silvertop, went over from Minsteracres to Lartington Hall to consult with Sir John Lawson and Mr. Maire as to what should be done. It was decided at that meeting to apply to George Baker, Esq., of Elemore, near Durham, for a lease of Crook Hall. Nevertheless, on the 26th May, Bishop Gibson went to York again to consult Sir John Lawson about the erection of a new college as a substitute for *alma mater* which he was fully determined to provide. Thus a great part of the summer of 1794 was spent in correspondence, in consultations, and in riding about to various places in the counties of Durham, Northumberland, and Yorkshire, in search of a suitable house and locality. The neighbourhood of Gainford was explored, the old mansion house of Newton Cap near Auckland was visited ; another at St. Helen's, Auckland, a third at Bishop Middleham, and a fourth at Hilton, near Sunderland. Crathorne, near Yarm, and Croft-upon-Tees, besides other places, were also visited, but objections of one kind or another were made to each of these places. The month of September was once more at hand, and still no place was selected for the students to be sheltered. His lordship was therefore again strongly advised to accept of Crook Hall, and he at length decided on that neglected mansion. Much was wanting to make the house fit for the reception of the students, and as the school, at Tudhoe was too small and inconvenient even for a temporary abode, the students under Dr. Lingard were ordered on the 9th of September to remove to Pontop Hall, near Lanchester, two miles from Crook Hall, the mission-house of the Rev. Thomas Eyre. There they assembled as a humble beginning of the new college, and on the 22nd were joined by Mr. John Bradley. The community, consisting entirely of Douay professors and students, was composed of the Rev. Thomas Eyre, in the office of president, Mr. John Lingard, not yet in orders, vice-president, Mr. John Rickaby, in Douay class of moral philosophy, Mr. Thomas Lupton, in rhetoric, and Messrs. Thomas Dawson, Thomas Storey, John Bradley, and Thomas Cock, in poetry. In the meantime Crook Hall was being prepared for their reception, and on the 15th of October they took possession of it. The Rev. John Bell was sent for from Minsteracres to become prefect of discipline. Since his escape from Douay, in April, 1793, he had been tutor to the sons of Mr. John Silvertop. He arrived at Crook on the 7th November, and was followed three days later by his pupil Henry Silvertop, who had left Douay on the 5th May, 1792, and ultimately assumed the name of Witham when he succeeded to the Lartington estates. Dr. Gibson also wrote to Old Hall Green for the removal to Crook Hall of those Douay students who belonged to the Northern District. These were Charles Saul, Edw. Monk, Rich. Thompson, Thos. Gillow, Thos. Penswick, and George Leo Haydock. With the exception of the last, who arrived at a later period, these gentlemen reached Crook Hall before the end of the year 1794. Thus by Oct. 19 were collected together 14 of the Douay students to continue the work of the parent college, of providing for the succession of the English priesthood. Their president, the Rev. Thomas Eyre, was well acquainted with the system of teaching and of discipline at Douay, having filled there in succession the offices of professor of syntax and poetry, and general prefect, previous to his twenty years of missionary work in the north. Hence he organized the new community in strict accordance with the rules and constitutions of the mother house at Douay. It was the ambition and endeavour of the bishop and the entire community to reproduce exactly in the new college their lost *alma mater*, and so well was their succession to Douay understood and recognized, that in the first announcement of Crook Hall as a college in the Laity's directory, it was only necessary, in speaking of the pension of the students, to write, " Terms—*as before.*"

Ordinations were held at the college in Dec., 1794, by Bishop Gibson, at which the following were ordained ;—John Bell and Robert Blacoe, priests ; John Lingard and James Worswick, deacons ; and Thomas Penswick, Richard Thompson, Thomas Gillow, Charles Saul, and Edward Monk, sub-deacons.

There were still at Old Hall eight students belonging to the Northern District, when their twenty-six companions arrived from their prison at Doulens, on Mar. 2, 1795. Of the liberated students, James Swinburne, John Penswick, Thomas Berry, Matthew Forster, and Robert Gradwell, repaired to Crook Hall, and these, together with Thomas and George Leo Haydock, raised the total number of Douay students who went to Crook to twenty-two. It has been already shown, under the account of Old Hall, that the two bishops even yet had not abandoned their desire to found a general college in the north for both districts. It was only after the inspection of Thorp-Arch on the 28th of April, 1795, and the subsequent difficulties about the purchase money that it was determined to go on with the two existing establishments—Crook Hall as the direct continuation of Douay, and Old Hall Green as the college for the Southern District.

Mr. Haydock shall now narrate his first experiences at Crook Hall.

"Crook Hall, near Gateshead, Bishopric, Monday 18 Jan., 1796. Dearest Mother and Sister—Thinking myself bound in duty as well as love to give you the first account of our journey

N

and safe arrival at Crook Hall, I allow myself no great respite till I have fulfilled this primary obligation, as you may easily judge from ye date of this letter.   On ye 17th of January Crook opened its welcome doors to us, and we were brought in amidst the hearty congratulations of our friends and ancient school-fellows.  We had, indeed, to wait about three quarters of an hour before we could get admittance, because they were all at evening prayers, or what we commonly call vespers ; for you must know that necessity had driven us into Sunday before we could well make an end of our travels.   And now to satisfy your curiosity I shall inform you how we passed our time from Wednesday, the 13th, when we took our departure from Tagg town, till ye present time, when I have just spent one day in ye old Douay customs, for Crook aims to come as near them as circumstances will allow.

"Lancaster greeted our eyes about four in ye afternoon, and made us heartily welcome till half past twelve ye following day, at Mr. Caton's as you may easily suppose.   They paid us every kind attention that could be desired, and were very importunate for us to stay ye following night, but we thought ye stay we made sufficient.   We called upon Dr. Rigby [the priest at Lancaster], and went to see ye castle and all ye beautiful places in the town.   At parting Miss Mary filled our pockets with home-made ginger-bread, which was very good and serviceable during ye remainder of ye journey.   We then passed on very comfortably thro' Hornby, and giving a look over that castle went forward by Kirby-Lonsdale to Setberg, where we supped and took a bed.   At seven ye next morning we began a journey rather less expensive, for we had only to give a shilling per mile after we left Setberg.   The country all ye way is very romantic, wild and stoney, fit only for grazing ; nor did we see a corn field for above thirty miles together, nor one mill from Lancaster to Durham.   We soon left Kirby-Stephen behind us, and, breakfasting at Brough, rode with great expedition thro' Bowes, and

over Stain Moor to Barnard Castle, a pretty, fine town, and remarkable for ye ruins of the castle, which we scampered up a
very steep hill to see. There we were obliged to stop about two
hours for a chaise coming from Greta-Bridge, which arrived at
last with one of Lord Darlington's servants to drive it. We
immediately posted forward by West Auckland and St. Helen-
Auckland, where after we had gone past I recollected ye nuns
from Lierre [Teresians], and one of our old masters, Mr. Roby,
dwelt, and my brother was so desirous to see them, that he rode
back three miles that night with ye return chaise, and walked to
Bishop Auckland the next morning, where Gradwell [Robert,
afterwards bishop] and I staid all night. On his coming up we
had ye curiosity to go and see one of ye bishop of Durham's
palaces, and indeed did not repent of it, for it is by far the most
magnificently ornamented that ever I saw. We then breakfasted,
and in a short time arrived at Tudhoe, where Mr. Storey and
Blacow keep a school. We staid dinner with them, and had ye
pleasure of Mr. Storey's company in ye chaise with us to Durham, where ye grand cathedral and abbey almost necessarily
drew our attention. It was now late in ye evening on Saturday,
and ye roads being described excessively bad we thought it
better to hear Mr. Storey's mass ye next day, and so proceed to
Crook Hall. Upon trial the roads fully answered, or rather much
surpassed, ye description we had received of them, but as good
fortune would have it, our driver had never been that way, so
that, tho' it exposed us to the trouble of enquiring ye way out,
yet it got us a conveyance, which, otherwise, we should perhaps
have found some difficulty to have done. At last after much
merriment, and some danger of our necks, we got into Paradise-
Lane, a name given it on account of its inconceivable badness,
for it is worse even than Hyles-Lane [in which the chapel of
Cottam is situated]. There ye horses were not able in one place
to draw us forward, so we got out and scampered over whins
and dirt for a little way, till we got in again and rode in state up
to Crook Hall, about a quarter after three o'clock.

"After the usual salutations of our friends, we paid a visit to Mr. Eyre, ye president, who behaved very courteously and desired us to get dinner. So we did, and then began to pursue ye duties of ye house. I shall tell you what they are. At six o'clock in ye morning we get up, and at ye half-hour we go and meditate till seven ; then Mass ; afterwards study till ye quarter to nine. At half-past nine, we go to school for an hour and a half; at one, dine ; at three, go to study ; at seven, prayer till supper ; at quarter-past nine, second prayers ; and thence immediately we may repose our weary or lazy limbs on a pretty hard matrass, and sleep if we can. Our living is very good, as much as I can tell you of it from report and ye little experience I have already had of it ; our drink is very much like your small drink, but not sour, so we can do very well with it. We have two play-days a week, and are in number twenty-eight students and masters.

"And now I shall tell you how much we each expended on ye journey, for it was much less than I expected at setting out. It was just about £3 3s., or 6d. per mile for 121 miles, ye exact length of our journey. Nothing material was damaged on the way ; only some drawing-paper which I had in ye great box was rather injured by ye rain, but that was very trifling, for I had fortunately left ye greatest part of it at ye Tagg in my drawer. I need not desire you to air it from time to time ; you will do it, I doubt not. We are much better provided for here than at Old Hall. The exterior of the house might be made very elegant, and ye rooms are far from being bad. I have three partners with me in a room, and so has my brother in another. I shall send you ye picture of ye house some other time, but for ye present I am not able, as I think you would choose rather that I should quickly answer your demand of a letter. I shall also write to James and Peggy as soon as possible. Uncles, aunts, and all other friends about Tagg will, I hope, be satisfied with this, for I must tell you frankly that I do not intend to write many letters without great necessity. You will perhaps be so kind as to inform Mrs. Slater, Tempest, &c., of our safe arrival, if it be convenient, and present our kindest and most sincere compliments to them and all other friends. You know I have a particular esteem for Mrs. Woodcock and family, so they must not be omitted. Give our duty and thanks to Mr. Lund for his kind favours, and tell him that to understand our regulations I must refer him to those of Douay, where he will find them pretty exactly drawn out. You know what to say to our dear uncles and aunts without my telling you ; in short, I leave all other compliments to your direction.

" I have just been with Mr. Eyre delivering our commission, and I thence took occasion to tell him the condition upon which I understood we came hither, viz., that upon ye delivery of that sum of money, all other necessaries were to be furnished us by the superiors, which he acknowledged was ye statement Mr. Wilson had given him of ye question, so I hope we shall have little to trouble you for during our stay here. But God knows how long it will be, for it is not doubted but ere long we shall have a removal [in allusion to the intention of establishing a general college for the whole country at Thorp Arch, or else-where in the north].

" You will, if you please, give my uncle the money you receive for me at Candlemas, which will reduce it to £12, and the rest as soon as you get it (unless needed other ways). You may also make use of ye cloth I left behind whenever you think proper. I must now beg leave to conclude with ye sincerest testimonies of love, remaining, along with my brother, dear mother and sister, yours—G. L. HAYDOCK."

The next letter is from Thomas Haydock to his brother James at the Tagg, endorsed : " In case of absence, to be sent to him at Trafford House, near Manchester. To be delivered to him with all possible haste." Poor Tom did not accompany his brother George to Old Hall, but went to the English College at

Lisbon, and now was making a third attempt to become a priest
at Crook Hall. Referring to this subject in later years, his
brother George, writing to Dr. Gillow, says that he was advised
to retire from the college. "Some one had written that he was
funny, and Mr. Eyre asked me if I thought he would do for a
priest? I replied : ' It was not for me to say ; he had done nothing at least to disqualify him there, and ye bishop, Dr. Gibson,
had authorised us to come, and thus he would have lost his time
and money.' ' Oh,' said Mr. Eyre, ' when I go into ye grounds,
I always see a crowd about Thomas laughing, and such generally
end in ye asylum !' So after defending ye thesis, my brother
went and taught school at Manchester, and then engaged in
printing Catholic books, generally to his loss, and has cost me
about £3000. My brother James was much displeased, and Mr.
Rayment [Rev. B., an excellent judge] thought Thomas would
have been ye best of us three."

"Crook Hall, June 1, 1796.

"    . . . . You say my vocation appeared to me true and
solid. I assure you it did, otherwise I hope I have more grace
than to enter upon ye ministry. It is dreadful at ye best, and
doubly so to those who enter upon it dubiously inclined. A
priest must necessarily lay aside all ye gay pleasures of life,
therefore I don't think I meant to have entered ye ministry *on
that account;* nor for ease, because I think I could have more in
some easy business; nor for honour, because little is ye honour
of a priest regardless of his duty.; nor for a livelihood, because I
am pretty certain I could get a better by other means. It rests
therefore that my intention at best was good, for I should detest
myself were I to harbour any other sentiments in entering ye
ministry but those of the honour of God, ye service of my neigh-
bour, &c. It remains for me, therefore, to say that if there is
any fault, it must be in imagining myself to have sufficient piety,
strength, and resolution to fulfil my intentions. This I always
meant to leave to the determination of friends, judges, and even

enemies, but I hoped they would have been more candid than to have attacked me *incognito*, so as to leave me no opportunity of offering what I had to say. I pronounce it once more, 'tis some priest who has always worn ye appearance of friendship who has given me ye stab. He has given it in the dark, like a black-hearted traitor, for if it proceeded from conscience, why afraid to be known? Did he fear my resentment? He who ought to die rather than betray his conscience, did he fear ye persecution of ye persecuted? But if his intentions were to render me miserable, I thank God it is out of his power. Priest or no priest, I am perfectly content. If priest, I trust in God for protection and strength in prosecuting all duties; if rejected, ye world is open, and ye world belongs to God.

" I've got a good deal to say to Mr. Wilson, but as I'm going to write to him, I will save you ye trouble of telling him things which I mean to inform him of in my letter to him. He will, I make no doubt, inform me of all that is said against me, and I hope I can give a good answer to all. Good God ! what scene of trouble and misfortune have I stored up for myself since leaving Douay. I can't look back, but giddiness seizes my head, and I'm lost in labyrinths of surprise and amazement. I was inexperienced, but every day serves to learn me ye great end, indeed ye only lesson that concerns men, viz., that all on this side of ye grave is vanity and shadow, and all beyond is substance.

" With regard to news about us and Old Hall, we know next to none. You will no doubt have heard that Bishop Berington intends joining Oscott School with Old Hall. Crook is up to the ears in debt, and Mr. Eyre has informed ye bishop in sundry letters that he would undoubtedly break up immediately after ye defensions in case supplies did not come. The debt amounts to upwards of 400 pounds, but Mr. Gibson at last has answered that he is coming to Crook shortly with plenty of money to defray our debts. Mr. Eyre, however, has desired him to defer his

visit till ye defensions, when it is conjectured he will give orders.
Our family consists of 29, inclusive of three maid-servants.
George is very well, studies hard, and promises to defend
well. I hope, if at Crook then, to give satisfaction also with
regard to my studies, though I think I could have done it much
better if this affair had not come upon my hands to disturb me.
The treatises to be defended are *De Gratia* and *Actibus humanis.*
George and I have nearly written these 2 vols. I mean to
write ye whole course if I remain here. You know my temper ;
you will hear what is said, and I desire you to give me your advice sincerely as you think. If you think it better for me to
leave, I look upon ye disgrace as trifling, yea, none at all—I
should still enjoy your friendship and George's, and if successful
should have provided a pretty retreat for you, George, and myself, to spend ye evening of this life, and fit us for another. If
you think I shall suit for ye mission, if no obstacle prevent me,
I will go on in God's name and lay all other thoughts aside.
Reflect well on this for I shall undoubtedly follow your advice
to whither way it inclines. Use dispatch that I may be at
case. Since I sent ye letter to you I have gained a good knowledge of arithmetic, but this will not be useless whatsoever
happens. Mr. Yates and Mr. Worswick, as likewise all your
friends at Crook, desire their compliments. Mr. Worswick desires you to come and stay with him some time at Newcastle
If you could I'm sure you'ld be welcome and might have an
opportunity of seeing all old acquaintance. Mr. Smith is absent
for a few days, but I will tell him your order when he returns.
You will give George's and my compliments to whom you think
proper. I cannot finish the letter to Mr. Wilson this post, for it
is going off now, but I will send it ye next.—Yours, &c.,

"THOMAS HAYDOCK."

Shortly after this Thomas Haydock withdrew from the
college, and opened a school at 42 Alport Street, Manchester.
He issued a neatly printed card, with an appropriate engraving,

announcing that "he intends teaching the following branches of useful and ornamental knowledge, Greek, Latin, French, Portuguese, Spanish, Italian, &c." In 1799 he threw himself heart and soul into the business of printing and publishing Catholic books at a cheaper rate than could then be obtained. In a letter to his brother George, dated 16 Tib Lane, Manchester, June 27, 1799, he gives á list of works printed and in prospect, which is really surprising in extent. There is no doubt that Thomas Haydock did very much to raise the position of Catholic literature in this country. Several of his publications were of his own translation, and others were edited by him. It was in this letter that he announced the completion of the engraving of Douay College, drawn by himself, "and though it does not answer my expectations (this apart), yet I think it is worth 6s., the price of the subscription, particularly when it is considered that, exclusive of the merit of the engraving, it is the representation of a place which is cherished by everyone who has been there." In the following September he tells his brother that he still goes on with his school as usual, which brings him in at that period after the rate of 132 guineas a year.

## Haydock's Douay Bible and Testament.

"You shall draw waters with joy from the Saviour's fountains."—Is. xii. 3.

IN the year 1806, Thomas Haydock conceived the idea of publishing a new and correct edition of the Douay Bible and Testament, supplied with a large body of notes selected from various commentators, with historical desertations prefixed to each book, and concise lives of the evangelists, tables, index, &c. The Rev. Benedict Rayment of Lartington, near Barnard Castle, proffered to assist him in the undertaking, but afterwards withdrew from the task. He therefore persuaded his own brother, George Leo, then at Ugthorpe, to write and select the notes. In his letter to him of Nov. 5, 1806, he says that his original intention was to commence in the spring, "but having altered the time for the appearance of the first number to the beginning of Aug., 1807, I hope you will have sufficient time both to digest the plan and furnish useful notes." He then gives his ideas as to how the work should be carried out. In this letter he also says, "I had nearly forgotten to tell you that I am preparing for the engraver . . . The Tree of Life. . . I mentioned this to my brother (James) lately, and he told me for the first time that you had something of a similar nature in your pericranium, and I have now your letter before me. I will send you Ward's old Tree, same, I believe, as Mr. Lund's, for inspection, alteration, and ad-integration, *i.e.*, to bring it up to the present time." This George afterwards completed, and it was published by Thomas in one large sheet in 1809. Pius VII. honoured the work by his acceptance of a copy, which still hangs on the walls of the Vatican.

In the meantime Thomas Haydock went over to Dublin to collect some large and long outstanding debts; married an Irish lady, Miss Mary Lynde; and opened an establishment in that city. In a letter to Dr. Gillow, his brother George says he was easy-going and got himself into great difficulties in consequence; "we had also at Douai and Old Hall Green a sly fellow, T. Cook, who had been a Methodist, and leaving afterwards, got to be employed by my brother Thomas, and ran away with above £20, as most of his canvassers, or caterpillars, did." When Thomas Haydock returned to Manchester in 1810, he was surprised to find that another Catholic printer, Mr. Oswald Syers, taking advantage of his absence, had made preparations for printing a new edition of the Bible and Testament. This work was actually commenced in March, 1811, in small folio, and was finished in 1813, having received the support of a number of priests who supposed that Haydock had given up all thoughts of publishing his Bible. On Jan. 22, 1811, Thomas Haydock issued a circular to the clergy explaining the reason for the delay in the appearance of the Bible, complaining of the advantage taken by Syers, and appealing to them for their support. The first sheet of the great work in folio was put to press on July 11, in that year, and for some time it appeared in fortnightly parts, at 1s. each, but afterwards the numbers were issued weekly. The first impression was 1500 copies, but as subscribers soon multiplied, it was deemed advisable to print a second edition, which was executed at Haydock's establishment in Dublin in 1812, etc. The press-work occupied three years and two months, the last sheet being worked off on Sep. 11., 1814, although the title-pages bear earlier dates. This undertaking turned out very unremunerative to the enterprising publisher, and brought about his ruin. He gave a bond as security for the payment of an advance for the purpose of printing the Bible to a certain John Heys, of Manchester, whose terms were hard, and himself very awkward. Poor Haydock was obliged to issue a circular, in 1814, warning the public against certain numbers issued from his nominal office in Manchester, "which during his absence in Ireland have been printed with an inaccuracy and a suppression of many essential notes that have justly caused the disgust and indignation of his brother, the Rev. G. L. Haydock, who has engaged to compile the same." Heys was declared a bankrupt, and Haydock's bond was entered up and his property sold by auction in 1818. On the 31st. of Oct., in that year, poor Tom wrote from Dublin to his brother George in very low spirits, informing him that—"three hours hence will find me a prisoner for debt; alas! not contracted by myself, but for which I must suffer the consequences of an imprisonment to continue at least 3 months and 21 days. Wogan, dead near two years ago, supposed to be worth £80,000, died insolvent. Fitzpatrick (dead only last Friday) supposed to be also immensely rich, has only left about 6s. 8d. in the pound in effects to answer numerous demands. These were the two most eminent in the Catholic [publishing] line. How must I then have been able to succeed where these two Goliaths of the trade have failed?" Subsequently he found that his manager and clerk in Dublin had wronged him during his absence in England to the extent of £3000 and upwards. After his release from the debtor's prison, he commenced again in Dublin, where he printed many valuable works. On Oct. 19, 1823, he had the misfortune to lose his wife. Writing to his brother on the 28th Oct., he says, "all the calamities of my hitherto chequered life are mere playthings in comparison with this last sad visitation. But God's will be done."

> " The flower is shed, and the spring is fled,
> And he wanders alone at the close of the day ;
> And the sleety hail, in the moonshine pale,
> Glistens at eve, on his locks of gray."
>
> *Rising of the North.*

At length he was obliged to abandon his publishing business, and settled in Liverpool about 1833. It was there he lost his only child, George, who was born at Dublin, Feb. 6, 1822, and died Jan. 29, 1840. Subsequently he retired to Preston, where he spent the remainder of his days. There the old man died Aug. 25, 1859, at the patriarchal age of eighty-seven, and was interred in the family grave at Newhouse Chapel.

> " There—broken heart—farewell !
> The pang is o'er—
> The parting pang is o'er ;
> Thou now wilt bleed no more,
> Poor broken heart, farewell ! "
>
> *Thomas Moore.*

## 𝔗𝔯𝔞𝔣𝔣𝔬𝔯𝔡 𝔥𝔬𝔲𝔰𝔢.

" Lo I where the glist'ning stores disclosed to-day,
By chemic art, assume more potent sway ;
Now in extended sheets secure the pile,
Now lend the faded face delusion's smile :
Now vaunting, mimic the carnation's bloom,
The canvass swell, or gaily robe the room."

*Maude.*

WHEN the Rev. James Haydock came on the mission from
Douay, in 1792, he was placed at Trafford House, as chaplain to
John Trafford, Esq. The chapel attached to the mansion was
not very large, but sufficient to accommodate any number of
the congregation likely to assemble in it at one time, for Mr.
Haydock's mission stretched over Barton, Eccles, Pendleton,
Pendlebury, Patricroft, Stretford, Sale-Moor, and Altrincham.
Though so extensive, this district is supposed only to have con-
tained some 300 Catholics.

In a letter dated July 21, 1801, addressed to his brother
George at Crook Hall, he says that he has had the pleasure of
seeing Mr. Lingard and Mr. Thompson, but could not prevail
upon them to pay him a visit at Trafford. He adds "Amongst
many other inquiries there were some which regarded my dear
George. The accounts were all in your favour. I was informed
that you enjoyed a good state of health, were very attentive to
ye duties of your station, and an assiduous compiler as well
as composer. The information I received respecting your
learned labours somewhat astonished me. I had no idea that
a Haydock was ever born to shine in ye literary department ;
experience has convinced me that I never was, and from myself
I have been led into an unfavourable conclusion respecting one
so nearly related to me. Though I may be allowed to regret
that I was either never made for learning, or that learning was
not made for me, yet I cannot but confess that I derive some

satisfaction from ye idea that my brother has been more fortunate." James Haydock was full of humility, and always underrated his abilities. Dr. Kirk assures us that he was not only a laborious and zealous missioner, but a learned man. This long letter of advice to his brother as to the course he should pursue to attain real learning, certainly displays a practised mind, and coincides with Dr. Kirk's description. He had been for some years prefect of the study-place at Douay, and taught catechism, in which branch of his duty he excelled. There are several other letters from him, which bear out the same character, but they are not to the present purpose.

After being at Trafford House for about fourteen years, he removed to Lea Chapel, near Preston, in 1807. It is said that he was so annoyed by the Trafford Volunteers assembling and parading around the house that he got the Bishop to remove him. He exchanged missions with the Rev. James Smith, whose brother William had married one of the daughters and coheiresses of Mr. Haydock's cousin, Robert Haydock of Leach Hall. Mr. Smith retired from the chaplaincy after some little time, in ill-health, and was succeeded by the Rev. Thomas Sadler. It was during his chaplaincy that the foundation-stone of a school in connection with the Mission was laid in 1822 by the late Sir Humphrey de Trafford, then a mere boy, and near this site, where once stood a blacksmith's shop, a Catholic cemetery was opened shortly afterwards. In 1827 the old Chapel at Trafford was pulled down, and re-erected near Dumpling-lane, Barton, at the back of which was the presbytery. Mr. Sadler died October 4, 1830, and was buried in the cemetery at Barton. He was succeeded by the Rev. Hen. Newsham, who spent the first three years of his priesthood here. Then followed the Rev. Messrs. Ball, Westhead, Hill, and lastly, about 1846, the present respected pastor, the Right Rev. Mgr. John Canon Kershaw. In 1856 the old school was replaced by another at Trafford, given by Sir Humphrey de Trafford, and in 1868 the present fine

church was erected by the same gentleman at a cost of something like £24,000.


## Lea Chapel.

" I have no hopes but one,
  Which is of heavenly raigne ;
  Effects atteynd, or not desird,
  All lower hopes refrayne."

*R. Southwell, S.J.*

Previous to the erection of this Chapel, in Lea Town, the
Mission was seated at Salwick Hall, but Mass was also said at
Ward's House, near the Hall, formerly the seat of a younger
branch of the Cliftons and afterwards of the Smiths, and at Moor
House, Newton-cum-Scales, the residence of George Gillow, who
had inherited it from the ancient Catholic family of Brewer.
When the Cliftons closed the Chapel at Salwick Hall, then
tenanted by the Gradwells, John Gradwell of Clifton, George
Gillow of Moor House, and James Smith of Ward's House,
purchased land in Lea, on which they erected the present
Chapel and presbytery. The Rev. Robert Wilson died at Salwick Hall, January 14, 1798, and his brother the Rev. Marmaduke
Wilson came from Appleton to wind up the Mission. He delivered the altar plate and vestments into the charge of Mr.
John Gradwell for the new Mission at Lea. Mr. Clifton claimed
them and contested the matter in the ecclesiastical courts at
Chester, but was defeated by Mr. Gradwell, who, it is said
maintained the suit at his own cost. The new Chapel was
purposely placed just outside Mr. Clifton's influence. It was
opened in 1800, and the Rev. James Smith, third son of James
Smith of Ward's House (where Mass was said in the meantime),
superintended the erection and was appointed pastor of the Chapel.
He was born December 25, 1775, and was educated with his

brother, the Rev. Thomas Smith of Croxdale, Durham, at the
English College at Valladolid.   As we have seen he exchanged
missions with the Rev. James Haydock, in 1807, and died in
retirement at Manchester, January 26, 1827.

On April 13, 1809, Mr. Haydock wrote to his brother George
at Ugthorpe, near Whitby ; "I sit down to my paper in order to
repay you ye tribute of gratitude and respect so long and so
justly your due . . . . At last I have deferred till a time in
which I do not find myself in good order for writing, being
rather unwell, and having, I think, a bad cold hanging over me.
But write I must, and my good George must pardon me for any
faults which may occur in ye letter."   He then refers to George's
purchase of land and preparations for building a Chapel at
Ugthorpe, of which he had received plans.   According to request
he passes his opinion upon the drawings.   "It is, I believe, upon
a plan which has spoilt most of ye new chapels which have of
late been erected, particularly those in Yorkshire.   In all plans
intended either for a speaker or an audience, height is essential
for ye ease of each.   Breadth always gives beauty, and brings
you nearer each other.   I have not spoken to one priest who
does not wish his chapel at least to be something higher.
Height is wanting at Cottam.   Mr. Carter would have had ye neatest
and most elegant chapel (at Newhouse) I ever saw, barring that
at Trafford, had it only been higher.   The fault in mine is being
too small.   Mr. Irving has begun a new chapel and house (at The
Willows, Kirkham), which in my opinion will be complete."
He then offers his advice at great length and in detail, and goes
on—"In aid of so noble an undertaking you might have expected something handsome from us.   But my being in a
similar situation to yours in point of expenses to be laid out on
improvements and building, we could not well do more.   I shall
have a gallery to build, and everything that belongs to an altar,
with ye altar itself, are all to be furnished.   Add to this a house
to furnish, and furniture to buy."

This was his last letter; he was seized by the epidemic which afflicted his flock, and on April 25, 1809, he died in the prime of life, aged 43, truly, as George Leo Haydock calls him a martyr of charity.

> " Joy, joy for ever ! my task is done—
> The gates are pass'd, and Heaven is won."
> *Thomas Moore.*

Two days later his brother Thomas wrote to George Leo at Ugthorpe, " Little did I think when I despatched my last letter and gave you hopes of our dear brother's recovery to have to write to you again announcing his death. This fatal event took place on Tuesday about noon. I received a letter by the coach-man late last night, and a duplicate this morning by the post but without any particulars. The letters were from John Marsh, and my dear brother will be buried to-day (at Newhouse). I will not dwell on our irreparable loss to one who knows so well how to feel its weight. To myself, indeed, I may term it truly irreparable, for surely no brother ever did more for another, both by words and deeds, than he has done to me. This consideration ought to calm our extreme grief, that as he always led a good and truly pious life, we may reasonably hope he has concluded the same by a happy death. The impression made on me I am unable to express, but I either don't know myself, or his good-ness and bright example will ever dwell before my eyes and have their due influence over my every future action. Farewell my dearest and now only brother, I shall visit my mother's in a few days, and will there write you every particular."

o

## Formby.

"Its altar fallen, in ruins lie
    Its walls grown to decay ;
    Its very burial mounds are gone,
    Its monuments away !"
                —*Gilfillan.*

IT seems that there was a prospect of George Leo Haydock being appointed to Formby, some time before he left Crook Hall in 1803. A letter to him from his relative, the Rev. Thomas Caton, then chaplain at Townely Hall, gives some curious information about the Formby mission, to which we have added a few notes. It is merely dated, " Burnly Wood, May 30," and he does not give the date of his being at Formby, but as he was at Culcheth from June 11, 1791, to June 29, 1792, it was probably between that time and his going to Townely. He went to Cottam, July 24, 1812, and died there August 14, 1826.

" I was in hopes ere this you had got possession of Hornby, as the bishop would not give it to either of the Worswicks, and the reason was that being so near their relations, they would either be constantly at Lancaster, or the relations would be at Hornby. Both father and mother asked the bishop when dining with them for the place for one of the sons, but he was resolute. As to Formby, it would do very well if you wish to farm and to be among a set of humble, well-meaning people. The congregation at Easter is about 250 ; great numbers of children, but not employed in any manufactory, so that any day or hour they come for instructions. I had 80 at Catechism every Sunday, and about 15 of the oldest every Wednesday and Friday evening at my house for instructions. The people are a blunt, honest people, and as old Bordley [Rev. Simon George, the eccentric missioner and schoolmaster at Aughton] calls them, 'a loving people'; but you must lord it over them, or at least keep a high hand, and not be too easy with them, or they will be masters of you. They are a people, if they see you wish their good, you may mould as you please. I was happy in the extreme, had the congregation been about 100 fewer. There are no rich people, and none very poor like what we find in the weaving countries. The house and ground is rented of a Protestant clergyman, and the ground will clear the house rent. He lives at Formby, is a most agreeable young man, and will do anything for you that you could wish [Rev. Richard Formby, LL.B.,of Formby, whose father was apparently the first Protestant of the family]. Neighbours are Mr. Buller, at Ince, three miles off [Fr. John Buller, S.J., died at Ince in December, 1811], Mr. Taylor, Crosby, four miles off [Dom Charles Boniface Taylor, O.S.B., died at Crosby in April, 1812], Mr. Gregson, at Sephton, about five miles off [Dom Rich. Vincent Gregson, O.S.B., died at Sefton in Sept., 1800], Mr. Johnson, at Lydiate, three miles [Fr. Robert Johnson, S.J., left Lydiate in 1821], Mr. Crook, a very sensible and agreeable young man at Ormskirk, seven miles [Dom Rich. Joseph Crook, O.S.B., died at Ormskirk in January, 1800], and about two miles further on the Preston road, Mr. Kellet, out of your neighbourhood [Rev. Hen. Kellet of Burscough Hall, died there Aug. 14, 1808, whose relative, Rev. Richard Kellet, was the son of Robert Kellet, of Woodplumpton, and Elizabeth, his wife, daughter of Robert Haydock of Leach Hall].

"The income as well as I recollect :—

| | | | |
|---|---|---|---|
| Benches . . . . . . . | £24 | 0 | 0 |
| Interest of money left by a Mr. Blundell | 5 | 0 | 0 |
| The Grange money . . . . | 5 | 0 | 0 |
| The old chapel rent . . . . | 3 | 3 | 0 |

3 F

Interest of Mr. Bastwell's money  .  .  £5  0  0

[The Bastwells were an old Catholic family of Augh
ton, one of whom, John, was outlawed for recusancy in 1680.  Mr. James Bastwell, of Ormskirk, gent., and Mary, his wife, were benefactors to the chapel of St. Anne, Ormskirk,
and their anniversaries are noted on May 3
and Feb. 9.  James Bastwell gave £1050 for
ecclesiastical education in the Northern District, £772 7s. 6d. of which now forms a fund
at Ushaw College, of which the priest at Aughton, the Rev. James Dennet, claimed the nomination.]

Money paid by the Jesuits yearly  .  .  2  11  6
*Eleemosyna missorum* that you may depend on  8  8  0
                                            ——————
                                            £59  7  6

"The rent of your house and ground is £24, or as I had it, £8
for the house alone without any land, but if you have the
ground it will, I think, bring you in free.  The bench money is
paid very regular, quarterly, all the other yearly, sent without
any trouble.  The old chapel has undergone some repairs lately,
so that I believe it will take the interest money a year or two to
pay the expense.  Your congregation will lie very compactly
about you; there is no need at all of a horse, unless for your
own private satisfaction, a mile and a half being the farthest
you have any off.  The house is, or at least was, entirely furnished, so that I had not a farthing to lay out when I went,
which is a great object for a beginner.  Should you go I shall
certainly pay you a visit, though you won't me.  Would I live
in a gentleman's house but he should allow me a horse!  Let
me know if you go.  I remain, sir, yours sincerely, T. CATON."

Alt Grange, commonly called The Grange, in Little Altcar,
adjacent to Formby, was formerly the granary belonging to
Whalley Abbey, when the manor was held by the monks.  It

lies among the sand-hills upon the shore, and was originally a place of some importance, as it always contained a chapel.

In 1716, Thomas Smith, high-constable of West Derby, reported to the Commissioners for forfeited estates that at "Grange, near Formby, [is] one Mr. Wolfall, who is reputed to exercise his functions as a popish priest at a place called New-hall, in West Derby. At Formby there is a certain building erected in the reign of James II. intended for a popish chapel, and now a dwelling-house, but the rent is received by a popish priest commonly reported : yearly value £1 10s."

The Rev. Thomas Wolfall, younger brother of Richard Wolfall, of Wolfall Hall and Moor Hall, Esq. (the last of his family), was ordained priest at the English College, Rome, in 1699, and used the *alias* of Butler on the mission. He served The Grange, and died there in 1720. His predecessor in the mission was the Rev. Edward Molyneux, of the family of Molyneux of The Grange, probably immediately descended from that of New Hall. Between 1626 and 1633, the names of John Molyneux, of The Grange, gent., and Margaret his wife, regularly appear in the recusant rolls. In 1667 Mrs. Molyneux was a widow, and with her son Edward and his wife Katherine paid the usual penalties for their religion. Mr. Nich. Blundell, of Crosby, tells us that the Rev. Edward Molyneux was born at Alt Grange, was ordained priest at Douay, and for 38 years was a most laborious missioner in Formby, Crosby, and the locality, having under his charge at the time of his death more than 800 penitents, besides children. He resided with his brother Richard at The Grange, a property held by his family for many generations under long leases from their kinsmen the Viscounts Molyneux of Sefton. He was found dead on the sands, Apr. 2, 1704, his death having been occasioned, according to tradition, by a highwayman. On the following night, about ten o'clock, he was buried in the old Catholic cemetery at Harkirk. Shortly after the death of Mr. Molyneux, Thomas

Tickle by his spiritual will, dated Aug. 26, 1704, left £30, part of a charitable bequest of £100, to the mission at The Grange, then served by Mr. Wolfall. After his death, in 1720, no priest is mentioned as resident at The Grange. It was probably served for a time from New Hall, for Richard Molyneux, by spiritual will dated Feb. 15, 1734, bequeathed £100, or £5 per annum, to the secular priest officiating at The Grange or New Hall.

Though part of Formby came within the Grange mission, the Jesuits possessed the ancient chapel referred to in Mr. Caton's letter. In 1701, Fr. Richard Foster, S.J., was the missioner, but he resided at New House, in the Car-houses in Ince Blundell, which the Society erected in that year with the intention of keeping a boarding-school, though this design was never carried out. Fr. Foster died at New House, May 9, 1707, aged 35, and was buried at Harkirk. His receipts for serving Formby amounted to £16, being £6 allowed by the Society, and £10 contributed by the congregation. Fr. Christopher Burton afterwards attended to the mission, and after him Fr. William Clifton. Thus the mission continued to be served from New House until 1740. Mass was also said in the chapel at Formby Hall, till the Formby family apostatized, or was robbed of its faith, about this time. It is not improbable that the hall chapel was occasionally served by the secular clergy, for the Formbys were educated at Douay College. Anyhow, in 1740, the Rev. John Debord *alias* Davison, a Douay priest, was serving the secular mission in Formby from Moor Hall, then the seat of the Stanleys, who had succeeded the Wolfalls. In that year it was arranged that the Father at New House who served the Jesuit chapel in Formby should permanently reside there, and in December of the same year Mr. Debord removed to Esh, co. Durham, though his successor at Moor Hall, the Rev. Thos. Wareing, also served in Ince and Formby till about April, 1744. New House was finally given up after the death of Fr.

William Clifton, S.J., in 1749, aged 71, who had served Formby for thirty years. He was succeeded by Fr. Francis Blundell, S.J., who found the income at Formby to be £20. He remained at the mission till his death in 1779, aged 62. He was the son of Richard Blundell, of Carside, in Ince Blundell, and his wife Elizabeth, daughter of Richard Tickle, of Ince Blundell and Altcar.

The Blundells of Carside were a junior branch of the Blundells of Ince Blundell Hall. Through their settlement in Preston, in the latter half of last century, they have been confounded with the ancient family of Blundell resident in that town for centuries. Their names, however, appear in the recusant rolls throughout the whole period of persecution. Richard Blundell, of Ince Blundell, yeoman, and his wife Cicely, were fined in 1633 and subsequent years, as likewise Henry Blundell, of the same, and Margaret his wife. Laurence Blundell and Ellen his wife occur in the roll for 1667, and Laurence again appears in that for 1679. Richard Blundell, of Carside, registered his estate as a Catholic non-juror in 1717; his will is dated 1730. He had sons, Laurence, Richard, and Francis the Jesuit. Richard settled as a corn-merchant in Preston, and died in 1772. He was succeeded in his business by his son John, who handed it over to the Gradwells in 1802, went to Ireland, erected flax mills at Navan, and died in 1810. His daughters, Elizabeth and Mary, were the mothers respectively of the Very Rev. John Canon Worthy, V.F., of Euxton, and the Right Rev. Bernard O'Reilly, Bishop of Liverpool.

Fr. Blundell was succeeded at Formby by his nephew, the Rev. Francis Blundell, son of Richard, of Carside, and his wife Helen, daughter of John Chadwick, of Birkacre, Chorley, gent, and sister of the Rev. John Chadwick, V.G., of Weld Bank. Mr. Blundell was a secular priest ordained at Douay, and as the Society had been suppressed in 1773, the ex-Jesuits handed Formby over to the sole charge of the secular clergy. The congregation about this time was returned by Vicar General Chadwick at 350 communicants, probably an error for 250. Mr. Blundell found no fund for the maintenance of a priest except £2 11s 7d, the interest of £86, paid by the ex-Jesuits, and the money left by his uncle. The latter consisted of two amounts ; of the first, £250, one hundred subsequently, in 1801, was expended in discharge of a debt incurred in fitting up the new chapel, as alluded to by Mr. Caton, and the second consisted of the reversion of £100 bequeathed to Fr. Blundell's housekeeper. Mr. Blundell removed to Stonyhurst after some years, and died in 1792. Mr. Miller succeeded him at Formby, and was there on Oct. 10, 1784, when Bishop M. Gibson confirmed 73 persons, the congregation being estimated at 250. He apparently was succeeded by the Rev. Thomas Caton. How long he remained is not stated. A new chapel was erected and opened in 1798, on the site of the ancient chapel mentioned in Mr. Caton's letter, which had belonged to the incumbent of Formby from time immemorial. The next priest found at the mission was the Rev. Joseph Maini, who came in 1806 from Leyburn. In 1818, the number of his congregation was put down at 650. He left in 1834 for Yealand, and was succeeded by the Rev. John Smith, who retired in ill-health in 1852, and died May 24, 1853. The Rev. Thomas Crcwe took charge in 1852, and died at Formby Aug. 21, 1862, being succeeded by the present missionary-rector, the Very Rev. James Canon Carr, V.G., President of St. Edward's College, who now has the assistance of his nephew the Rev Wilfrid Carr. In 1864, a fine church was erected on a new site.

## Ugthorpe and Whitby.

"For there is joy both true and fast,
 And no cause to lament,
 But here is toil both first and last,
 And cause oft to repent."

*Fr. Nicholas Postgate's Hymn.*

In 1796 George Leo Haydock received minor orders at Crook Hall at the hands of Bishop William Gibson. In the following year he was admitted to the diaconate, and, after defending his *theologia universa* with great applause, was ordained priest on Sept. 22, 1798. For close upon five years he was retained in the college as a professor, and during that time, Dr. Kirk informs us, was an incessant reader of the fathers, divines, and biblical annotators. On Feb. 5, 1803, he took possession of the mission at Ugthorpe, near Whitby, a poor mission in Yorkshire, where his salary at first was but £27 a-year. It was known by the *sobriquet* of "the Purgatory of the mission."

Here resided the holy martyr Nicholas Postgate, who was put to death for the faith, at York, Aug. 7, 1679.

"Nor spar'd they father Posket's blood,
 A rev'rend priest, devout and good,
 Whose spotless life in length was spun
 To eighty years, and three times one.
 Sweet his behaviour, grave his speech,
 He did by good example teach.
 His love right bent, his will resign'd,
 Serene his look, and calm his mind.
 His sanctity to that degree
 As angels lived, so lived he."

*Ward, England's Reformation.*

The poet speaks feelingly, for he was intimately acquainted with the good old man. For upwards of fifty years he had assiduously laboured in this his native locality, converting hundreds by word and example, and contentedly living in wretched huts on Egton Moor and at Ugthorpe. He was a man of no mean literary attainments, and possessed a refined taste for poetry. Perhaps it was during that dreadful period when he was hunted about from place to place, through the fanatical persecution which the insidious Earl of Shaftesbury raised by means of the impostor Oates and his *confrères*, that he penned the following two stanzas in his beautiful hymn to Jesus:

> "And thus, dear Lord, I fly about
> In weak and weary case,
> And like ye dove Noë sent out,
> I find no resting-place.
>
> "My wearied wings, sweet Jesus, mark,
> And when thou thinkest best,
> Stretch forth Thy hand out of ye ark,
> And take me to Thy breast."

At length the venerable man was apprehended at the house of one of his parishioners at Little Beck, near Whitby, and was with his harbourer committed to York Gaol. His trial and condemnation for exercising his priestly functions quickly followed, and thus he obtained that rest, that glorious crown of martyrdom, for which he had so ardently prayed.

> "But now my soul doth hate ye things
> In which she took delight,
> And unto Thee, ye King of Kings,
> Would fly with all her might."

The martyr's immediate successor at Egton Bridge and Ugthorpe seems to have been the Rev. John Marsh. He was a priest "of excellent wit, parts, and zeal," says an ancient record, and being banished London by Dangerfield, one of Oates' accomplices, fled to Lancashire, and then "humbly betook himself to the most desolate and laborious place in Yorkshire." His abode was chiefly at Egton Bridge. He was followed by the Rev. George Bostock, *alias* West, who resided in the house of Richard Smith, gent., the representative of an ancient Catholic family seated at Egton Bridge. This worthy priest was here when Bishop Williams made his visitation in May, 1728, when eighty-four persons were confirmed, but died on the following Sept. 17th.

Shortly after, the Rev. John Monnoux Harvey, *alias* Rivett, who had opened a boarding-school in London in 1729, or the following year, transferred his establishment to Ugthorpe. His venture had met with considerable success in the capital, and consequently had attracted the vigilant eyes of sensitive Protestants. In 1733, attention was called to the school and its energetic master in a little pamphlet entitled " The present state of Popery in England." The penal laws were still in force against Catholic schoolmasters. The very idea of anyone daring to provide Catholic education for the sons of Catholic gentlemen was an outrage on society ! Such audacity could not be tolerated ; it was inconsistent with the glorious principles of liberty and the rights of conscience as understood by the upholders of the free and enlightened Church established by law ! Poor Harvey, therefore, had to fly to the most out-of-the-way place he could find. He re-opened his school at Ugthorpe, with what success does not appear, and so continued till after the Stuart rising of 1745. The defeat of Charles Edward was an incitement for another burst of persecution, more vigorous than any that had been witnessed since the discomfiture of the Chevalier de St. George in 1715. Towards the close of 1745, Mr. Rivett, the name by which Mr. Harvey was generally known, was apprehended and brought before three justices of the peace, charged with being a Popish priest and keeping a school for the education of children in the Popish religion. This he acknowledged, and as he refused to take the prescribed oaths, by which he would have abjured his religion, he was committed to York Castle. In the following March he was tried at the Lenten assizes with Sir William Anderson a Valladolid priest, "for that, being Popish priests, and, little regarding the laws and statutes of this realm, and not fear-ing the pains and penalties therein contained after the 25th of March, 1700, to wit, the 8th of Sept., in the nineteenth year of George II. (1745), did say Mass at Craythorne and Ugthorpe, and that office or function of a Popish priest did use and exercise in contempt of the said Lord the King and his laws." After some time Mr. Harvey obtained his release from prison, and seems to have withdrawn at once to London.

In the meanwhile, the Rev. Thomas Shepherd, a newly-ordained priest from Douay, took charge of the mission at Ugthorpe for a short period. In 1747, the Rev. Edward Ball arrived, and possibly he may have re-opened Mr. Harvey's school. He remained there till 1757, and subsequently became a professor at St. Omer's College. It is not certain that there was a resident priest at Ugthorpe between Mr. Ball's departure and 1767. The former pastor, the Rev. Thomas Shepherd, may have attended the mission from Egton Bridge. In the latter year, the Rev. John Bradshaw came from Douay, and in 1768 opened the chapel which was still in use in Mr. Haydock's time. In Oct., 1773, when Bishop Walton made his visitation, Mr. Bradshaw returned his congregation at one hundred and seventy communicants. After a few years he was succeeded by the Rev. Thomas Ferby, who remained till 1777, and was followed by the Rev. John Marsland, who came from Scarborough. Mr. Marsland probably remained till 1787, when the Rev. Henry Dennett took charge of "the Purgatory of the Mission," as he characteristically termed it. After a durance of twelve months the sturdy Lancashire priest was released, and from that year, 1788, Ugthorpe seems to have been served by the Rev. Thomas Talbot from Egton Bridge, till the arrival of the Rev. George Leo Haydock in February, 1803.

Soon after Mr. Haydock's arrival at Ugthorpe, the annual income of the mission was increased by £15; ten pounds bequeathed by Rowland Conyers, Esq., who died Apr. 28, 1803, and the remainder by the Rev. Mr. Tootell, a relative of the Rev.

Hugh Tootell, *alias* Charles Dodd, the church historian. Mr. Tootell, says Mr. Haydock in a letter to Dr. Gillow, called himself a "full-bottomed Lancashireman," a term which will be appreciated by those acquainted with the plain, sterling characters of the old-fashioned priests of that county. His niece, Winifred Tootell, afterwards rented Tagg Cottage on Mr. Haydock's estate at Cottam. He found the old chapel at Ugthorpe, in use since 1768, in a very dilapidated condition. It was situated in the upper part of a thatched cottage, the rooms underneath serving as the priest's house. It was very similar to Thomas Ward's description of Fr. Postgate's residence—

> "A thatched cottage was the cell
> Where this contemplative did dwell,
> Two miles from Mulgrave castle 't stood,
> Shelter'd by snow-drifts, not by wood ;
> Tho' there he liv'd to that great age,
> It was a dismal hermitage.
> But God plac'd there the saint's abode,
> For Blackamoor's greater good."

Mr. Haydock has left several interesting sketches of this old place as he found it in 1803. In the October of that year he replaced the thatch with tile, and otherwise improved the place. It was not long, however, before he began to contemplate the erection of a new chapel. On September 16, 1808, he sent plans of the proposed chapel and house to his brother James at Lea. In this letter he says: "I have been at Loftus every month since May, but only one has offered to become a Catholic! Pray that God may touch their hearts, and enable me to speak in such manner as to be of service to them. The last time I was there I lodged in ye same room with an old man whose wife had just before made an end of her life, first, by cutting her throat, secondly, by hanging herself, and thirdly (ye string breaking), by water, as she fell into a pail of water, and some say was drowned. I had seen her a month before, and had observed to ye old man, he and his wife would live well on some bacon which I saw hanging. He misunderstood me, and thinking I was asking him if he never invited his wife to come to prayers, 'Oh,' said he, 'it is all in vain. I have asked her often.' Poor soul! she was of a most dark countenance, and advanced in years. . . . Your alterations must be very trifling at Lea, so that I hope they will not divert ye channel of your generosity altogether from Ugthorpe. I calculate ye new buildings, &c., will cost between three and four hundred pounds. .   . I enjoy very good health, and am in hopes of being more comfortable a great deal when I get into ye other house, which, I suppose, will be soon after this time next year. Pray for me that I may not be so much attached to Ugthorpe as to forget heaven . . . . Farewell."

In 1810, the new chapel and house were opened, numerous drawings of which, both coloured and plain, were sent by Mr. Haydock to his relations. On August 2 of that year, he writes to his mother : " I was highly pleased at ye receipt of your kind letter to find that you were at last got out of the stocks, and that ye letters of administration [to the estate of his brother James, who died intestate], were at last obtained, though ye expense for them, or for ye mistake of your ignorant parson in writing our name wrong, seems quite exorbitant, and I cannot be persuaded that it is authorised by ye law." This refers to the parson having written the name as it was generally pronounced, *Haddock.* " I do not see how you could have acted better than you have done, but ye lawyer and ye parson (or surrogate, as he is called) might undoubtedly. However, they are bad people to deal with in money matters, and if you think you can get no good by speaking to them, or to another lawyer, you may let them rest in peace for the present, and make restitution if they can when their conscience will prick them to conviction." . . " I went ten days ago to see Mr. Coghlan [Rev. William, second son of James Peter Coghlan, the publisher], who was on ye point of leaving Scarborough, and is now, I suppose, settled at Burscough Bridge [Burscough Hall Chapel, Lancashire]. You will probably see him at ye meeting. Mr. [Rev. John] Woodcock went along with me, and joins me in love and duty to you and his relations. I think I shall be able to spend a few weeks with you soon after Easter next better than now, and then we can settle all. . . I expect ye masons next week to continue with me till they have finished or nearly so at least."

In the meantime, Mr. Haydock's uncle, William Cottam, died February 12, 1804, in his 85th year. He bequeathed £3000 to pious uses, of which the college at Crook Hall received about £2200; the Rev. William Irving, of Mowbreck Hall, some three or four hundred for his new chapel at The Willows, Kirkham; Sister Stanislaus Haydock, O.S.A., £200 for her convent; and the remainder for other religious objects. A part of his estates was left to Miss Haydock and her three brothers. His sister, Miss Elizabeth Cottam, George Leo's godmother, died October 14, 1806, aged 86, and his brother, James Cottam, died January 9, 1811, aged 72, the last of his family. Old William Cottam died of the stone, and just before his death made three wills within ten days, written by the Rev. William Irving, his director. Bishop Gibson wrote to Mr. Haydock that his "two uncles were the greatest benefactors of ye college." The will was so worded, and written under such circumstances, that all the bequests might have been set aside. Indeed, the Rev. Thos. Eyre, the president of Crook Hall, said he would give nothing for it. The Haydocks, however, waived their claim, and said nothing about it. Considering all this, Mr. Haydock, at a later period, not unnaturally felt that he was harshly dealt with by his superior, the Rev. Thomas Sherburne, *vere* Irving (brother to Mr. William Irving), then V.G. in Lancashire to the Vicar Apostolic of the Northern District.

Mr. Haydock continued at Ugthorpe until July, 1816, when he was ordered to reside at Whitby in succession to the Rev. Nicholas Alain Gilbert, a learned and zealous French refugee who had established the mission, and had returned to France Aug 20, 1815. From that date the mission had been served by Mr Haydock from Ugthorpe. For the first year after his arrival in Whitby, he served Scarborough alternately with Mr. Woodcock of Egton Bridge, and afterwards Ugthorpe in like manner for ten years. The chapel at Whitby, situated in Bagdale, was erected by Mr. Gilbert, and opened April 10, 1805. It was then considered a handsome erection, built of stone, furnished with an organ, and capable of holding 300 persons. Mr. Haydock found a debt of £1000 upon it, which he reduced by £340.

After paying a visit to The Tagg, Mr. Haydock writes from Whitby to his mother and sister, Oct. 3, 1818: "Being now at the term of my peregrination, I can sit down with pleasure to inform you of ye particulars. I came just in 'pudding time' to Broughton Hall [co. York, the seat of Stephen Tempest, Esq.], where I spent ye following rainy day and the next night. We played at cards both nights, and I won enough to defray all ye subsequent expenses of my journey. Bravo! Poor Mr. Pugh [the chaplain], who had been represented as so morose, was quite engaging, though losing 15s. one night would have almost tempted any one to put on a sourer countenance. How seldom do we receive a proper account of people's character! We judge from love and hatred. The rev. gentleman seemed to me quite friendly enough with ye family. There were no ladies. I was sorry not to find Catharine at home [she married in 1825 John Nic. Coulthurst, of Gargrave, Esq.]. She would have gone with her sister to New Hall [convent, Chemsford], but ye doctor judged it unsuitable for her arm. Hence all but Monica [Mr. Tempest's youngest daughter] would be at home this Saturday. Next Tuesday will be Catharine's sixteenth birthday. If I had been a week later, I should have fallen into it, and I should have been able to rest at Ugthorpe, as next Sunday I must say prayers there. But perhaps all is as well according to ye present arrangement, as this is a time of indulgence, which I should otherwise have missed. I was much pleased with the grandeur of Broughton Hall, though much inferior to Trafford [Mr. Tempest's fourth son Henry married in 1829 the second daughter of Thomas Joseph Trafford, of Trafford Park, co. Lancaster, Esq.]. I left it on Thursday at ten o'clock, and pro-ceeded on a most dismal and rough road to Ripon, thirty miles, ye same I travelled over in 1811, when my borrowed mare fell about halfway at Fellbrook. I could not exactly point out ye place. No great improvements seem to have taken place there. I have bid an eternal adieu, I think, to that road. On Friday morning I set out at six o'clock, and travelled very pleasantly fifty miles, reaching Ugthorpe about seven. I found all well except John Chapman, who complained of a great pain in his back. I left him in bed on Saturday at ten o'clock, and went to get a person to bleed him, proceeding afterwards to Mr. Woodcock's [at Egton Bridge] to deliver his £25. He was well, and desired his love to his sisters and compliments to you. To-morrow he proposes going to Scarborough to be absent about ten days. After dinner, at two, and drinking a bottle of wine, I set off for Whitby, and was more than usually tired when I arrived about six, as I began my journey too soon after dinner, and had a great-coat. All was in good order at my return. I had a piece of your gingerbread to treat our friends at Ugthorpe and Whitby. They all join in compliments to you, and would have rejoiced if you had accompanied me. I hope you will come when you can make it convenient and find a proper tenant for our immense estates! From ye foregoing narrative you will conclude that I had a very pleasant journey, as usual. I hope you will be favoured in like manner when you take courage to try again. I found a letter from Mr. Gilbert waiting. It con-tained no news, only that he was busy on ye missions and very cheerful, living at ye time at ye bishop's palace at Finisterre. I must now think of my missionary duties, and begging my best

P

respects to all friends as if named  .  .  .  yours for ever, G. L.
HAYDOCK."

A few years later, Mr. Haydock was relieved of the arduous
labour of attending to the missions of Ugthorpe and Scarborough.
In a letter to Dr. Gillow in 1849, he says : " I had the pleasure
of knowing your father, and accompanied your rev. brother,
Richard Gillow, in 1822, to take possession of his new mission as
my worthy successor at Ugthorpe and Scarborough [Dean
Gillow was ordained at Ushaw College on the preceding Dec. 21].
Unhappily his health would not permit him to stop above seven
months, and I was told by Rev. Nic. Rigby that we (Mr. Woodcock and myself) ' did not help him,' though I remember during
ye time that Mr. Woodcock was for four weeks visiting his
friends at Preston, I had to travel over 150 miles visiting ye sick
of Mr. Gillow's flock, and of ye seven who died in seven months
I attended four *gratis*.   We are on very friendly visiting terms
with Mr. Joseph Gillow [the Doctor's brother] and wife, the
daughter of Jane Haydock, my third cousin, when I go over
once a year to see my nieces."   On a letter to Mr. Haydock from
Richard Gillow, dated Ugthorpe, July 4, 1822, in reference to his
mission, Mr. Haydock has endorsed : " R. Gillow attended Jane
Powell, who died of scarlet fever, caught it and dyspepsy, so that
he could revisit Ugthorpe no more, and left Scarborough in Sept.
[1823].   G. L. H. had to travel 150 miles for him and Mr. Woodcock in six weeks *gratis*.   Yet, Nic. Rigby heard we did not
assist R. Gillow enough !  .  .  .   Mr. Gillow got a much better
place at Fernyhalgh, Lancashire, soon after Rev. Robert Blacow's death."   Thus Mr. Haydock resembled Chaucer's match-
less picture of "the pore parsoun of a toune," who, he tells us,
could in little things have suffiance :

> " Wyd was his parisch, and houses fer asundur,
>   But he lefte not for regn ne thondur,
>   In siknesse ne in meschief to visite
>   The ferrest in his parissche, moche and lite."

It was at Ugthorpe that he undertook, at his brother's request, the editorship of the Douay Bible and Rheims Testament, "with useful notes, critical, historical, controversial, and explanatory, selected from the most eminent commentators, and the most able and judicious critics." The Text professedly adhered to was that of Bishop Challoner, with all his notes, either verbatim or at least given in their full sense, accompanied by others, abridged and modernized, from Bristow, Calmet, Du Hamel, Estius, Menochius, Bp. Walmesley, Tirinus, Worthington, Witham, and others. To these the editor added his own original observations. The whole was published in three large folio volumes, enriched with many engravings, the last volume appearing in 1814. The characteristic of this edition is its new and copious annotations. It is generally allowed to be the most useful one issued in the English language, and it has passed through many editions both in this country and America. Archdeacon Cotton informs us that Mr. Haydock also composed a Paraphrase of the Psalms, in the years 1805 and 1806. This he intended to publish as an accompaniment to some "Biblical Dissertations," which it was proposed to print as a supplement to the Bible when finished. The design, however, was not carried into execution, and the MS. fell into the hands of Dr. Cotton after Mr. Haydock's death. It consists of 4 quarto vols., entitled "The Psalms and Canticles in the Roman Office, paraphrased and illustrated, with some choice observations of F. de Carrieres, Calmet, Rondet, &c., by George Leo Haydock." He likewise wrote a "Treatise on the various points of difference between the Roman and Anglo-Catholic Churches," which is still in MS.

His pen was never idle ; almost every volume of his immense library contained annotations in his own handwriting on the fly-leaves and margins. He passed his observations upon almost every subject, and amassed a pile of notes, "which," as he remarked to Dr. Gillow, "if some curious antiquarian fall upon a century hence, may surprise or amuse him, and perhaps posterity, as what you seem to be attempting may do also." The late Mr. Alderman Brown, of Preston, possessed two volumes of his miscellaneous extracts, and original pieces written in Hebrew, Greek, Latin, French, and English. Some of his poetical pieces are said to exhibit no mean power.

Besides his "Tree of Life," previously alluded to, Mr. Haydock published, whilst at Whitby, "A Collection of Catholic Hymns," "A Key to the Roman Catholic Office," "Conflicts of Religion," "A New Collection of Catholic Psalms, &c.," and "Prayers before and after Mass." He also edited the Rev. N. A. Gilbert's "Method of Sanctifying the Sabbath Days at Whitby, Scarborough, &c." He frequently communicated with the public press, and occasionally was engaged in controversy.

On June 23, 1827, the Rev. Nicholas Rigby* succeeded Mr. Woodcock at Egton Bridge, and relieved Mr. Haydock of the mission at Ugthorpe, but declined to acknowledge the debt of about £284. Mr. Haydock naturally objected to this treatment after all he had done for Ugthorpe, the chapel having been chiefly paid for out of his own private purse and the pockets of his relatives. During no part of his missionary career could he have lived upon the income he received from his poor flocks, and maintained his position, had he not possessed an independent fortune of his own. He differed with his superiors as to the justice of making him responsible for the debt, as they claimed the property. Besides this, he also complained of another decision affecting the mission at Ugthorpe. When he left Ugthorpe to reside in Whitby, " ye beginning of sorrows, 1816," Dr. Gillow (senior), the president of Ushaw College, informed him that a letter had been received by John Lawson and Wm.

* A few days after these papers were finished the writer observed the notice of Mr. Rigby's death in the papers. He died at the presbytery, Ugthorpe, Sept. 7, 1886, aged 86. He was born at Walton, near Preston, in 1800, and was educated and ordained priest at Ushaw College. His mother was Mary Cardwell, whose mother, Elizabeth, was daughter of James Sidgreaves, of Inglewhite Lodge, co. Lancaster.

White from Sir Harry Trelawny, requiring, or desiring at least, the £300 which he had given for the girls' poor-school at Whitby in 1811, to be transferred to Ushaw College for their education. " I thought this very strange," says Mr. Haydock, " but having no documents left, supposed ye donation had been conditional, and wrote to Mr. Gilbert [his predecessor in the mission], who said it was absolute, and he had paid for ye writings, and spent £20 on ye land purchased. In ye meantime Dr. Gillow said he would be content with £200, but when I sold ye land for £375 he insisted on £300, at which I expressed my surprise or indignation, and declined sending more unless forced by ye bishop. The president sent back ye letter, and, on receiving Mr. Gilbert's explanation, I and Mr. [Rev. John] Woodcock informed him, and ever since have required the money to be refunded. Sir Harry had fallen back to Protestantism in 1815, but died a Catholic in Italy in 1834, and ye president's successors might surely have gotten ye money from him. I can see no right that ye college has to it." In a later letter to Dr. Gillow (junior), in 1849, Mr. Haydock says, " My desire for Mr. President [Mgr. Chas. Newsham] seeing ye letter was that he might know that my conscience is not still at rest about ye £200 gotten in 1816 by ye college from Whitby girls'-school. I asked simply, as I have done *usque ad nauseam* from ye different bishops and presidents since, ' can an absolute donation be recalled, particularly in such circumstances?' Sir H. Trelawny in 1811 agreed to pay for a piece of land which cost £300, hoping that ye present Whitby Chapel might be turned into a school, or one built upon ye land. His young daughter (a convert at 13, and ye occasion of his becoming a Catholic and throwing up his livings) was teaching at London, and there was some talk of his coming to Whitby. Sir Harry came to see Ugthorpe *old* chapel, if it would do for him as a sort of monastery, and put me to some expense in vain. Hence I supposed that ye donation had been conditional when I sent the £200, with which Dr. Gillow said he would be content, though Sir H. Trelawny had agreed to pay ye college £300 for two boys from Whitby. When I heard from Mr. Gilbert soon after, I found that Sir Harry had relapsed to act as a parson awhile, and that ye donation was absolute."

These cases of conscience troubled Mr. Haydock very much, and he could never bring his mind to submit to what he felt absolutely convinced were wrong decisions. These matters would not have been treated here if allusion to his differences with his superiors had not been made with such frequent publicity. He complained of the various decisions, and demanded some reason for them, which he never satisfactorily obtained.

Bishop Penswick, in a letter to Mr. Haydock, dated, Liverpool, Aug. 16, 1828, says, " No doubt you have brought your judgment to harmonize with your feelings, and thus your resolves are deemed to be proper, but, were your council to be sought on a similar occasion, you would pronounce it dangerous in another to decide when under the influence of irritation. That you have received great provocation I will not deny, at the same time I see much to be lamented and much to be censured, both in you and in Mr. N. Rigby. He shows too little respect for superiority of years and experience, and you are very blameable for the asperity with which you have treated him." Eventually the bishop judged it best to remove Mr. Haydock, and appointed him to Westby Hall, in Lancashire, in spite of the petition of his congregation that he should be allowed to remain at Whitby. He left Whitby on Sept. 22, 1830, to take possession of his new mission, and though he only remained for a short time at Westby, his connection with the place will serve for the introduction of a brief account of that ancient mission.

## 𝔚𝔢𝔰𝔱𝔟𝔶 𝔥𝔞𝔩𝔩.

" No more the voice of feasting is heard amid those halls,
The grass grows o'er the hearthstone, the fern o'ertops the walls."
                                                    *L. E. Landon.*

The old hall, now a farmstead, is situated between Kirkham
and Lytham. It ceased to be occupied as a residence of the
manorial lords, the Cliftons, either after the death of Cuthbert
Clifton, a colonel in the royalist army in 1641, or during the
lifetime of his brother, Sir Thomas Clifton, who was created a
baronet in 1662, and died in 1694. The Cliftons maintained a
priest at Westby throughout the days of persecution. If he
was not at all times resident in the hall, owing to the surveillance
of the pursuivants, he was not far distant, and perhaps sometimes there was more than one priest attending to the wants of
the district. About 1585 the council was informed that " ffather
Robinsonne [is] wᵗʰ Mr. Cliffetonne of Molbricke [an error for
Westby] or wᵗʰ Mʳⁱˢ Tildestley at Standesaker " (*Dom. Eliz. voL
clxxxv. No.* 85, *P.R.O.*) The Rev. T. E. Gibson, in his history of
Lydiate Hall, quotes a document in the Harleian MSS. : " 1586
—Richard Brittain, a priest receipted in the house of Wm.
Bennet of Westby about the beginning of June last, from whence
young Mr. Norrice of Speke conveyed the said Brittain to the
Speke as the said Bennet hath reported. The said Brittain
remayneth now at the house of Mr. Norrice of the Speke, as
appeareth by the deposition of John Osbadilston (by common
report)." This was the presentment of the Vicar of Kirkham.
The Bennets remained a good Catholic yeomanry family for
long after this date. Thomas Bennett de Westby in Plumpton,
was a recusant in 1638, and William and Robert Bennett and
their wives appear in the recusant rolls between 1667 and 1679.
The names of the various members of the Clifton family, from

the age of sixteen upwards, of course appear annually in the rolls. Dom Gervase Gray, O.S.B., died at Westby Hall. April 6th, 1641. His real name was very likely Gervase Clifton. Edward Robinson, a roundhead major, had taken possession of the hall in that year, and the cavaliers made an unsuccessful raid on the place, and a good deal of skirmishing was the result. Perhaps this had something to do with the good Benedictine's death. Towards the close of the 17th century, Fr. Edward Barrow, S.J., a native of Westby, had charge of the mission. On the 15th Jan., 1716, after the unsuccessful attempt of the Chevalier de St. George, Fr. Barrow was convicted of recusancy at the Lancaster Sessions, and was declared an outlaw. Mr. Chambers Slaughter, the accountant-general to the Forfeited Estates Commission, was very anxious to catch him, and the description he gives of his proceedings to the commissioners reads like a romance, or a thrilling narrative of a priest-hunt in the days of Elizabeth.

Preston, Feb. 17, 1716.—" I had a message yesterday that Barrow, ye priest sometime since advised ye off, was selling his household goods and making off, so I went last night in the evening to have a watchfull eye on him, but found all quiett, and am again assur'd there is good quantity of plate for ye use of Chappell, and not only this but of two more within 4 miles. This I gather'd from one of ye dragoons who was of those congregations about 4 years since, but now a true protestant, and was privy to all those secret places, which made me so desirous of an order for these purposes. And they are now like to march before I can have your answer. It is very probable that both parchments and papers might be found on a diligent search that might cause good discoverys in all other houses."

Preston, Feb. 26, 1716.—"I have received the warrant to search Barrow's house, who is both a priest and outlaw'd ; I shall do my best to secure what he has, but as everything remains about him very quiett, and he absconded again last week, I would gladly he should returne home first, being only att Mr. Clifton's [at Lytham], for I have constant notice where he goes.'

Preston, 8 Mar., 1716.—"I was yesterday at Westby Hall, but could not find the priest, tho' I am pretty confidant he is not far, nor does he absent himself long at a time, the larder and cellar being well stored and of the best, and only one domestic appearing, who, as in all these cases knows nothing of the matter, notwithstanding an old clock, the linnen and pewter, and, if any good furniture, was all made off or hid the night before ; there is nothing of any vallue remaining, only some necessary utensils below stairs, which may sell for something among the country people. But making a very narrow search, up two pair of stairs in the Chappell, and sounding the walls of the chimney, I found an entrance about 20 inches square painted as brick worke, which could not have been distinguished by the eye, but striking a spitt into several places I accidently struck through here, and found a large opening. The conveniences of a ladder there fixed, I went down, and removing some little rubbish discovered a large quantity of folio books, among which several MSS., a large gilt head of St. Ignatius, some altar linnen, and a crucifix ; then I came to some more rubbish, but sounding for a bottom with a large spitt, could find none, so conclude it goes to the bottom of the house. It being late I charged the constable with one man more and my own servant to abide there in the house. I nailed upp two doors to prevent more passages than one, so came home last night about nine o'clock. . . . . This morn ye sheriffe (Mr. Robarts) is gone to take care, and this afternoon I design to go myself againe with some workmen to assist, other ways would be impossible to come att the bottom. There being likewise two places more that I suspect from the hollowness. Some expenses I must be in at on this and such like occasions, but I shall be as good a husband for the publick as possible. There is a great quantity of hay, which I design to gett away believing severall things concealed there. All I hope to gett away too-morrow. I will not fail advising you again next post, being—Hond. Sirs, your most obedient humble servt, Chambers Slaughter. The maid at last own'd that everything was thrown in there upon notice of the defeat att Preston."

Preston, Mar. 10, 1716.—"Hon. Sirs,—Since my last I have been againe att Westby Hall with some workemen, and after a thorough search have not found anything besides the books, priests' vests, some altar and household linnen, and a large picture of ye Virgin Mary, which I suppose by the size cover'd the wall at the altar. There remain in the house all the kitchen furniture (pewter excepted) and other goods in the larder very good of the sort, but all of no great vallue, a quantity of hay, about, I believe, ten loads, and a great stack of turff. I have taken care of these things and shall attend your orders in relation thereunto . . . . The last instance of these people's disregard was last night coming thro' Kirkham. The people came out and forct in the two horses which were hir'd from thence to bring Barrow's books, &c., to Preston. But by the help of constable whom I charg'd, and some other assistance, I forct out the horses again, and brought off ye goods. The reason, I apprehend, must be disaffection. These things I think proper to hint to you being resolv'd to trouble ye Board with no more complaints."

Preston, Mar. 19, 1716.—"I do find by Mr. Shawe and Mr. Richardson that . . . Barrow is outlaw'd, and so shall proceed as you direct by appraizment, three days notice, and sale. The same was done att Manchester in the case of Gartside's goods, when Mr. Mosman and self were sworne appraisers, but nobody buying, I was forct to bid by another hand and take the goods in my possession, so that the Act was comply'd with. If you'l have the goods putt up to publick sale againe at Liverpoole it shall be done forthwith." (*S. 54, Forfeited Estates, P.R.O.*)

Fr. Barrow, like his grand-nephew, the Rev. John Barrow, of Claughton, possessed extraordinary force of character. He was a famous hunter, and used to follow the hounds with Squire

Clifton. Probably he was present with old Mr. Harris and the Rev. Richard Penketh at the famous Stonyhurst buck-hunt in 1712, recorded in song by Mr. Cottam, the schoolmaster at Hurst Green :—

> " No river, mount, or dale can stay
> His passage, but he finds a way
> Through all obstructions, past compare
> In hunting otter, buck, or hare."

He proved himself a match for Mr. Chambers Slaughter, and remained at Westby till his death in August, 1721, aged 61. His immediate successor was Fr. John Berington, *alias* Harper, S.J., chaplain to Wm. Hesketh, of the Maynes, Little Singleton Esq. Fr. Harper was likewise a keen sportsman. On May 31, 1712, Thomas Tyldesley, the Jacobite squire, records in his diary going to Layton Hayes, near Blackpool, to see a race between Fr. Harper's mare and that of the Rev. Nicholas Sanderson. "A greatt deall of good company" assembled to witness the contest between the worthy Jesuit and secular priests. Nicholas Sanderson was an old school-fellow of the diarist, first at Lady-well, Fernyhalgh, and afterwards at St. Omer's College. Eventually, he was ordained priest at the English College at Rome. Tyldesley does not state the result of the race, but it is not unreasonable to assume that the Jesuit proved his superiority as a trainer, for Nick's nephew and namesake sent his son to St. Omers' and the family ever afterwards remained staunch to the Society. The Rev. William Winckley, subsequently rural-dean of Leyland Hundred, was present at the race, and accompanied the diarist to Mr. Clifton's at Lytham after the sport was over. A little later, on June 18, the Jacobite company again met at Lytham Hall, and after dinner Fr. Harper once more entered his grey mare, " 14 and an inch," to contest the same course with Sir Francis Andrews, Bart., James Singleton of Raygill, the diarist's son, Edward Tyldesley, and the young lord of Rawcliffe.

Richard Butler, of whom unhappily the last three were so soon to stake and lose their estates in the Chevalier de St. George's dash for the throne in 1715.

When Bishop Williams made his visitation of Lancashire in the beginning of 1729, the Westby congregation was included in that of Lytham under Fr. John Bennett, and 247 were confirmed at the hall. In 1741, Fr. Bennett removed to Highfield, near Wigan, and Fr. Harper took his place at Lytham Hall, where he remained till his death, August 28, 1743, aged 70. Fr. Roger Leigh, S.J., who entered the Society in 1728, came from Liverpool to Westby when Fr. Harper left. During Fr. Barrow's troubles, and probably for some years afterwards, William Lathom was the tenant-farmer of Westby Hall. The Lathoms were connections of the Leighs of Aspull, for Fr. Roger Leigh died at the house of his nephew, Thomas Lathom, in Wigan Lane, Jan. 29, 1781, aged 73. Fr. Roger was apparently the son of James Leigh, of Aspull, son of Roger Leigh, of the same place, both non-jurors in 1717. In or before 1745 he was succeeded by Fr. William Weldon, *alias* Hunter, S.J., from Ince Blundell who died here in 1761. Fr. Thomas Cuerden, S.J., then took charge of the mission, which he retained until 1791, when he removed to Scholes, near Prescot, and died in 1793. On Sept. 21, 1784, Bishop M. Gibson visited Westby, and confirmed 78 persons, the number of communicants in the congregation being returned at 360. Some time previous to Fr. Cuerden's time, it was customary for Mr. Clifton's chaplain to say an early mass at Lytham Hall and a later one at Westby Hall. After Fr. Cuerden's removal, Westby ceased to be a Jesuit mission, the Society having been suppressed in 1773. From 1791 to 1820, the mission was served by Dom Richard Bernard Butler, O.S.B., grandson of Xfr. Butler, youngest son of Richard Butler, Esq., of Rawcliffe Hall, by his wife Catherine, daughter of Thomas Carus, of Halton Hall, Esq. Fr. Butler was succeeded by the Rev. Thomas Pinnington, who retained possession of the mission until 1830. It seems, however, that Dom Peter Athanasius Allanson, O.S.B., served at the chapel during a short period, probably immediately after his ordination in 1828. The Rev. George Leo Haydock took possession of the mission on Sept. 25, 1830. He only remained eleven months, and on Aug. 22, 1831, the Rev. John Dixon was installed in the mission, and remained until the Cliftons closed the chapel in 1845.

The income of the mission at this time, Mr. Haydock says, writing in 1847, amounted to about £100. "John Clifton paid for all repairs, several hundreds, while I was there. But in Aug., 1831, his son Thomas went over to ye Protestant church, and after some years shut up ye chapel, and my successor, John Dixon, got to Cottam happily. John Clifton died Mar. 23, 1832, near London, perhaps still a Catholic, and was brought to be buried at Lytham. His son, upon whose wife I once called, about June, 1831, was zealous for ye Protestant church. He had never been so for ye Catholic church, though educated at St. Cuthbert's College, and— marrying a Protestant clergyman's daughter, said to have been a Jewess, and both gamblers—probably neglecting a good conscience, easily made shipwreck of ye faith. May he return before it be too late. His son (John Talbot Clifton, who returned to the faith before his death) got awhile to be M.P. for North Lancashire, and talked foolishly about ye Protestant prayer-book, denying that there was any prayer for 'plenty' and against 'dearth,' being a protectionist. The Clifton family has injured ye congregation at Westby, which had just beautified ye chapel at £100 expense. The father of Thomas, and son of ye admired old squire, had formerly suppressed Salwick chapel, and had a lawsuit (in which he was cast) with Mr. Lund, &c., on ye death of good old Rev. Wilson. The judge said he might have been transported, and he was probably ye first who had thus acted towards his own church. He lived at variance with his wife Riddell (daughter of Thos. Horton Widdrington Riddell, of

Swinburne Castle), and all this tended to his ruin. We must pray for all benefactors—as ye family was long—and for enemies too."

The old chapel attached to Westby Hall stood at the western end of the building, and hardly a trace of it can now be seen. It was erected in 1741, and was formally opened on May 1, 1742. Like most of the other chapels in the Fylde, it was "up-steps." After its closure in 1845, the congregation was annexed to The Willows, Kirkham, but the rapid development of the Catholic population soon rendered the church there far too small for those attending it. Consequently, Dean Fred. Hines, of The Willows, purchased from Col. John Talbot Clifton, of Lytham, a site for a new chapel at Westby, a short distance from the hall. Miss Elizabeth Dalton, of Thurnham Hall, paid for the land; Miss Orrell, of Blackbrook, gave £500; Mr. W. Billington, of Kirkham, bore the entire expense of the chancel; Mr. John Hodgson, of Goosuargh, gave £100; and Mr. John Sidgreaves, of Lytham, a similar amount. The foundation-stone of the new church, which is dedicated to St. Anne, was laid May 31, 1859, by Bishop Goss, and on Aug. 26, 1860, it was opened. The design of the church is peculiar, being one of the bishop's ideas carried out by the younger Pugin. For fourteen months after the opening Dean Hines served the mission from The Willows, after which his curate, the Rev. William Ball, was appointed to take charge of it.

## The Golden Cagg.

"Though in the paths of death I tread,
With gloomy horrors overspread,
My steadfast heart shall fear no ill,
For thou, O Lord, art with me still;
Thy friendly crook shall give me aid,
And guide me through the dreadful shade."

*Addison.*

As Mr. Haydock did not cease to press his claims and to

dispute the justice of the various decisions of the arbitrators and of his superiors, the bishop suspended him on Aug. 31, 1831, from saying Mass and exercising his priestly functions. Mr. Haydock retired quietly to " The Golden Tagg," the title of endearment he gave to his home. In the autumn of the following year he addressed an appeal in Latin to the prefect of propaganda which he requested his old pupil, Bishop Gradwell, the late agent for the vicars apostolic at Rome, to transmit thither. But the bishop instead sent it to the superior against whom Mr. Haydock appealed. On Jan. 29, 1837, after Bishop Penswick's death, Mr. Haydock petitioned that he might be allowed to fit up an altar and say Mass privately at his residence, The Golden Tagg, and later, he a third time appealed to Rome direct. Shortly after he was informed by the vicar-general, Mr. Sherburne, "without any explanation," that he might go to the mission at Penrith.

Thus for eight years and a quarter the old man resided at The Tagg, devoting himself to study, with his books all around him, lining the walls, and piled in heaps on the floors.[1] His banishment was indeed long, yet he could afterwards say with Prospero :

> " Me, poor man ! my library
> Was dukedom large enough."
>
> *Shakespeare—Tempest, Sc. II.*

## Penrith.

> " At church, with meek and unaffected grace,
> His looks adorn'd the venerable place ;
> Truth from his lips prevail'd with double sway,
> And fools, who came to scoff, remain'd to pray."
>
> *Goldsmith—Deserted Village.*

After the so-called Reformation, and during the time when

---

[1] The sale of his library by public auction at Preston, by Mr. H. C. Walton, in July, 1851, occupied a week. It contained many curious Catholic MSS.

the penal laws were in vigorous operation, the ancient faith had still a few adherents in Penrith. Mr. Walker, in his history of the town, tells us that an entry in the parish register records that upon the 19th of June, 1681, five Catholics were summoned to appear before the chancellor at Penrith. This summons appears to have been disregarded, for an excommunication by the bishop of Carlisle, under the seal of the office, was shortly afterwards published, and the contumacious parties were denounced by the vicar as excommunicated, while several other persons who were summoned along with the Catholics, having made proper submission, were absolved, and their absolution publicly proclaimed. In 1717, the Catholics who registered their estates in the vicinity, were Henry Charles Howard, of Greystoke Castle; Joyce Mounsey, widow of Cuthbert Mounsey of Stainton; her son John, of the same place, yeoman; John Robinson, of Brockell Moor, in Lazonby; and Lancelot Garth, of Hesket, yeoman—all in the county of Cumberland; and in Westmoreland, John Huddleston, of Hail Grange, in Newbiggin, gent. The Blencowes, of Blencowe Hall, were Catholics at one period, Hutton John belonged to the Huddlestons, and the last of the Fletchers of Hutton Hall died a Catholic. But there is no record of where the Catholics of Penrith attended Mass.

Perhaps it was the Franciscans who served the district at this time, for it was Fr. Martin (à S. Carolo) Grimstone, O.S.F., who converted Sir Henry Fletcher, of Hutton Hall, co. Cumberland. The good baronet was the son of Sir George Fletcher by his wife, Alice, daughter of Hugh, Viscount Colerain. Betham calls him "a gentleman of great hopes and expectations." He was educated in the Protestant religion, but became a Catholic, and settled his estate of about £1,500 a year on a distant relation, Thomas Fletcher, of Moresby, Esq., reserving only a small competency for life. He then retired to Douay, and fitted up an apartment for himself adjoining the English Franciscan monastery dedicated to St. Bonaventure. There he died, May 19,

1712, in the 54th year of his age. He was buried on the north
side of the choir, before the high altar, in the beautiful conven-
tual church which he had just erected for the friars at his own
expense. It was solemnly consecrated by Clement, Archbishop
of Cologne, on the following Nov. 13. By a codicil to his will
Sir Henry left legacies to the amount of £850, which the commissioners for forfeited estates in 1716 declared to be for super-
stitious uses. The money was accordingly seized, as also " a
large altar, with other plate of Sir Henry Fletcher's," which sold
for £960. Of the latter sum, £225 was paid to the discoverer.

> " No marble decks thy grave to tell
> The tale of one I loved so well ;
> But Angel eyes thy vigil keep,
> And living forms come here to weep."
>
> *Phil. Hen. Howard, of Corby.*

On May 22, 1833, a large room situated on the south side of
the churchyard at Penrith, was opened as a chapel, which was
attended from Wigton by the Rev. John Dowdall, every fortnight. In the · following year, for a short time, Penrith
was similarly served by the Rev. John Kelly. In 1835,
or perhaps towards the close of the previous year, the
Rev. Henry Newsham was appointed to reside in Penrith,
but in 1836 he left and was succeeded by the Rev. James
Seddon, who resided with his mother in the town. In
1838 the Rev. John Fielding Whitaker took possession of
the mission. He did not stay many months, however, and
in 1839 the Rev. Patrick Phelan, a young priest just ordained, was placed at the mission. He was soon removed to St.
Marie's, Wigan, and on Nov. 22, 1839, the Rev. George Leo
Haydock arrived at Penrith.

Though advanced in years Mr. Haydock energetically laboured
for the establishment of the mission on a firm footing, and to
him and his influence the Catholics of Penrith are greatly indebted for the erection of their present chapel. There was
great difficulty in securing an eligible site, for the land which had

Q

been purchased, through the assistance of Henry Howard, Esq., of Corby Castle, was required by the Lancaster and Carlisle Railway Company. The mission owed its foundation to Lady Catherine Throckmorton of Carlton, in Yorkshire—to whose husband Cowper, the poet, dedicated some of his pieces—and Mr. Howard's son, the late Philip Henry Howard, Esq., was one of Lady Throckmorton's executors. She died Jan. 22, 1839, and a mural tablet was erected in the new chapel to her memory, as well as a handsome stained glass window, which informs us that she was the foundress of the mission. It was not till shortly before his death that Mr. Haydock succeeded in securing a new site, and in making preparations for the erection of the chapel. His congregation was of the poorest class, and but for his own private means he could not have lived out of what they were able to afford him. In spite of these circumstances he was ever mindful of the necessities of others. Amongst his papers is a letter dated Dec. 20, 1845, from the Right Rev. Mgr. Charles Newsham, president of Ushaw College, acknowledging the receipt of a donation of £100—£20 towards the new church, and £80 towards the education of poor students.

On Sept. 16, 1849, he wrote to The Tagg,—"I must confess I am not in my best fashion, and hence I have excused myself from saying afternoon prayers at ye chapel—ye first time these nearly ten years. Seeing the little fruit, I could not refrain from tears, particularly as the third Sunday in September is the feast of the seven sorrows of ye Blessed Virgin, and I could hardly get through ye *Stabat Mater*, which you may find most affecting at page 15 of the new Hymn Book which I gave you, *The most afflicted Mother stood, &c.* I had other subjects of sorrow to dwell upon. Last Wednesday week a tramp, 27 years old, who with her mother became serious (at my instigation perhaps) about six years ago, and who was at communion a month before at Cockermouth, where ye cholera is raging (as in many parts of

England and Europe), fell down on ye moor, and was found with her mother and brother by a gentleman. He gave them 1s. to get some brandy, and they were conveyed to a public-house about eight miles from Penrith. They were placed by the overseer, Wilson, in an outhouse intended for calves or pigs, without a door or a stool, on straw. The doctor did not think she would live twelve hours then, yet I was not informed till Saturday. . . . She wished very much to see me. Accordingly I hired a horse, and was two hours on ye road going. I set off at two and got home about seven, much shaken, though I went slowly." He then describes the illness with which he was seized, and of which he at first thought he should die. " But I must stay at my post, though unworthy and almost useless . . . Your snug parlour would not be comfortable if I thought I was not working while it was day for me—night is coming. My school-fellow, Rev. Thomas Gillow, four years older, has resigned on account of old age. Most at my time of life have indeed retired to prepare more immediately for eternity. Still, if God give ability He requires us to labour to ye end."

> " In all my wand'rings round this world of care,
> In all my griefs—and God has giv'n my share—
> I still had hopes my latest hours to crown,
> Amidst *Tagg's* humble bowers to lay me down."
>
> *Goldsmith—Deserted Village.*

Eight days before his death he again wrote to The Tagg,— " This day ten years ago I set off to come hither, and though near 76, I still continue pretty well, except occasionally having ye pain at ye heart or breast, chiefly when I walk rather fast." This was his last letter ; he died at Penrith on the 29th of Nov., 1849, and there was interred.

> " The good old man is gone !
>   He is gone to his saintly rest,
> Where no sorrow can be known,
>   And no trouble can molest,
> For his crown of life is won,
>   And the dead in the Lord are blest."
>
> *Doane.*

He was succeeded by his accomplished friend and relative, the Very Rev. Robert Smith, son of his cousin Jane Haydock, who erected the chapel, which was opened about seven months after Mr. Haydock's decease, and also built the presbytery, in great measure at his own expense. In 1860 he enlarged the chapel, which is a pretty piece of ecclesiastical architecture, enshrouded by trees in a lovely situation. Canon Smith had studied at Ushaw College and St. Sulpice, and for nine years after his ordination was chaplain at Haggerstone Castle. His correspondence with Mr. Haydock shows him to have been a man of deep thought and cultivated mind. He remained at Penrith until 1867, when he removed to Gainford, near Darlington, where he remained till 1869, in a declining state of health. After that he spent some time on the Continent, and a few years before his death opened a mission on Holy Island, whence he retired to Kyloe Cottage, Beal, close to the scene of his first missionary labours. There he died, Sept. 7, 1879, aged 67, and was interred at St. Ninian's, Wooler. While at Penrith he erected in the chapel a mural tablet to the memory of his relative, bearing the following inscription :—

"REV. GEORGE LEO HAYDOCK,
Priest of this Mission.
Nat : April 11, 1774.
Obiit : Nov. 29, 1849,"

*Tristitia vestra vertetur in gaudium.*

* * * * * *                    *Haydock motto.*

" My task is done—my song hath ceased—my theme
Has died into an echo ; it is fit
The spell should break of this protracted dream.
The torch shall be extinguish'd which hath lit
My midnight lamp—and what is writ, is writ,—
Would it were worthier ! but I am not now
That which I have been—and my visions flit
Less palpably before me—and the glow
Which in my spirit dwelt is fluttering, faint, and low."

*Childe Harold.*

THE END.

# INDEX AND ELUCIDATION

Claughton Estate, and assume the name of Brockholes, 69, 72. *Fam.*
of White Hill, 45, 58. *Wm.*, 23, prisoner in the Fleet, 32, 34. *Wm.*
69, 235.
Heton of Heton, 2.
Heys, Jno., 203.
Hiding-places, 5, 27, 34, 62, 232-3.
Higgison, Jennet and Roger, 68.
Highfield House, seat of Gerard fam., chap. 236.
Hill, Jno., pr. 206.
Hilton, Margery, *alias* Mag Shelton, the witch, 41.
Hines, Dean Fred., 238.
Hippesley, Sir Jno. Cox, 147.
Hodgson Joseph, pr., narrator of the seizure of Douay, 120, 122, 128-9.
      *Jno.* 238.
Hodsock Park, chap., 46, 49.
Hogarth, Bp. Wm., 127.
Hoghton. Adam 21, 65. *Alex.*, 19, 23. *Anne*, 15. *Ballad,* 8, 10. *Bottoms*,
      8-9. *Bryde*, 8. *Cath.*, 17. *Elis.* 8. *Fam.* of Hoghton, 1, deprived
      of its faith 20, 22, 65. *Fam.* of Dun Cow Rib 64, of Grimsargh 21, of
      Lea 22, of Park Hall 15. *Isabel*, widow of Gilbert Haydock takes the
      veil 1. *Jane*, 23. *Jno.*, assumes the name of Dalton, 16. *Mary* 18.
      *Mrs.* 20. *Motto*, 15. *Rich.* of Park Hall, 13 seq., 23. *Sir Rich.*, 5,
      8, 9, 15, 20, 36. *Thomas*, the exile, 7, withdraws to Antwerp 8 seq.,
      dies at Liége 17 seq. *Thos.*, the younger, slain, 20, 65. *Thos.*, pr.,
      and confessor 17 seq., 32. *Tower*, 7 seq., erected 9 seq., searched,
      19, 23, 31, 36. *Wm.*, 1. *Wm.* of Park Hall, 15. *Wm.* of Grim-
      sargh, 21, 65.
Holborn, Castle-street, mission. 130.
Hollowforth, 26. Mill, 73.
Holman, Wm. 170.
Holme Pierrepoint, 22.
Holmes, fam. 74. *Peter*, pr., 74. *Margt.*, 74, 77.
Holy Island, mission, 244.
Hopton, Sir Owen, lieut. of the Tower 28.
Hornby, mission, 133, 210. *Castle* 194.
Hornyold, Bp. Jno., 142.
Hothersall, of Hothersall, 2. *Hall*, chap., 63. *Jno.*, outlaw, 63-4. *Thos.*, 63-4.
Hough, The, mission, 57, 63, 69, 71.
Howard, fam., students at Old Hall, 171. *Hen. Chas.*, 240. *Hen.*, of Corby,
      242. *Philip Hen.*, M.P., 189, 241-2.
R